INVESTORS AND
MARKETS

Princeton Lectures in Finance

Yacine Ait-Sahalia, Series Editor

The Princeton Lectures in Finance, published by arrangement with the Bendheim Center for Finance of Princeton University, are based on annual lectures offered at Princeton University. Each year, the Bendheim Center invites a leading figure in the field of finance to deliver a set of lectures on a topic of major significance to researchers and professionals around the world.

Stephen A. Ross, *Neoclassical Finance*

William F. Sharpe, *Investors and Markets:*
Portfolio Choices, Asset Prices, and Investment Advice

INVESTORS AND MARKETS

PORTFOLIO CHOICES, ASSET PRICES, AND INVESTMENT ADVICE

William F. Sharpe

This work is published by arrangement with the
Bendheim Center for Finance of Princeton University

PRINCETON UNIVERSITY PRESS

PRINCETON AND OXFORD

Published by Princeton University Press, 41 William Street, Princeton, New Jersey 08540

In the United Kingdom: Princeton University Press, 3 Market Place, Woodstock,
Oxfordshire OX20 1SY

Library of Congress Cataloging-in-Publication Data

Sharpe, William F.
Investors and markets : portfolio choices, asset prices, and investment advice /
William F. Sharpe.
p.   cm.
Includes bibliographical references and index.
ISBN-13: 978-0-691-12842-9 (hardcover : alk. paper)
ISBN-10: 0-691-12842-1 (hardcover : alk. paper)
1. Portfolio management.   2. Securities—Prices.   3. Capital asset pricing model.
4. Investment analysis.   5. Investments.   I. Title.
HG4529.5.S53   2007
332.6—dc22   2006015387

British Library Cataloging-in-Publication Data is available

This book has been composed in Goudy and Swiss 911 Extra Compressed
by Princeton Editorial Associates, Inc., Scottsdale, Arizona

Printed on acid-free paper. ∞

pup.princeton.edu

Printed in the United States of America

3 5 7 9 10 8 6 4 2

CONTENTS

PREFACE

THIS BOOK IS based on the Princeton University Lectures in Finance that I gave in May 2004. The invitation to present these lectures provided me a chance to address old issues in new ways and to bring together a number of interrelated topics in financial economics with an emphasis on individuals' saving and investment decisions.

I am grateful to Professor Yacine Ait-Sahalia of Princeton, the series editor, and to Peter Dougherty of Princeton University Press for inviting me to undertake this project and for giving me valuable advice throughout.

This work follows a tradition with strong Princeton roots. In the first (2001) Princeton Lectures in Finance, Stephen Ross masterfully addressed the central issues associated with asset pricing. That work is now available as the first book in this series: *Neoclassical Finance* (Ross 2005).

In 2001 Princeton University Press published the first edition of John Cochrane's marvelous book, *Asset Pricing* (Cochrane 2001), which is fast becoming a standard text for its target audience—"economics and finance Ph.D. students, advanced MBA students, and professionals with similar background."

My goal is to continue down the path set by Ross and Cochrane, using a somewhat different approach and providing several extensions. However, this book differs substantially from the work of Ross and Cochrane in both approach and motivation. I am primarily concerned with helping individual investors make good saving and investment decisions—usually with the assistance of investment professionals such as financial planners, mutual fund managers, advisory services, and personal asset managers. This requires more than just an understanding of the determinants of asset prices. But for many other applications in finance, it suffices to understand asset pricing. For example, a corporation desiring to maximize the value of its stock can, in principle, simply consider the pricing of the potential outcomes associated with its activities. A financial engineer designing a financial product may need only to determine a way to replicate the desired outcomes and compute the cost of doing so.

Appropriately, Ross concentrated on the ability to price assets using only information about other assets' prices in his first chapter: "No Arbitrage: The Fundamental Theorem of Finance." The title of Cochrane's book indicates a similar focus, as does his statement in the preface that "we now go to asset prices directly. One can then find optimal portfolios, but it is a side issue for the asset pricing question."

However, to determine the best investment portfolio for an individual, one needs more than asset prices. To use the standard economic jargon, individuals should maximize expected utility, not just portfolio value. To do so efficiently requires an understanding of the ways in which asset prices reflect investors' diverse situations and views of the future. I thus deal here with both asset pricing and portfolio choice. And, as will be seen, I treat them more as one subject than as two.

Over the past year and a half I have benefited greatly from comments and suggestions made by a number of friends and colleagues. Without implicating any of them in the final results, I wish to thank Yacine Ait-Sahalia, Princeton University; Geert Bekaert, Columbia University; Phillip Dolan, Macquarie University; Peter Dougherty, Princeton University Press; Ed Fine, Financial Engines, Inc.; Steven Grenadier, Stanford University; Christopher Jones, Financial Engines, Inc.; Haim Levy, Hebrew University; Harry Markowitz, Harry Markowitz Associates; André Perold, Harvard University; Steven Ross, Massachusetts Institute of Technology; and Jason Scott, Jim Shearer, John Watson, and Robert Young, Financial Engines, Inc.

Finally, I express my gratitude to my wife Kathy for her support and encouragement. We are proof that a professional artist and a financial economist can live happily and productively together.

INVESTORS AND
MARKETS

ONE

INTRODUCTION

1.1. The Subject of This Book

THIS IS A BOOK about the effects of investors interacting in capital markets and the implications for those who advise individuals concerning savings and investment decisions. The subjects are often considered separately under titles such as portfolio choice and asset pricing.

Portfolio choice refers to the ways in which investors do or should make decisions concerning savings and investments. Applications that are intended to describe what investors do are examples of positive economics. Far more common, however, are normative applications, designed to prescribe what investors should do.

Asset pricing refers to the process by which the prices of financial assets are determined and the resulting relationships between expected returns and the risks associated with those returns in capital markets. Asset pricing theories or models are examples of positive or descriptive economics, since they attempt to describe relationships in the real world. In this book we take the view that these subjects cannot be adequately understood in isolation, for they are inextricably intertwined. As will be shown, asset prices are determined as part of the process through which investors make portfolio choices. Moreover, the appropriate portfolio choice for an individual depends crucially on available expected returns and risks associated with different investment strategies, and these depend on the manner in which asset prices are set. Our goal is to approach these issues more as one subject than as two. Accordingly, the book is intended for those who are interested in descriptions of the opportunities available in capital markets, those who make savings and investment decisions for themselves, and those who provide such services or advice to others.

Academic researchers will find here a series of analyses of capital market conditions that go well beyond simple models that imply portfolio choices clearly inconsistent with observed behavior. A major focus throughout is on the effects on asset pricing when more realistic assumptions are made concerning investors' situations and behavior.

Investment advisors and investment managers will find a set of possible frameworks for making logical decisions, whether or not they believe that asset prices well reflect future prospects. It is crucial that investment professionals differentiate between *investing* and *betting*. We show that a well thought out model of asset pricing is an essential ingredient for sound investment practice. Without one, it is impossible to even know the extent and nature of bets incorporated in investment advice or management, let alone ensure that they are well founded.

1.2. Methods

This book departs from much of the previous literature in the area in two important ways. First, the underlying view of the uncertain future is not based on the *mean/variance* approach advocated for portfolio choice by Markowitz (1952) and used as the basis for the original Capital Asset Pricing Model (CAPM) of Sharpe (1964), Lintner (1965), Mossin (1966), and Treynor (1999). Instead, we base our analyses on a straightforward version of the *state/preference* approach to uncertainty developed by Arrow (1953) extending the work of Arrow (1951) and Debreu (1951).

Second, we rely extensively on the use of a program that simulates the process by which equilibrium can be reached in a capital market and provides extensive analysis of the resulting relationships between asset prices and future prospects.

1.2.1. The State/Preference Approach

We utilize a state/preference approach with a discrete-time, discrete-outcome setting. Simply put, uncertainty is captured by assigning probabilities to alternative future *scenarios* or *states of the world*, each of which provides a different set of investment outcomes. This rules out explicit reliance on continuous-time formulations and continuous distributions (such as normal or log-normal), although one can use discrete approximations of such distributions.

Discrete formulations make the mathematics much simpler. Many standard results in financial economics can be obtained almost trivially in such a setting. At least as important, discrete formulations can make the underlying economics of a situation more obvious. At the end of the day, the goal of the (social) science of financial economics is to describe the results obtained when individuals interact with one another. The goal of financial economics as a prescriptive tool is to help individuals make better decisions. In each case, the better we understand the economics of an analysis, the better equipped we are to evaluate its usefulness. The term *state/preference* indicates both that discrete states and times are involved, and that individuals' preferences for consumption play a key role. Also included are other aspects, such as securities representing production outputs.

1.2.2. Simulation

Simulation makes it possible to substitute computation for derivation. Instead of formulating complex algebraic models, then manipulating the resulting equations to obtain a closed-form solution equation, one can build a computer model of a marketplace populated by individuals, have them trade with one another until they do not wish to trade any more, then examine the characteristics of the resulting portfolios and asset prices.

Simulations of this type have both advantages and disadvantages. They can be relatively easy to understand. They can also reflect more complex situations than must often be assumed if algebraic models are to be used. On the other hand, the relationship between the inputs and the outputs may be difficult to fully comprehend. Worse yet, it is hard if not impossible to *prove* a relationship via simulation, although it is possible to disprove one.

Consider, for example, an assertion that when people have preferences of type A and securities of type B are available, equilibrium asset prices have characteristics of type C; that is, $A + B \Rightarrow C$. One can run a simulation with some people of type A and securities of type B and observe that the equilibrium asset prices are of type C. But this does not prove that such will always be the case. One can repeat the experiment with different people and securities, but always with people of type A and securities of type B. If in one or more cases the equilibrium is not of type C, the proposition ($A + B \Rightarrow C$) is disproven. But even if every simulation conforms with the proposition, it is not proven. The best that can be said is that if many simulations give the same result, one's confidence in the truth of the proposition is increased. Simulation is thus at best a brute force way to derive propositions that may hold most or all of the time.

But equilibrium simulation can be a powerful device. It can produce examples of considerable complexity and help people think deeply about the determinants of asset prices and portfolio choice. It can also be a powerful ally in bringing asset pricing analysis to more people.

1.2.3. The APSIM Program

The simulation program used for all the examples in this book is called APSIM, which stands for Asset Pricing and Portfolio Choice Simulator. It is available without charge at the author's Web site: www.wsharpe.com, along with workbooks for each of the cases covered. The program, associated workbooks, instructions, and source code can all be downloaded. Although the author has made every attempt to create a fast and reliable simulation program, no warranty can be given that the program is without error.

Although reading C++ programming code for a complex program is not recommended for most readers, the APSIM source code does provide documentation for the results described here. In a simulation context, this can serve a function similar to that of formal proofs of results obtained with traditional algebraic models.

1.3. Pedagogy

If you were to attend an MBA finance class at a modern university you would learn about subjects such as portfolio optimization, asset allocation analysis, the Capital Asset Pricing Model, risk-adjusted performance analysis, alpha and beta values, Sharpe Ratios, and index funds. All this material was built from Harry Markowitz's view that an investor should focus on the expected return and risk of his or her overall portfolio and from the original Capital Asset Pricing Model that assumed that investors followed Markowitz's advice. Such *mean/variance analysis* provides the foundation for many of the quantitative methods used by those who manage investment portfolios or assist individuals with savings and investment decisions. If you were to attend a Ph.D. finance class at the same university you would learn about no-arbitrage pricing, state claim prices, complete markets, spanning, asset pricing kernels, stochastic discount factors, and risk-neutral probabilities. All these subjects build on the view developed by Kenneth Arrow that an investor should consider alternative outcomes and the amount of consumption obtained in each possible situation. Techniques based on this type of analysis are used frequently by financial engineers, but far less often by investment managers and financial advisors.

Much of the author's published work is in the first category, starting with "Capital Asset Prices: A Theory of Market Equilibrium under Conditions of Risk" (1964). The monograph *Portfolio Theory and Capital Markets* (1970) followed resolutely in the mean/variance tradition, although it did cover a few ideas from state/preference theory in one chapter. The textbook *Investments* (Sharpe 1978) was predominantly in the mean/variance tradition, although it did use some aspects of a state/preference approach when discussing option valuation. The most recent edition (Sharpe, Alexander, and Bailey 1999) has evolved significantly, but still rests on a mean/variance foundation.

This is not an entirely happy state of affairs. There are strong arguments for viewing mean/variance analysis as a special case of a more general asset pricing theory (albeit a special case with many practical advantages). This suggests that it could be preferable to teach MBA students, investment managers, and financial advisors both general asset pricing and the special case of mean/variance analysis. A major goal of this book is to show how this might be accomplished. It is thus addressed in part to those who could undertake such a task (teachers, broadly construed). It is also addressed to those who would like to understand more of the material now taught in the Ph.D. classroom but who lack some of the background to do so easily (students, broadly construed).

1.4. Peeling the Onion

Capital markets are complex. We deal with stylized versions that lack many important features such as taxes, transactions costs, and so on. This is equivalent to introducing some of the principles of physics by assuming away the influences of friction. The justification is that one cannot hope to understand real capital markets without considering their behavior in simpler settings.

While our simulated capital markets are far simpler than real ones, their features are not simple to fully understand. To deal with this we introduce material in a sequential manner, starting with key aspects of a very simple case, while glossing over many important ingredients. Then we slowly peel back layers of the onion, revealing more of the inner workings and moving to more complex cases. This approach can lead to a certain amount of frustration on the part of both author and reader. But in due course, most mysteries are resolved, seemingly unrelated paths converge, and the patient reader is rewarded.

1.5. References

The material in this book builds on the work of many authors. Although some key works are referenced, most are not because of the enormity of the task. Fortunately, there is an excellent source for those interested in the history of the ideas that form the basis for much of this book: Mark Rubinstein's *A History of the Theory of Investments: My Annotated Bibliography* (Rubinstein 2006), which is highly recommended for anyone seriously interested in investment theory.

1.6. Chapters

A brief description of the contents of the remaining chapters follows.

1.6.1. Chapter 2: Equilibrium

Chapter 2 presents the fundamental ideas of asset pricing in a one-period (two-date) equilibrium setting in which investors agree on the probabilities of alternative future states of the world. The major focus is on the advice often given by financial economists to their friends and relatives: avoid non-market risk and take on a desired amount of market risk to obtain higher expected return. We show that under the conditions in the chapter, this is consistent with equilibrium portfolio choice.

1.6.2. Chapter 3: Preferences

Chapter 3 deals with investors' preferences. We cover alternative ways in which an individual may determine the amount of a security to be purchased or sold, given its price. A key ingredient is the concept of marginal utility. There are direct relationships between investors' marginal utilities and their portfolio choices. We cover cases that are consistent with some traditional financial planning advice, others that are consistent with mean/variance analysis, and yet others that are consistent with some features of the experimental results obtained by cognitive psychologists.

1.6.3. Chapter 4: Prices

Chapter 4 analyzes the characteristics of equilibrium in a world in which investors agree on the probabilities of future states of the world, do not have sources of consumption outside the financial markets, and do not favor a given amount of consumption in one future state of the world over the same amount in another future state. The chapter also introduces the concept of a complete market, in which investors can trade atomistic securities termed state claims. Some of the key results of modern asset pricing theory are discussed, along with their preconditions and limitations. Implications for investors' portfolio choices are also explored. We show that in this setting the standard counsel that an investor should avoid non-market risk and take on an appropriate amount of market risk to obtain higher expected return is likely to be good advice as long as available securities offer sufficient diversity.

1.6.4. Chapter 5: Positions

Chapter 5 explores the characteristics of equilibrium and optimal portfolio choice when investors have diverse economic positions outside the financial markets or differ in their preferences for consumption in different possible states of the world. As in earlier chapters, we assume investors agree on the probabilities of alternative future outcomes.

1.6.5. Chapter 6: Predictions

Chapter 6 confronts situations in which people disagree about the likelihood of different future outcomes. Active and passive approaches to investment management are discussed. The arguments for index funds are reviewed, along with one of the earliest published examples of a case in which the average opinion of a number of people provided a better estimate of a future outcome than the opinion of all but a few. We also explore the impact of differential information across investors and the effects of both biased and unbiased predictions.

1.6.6. Chapter 7: Protection

Chapter 7 begins with a discussion of the type of investment product that offers "downside protection" and "upside potential." Such a "protected investment product" is a derivative security because its return is based on the performance of a specified underlying asset or index. We show that a protected investment product based on a broad market index can play a useful role in a market in which some or all investors' preferences have some of the characteristics found in behavioral studies. We also discuss the role that can be played in such a setting by other derivative securities such as put and call options. To illustrate division of investment returns we introduce a simple trust fund that issues securities with different payoff patterns. Finally, we discuss the results from an experiment designed to elicit information about the marginal utilities of real people.

1.6.7. Chapter 8: Advice

The final chapter is based on the premise that most individual investors are best served through a division of labor, with investors assisted by investment professionals serving as advisors or portfolio managers. We review the demographic factors leading to an increased need for individuals to make savings and investment decisions and suggest the implications of the principle of comparative advantage for making such decisions efficiently. We then discuss the importance of understanding the differences between investing and betting and the need for investment advisors to have a logically consistent approach that takes into account the characteristics of equilibrium in financial markets. The chapter and the book conclude with a discussion of the key attributes of sound personal investment advice and an admonition that advisors and managers who make portfolio choices should have a clear view of the determination of asset prices.

TWO

EQUILIBRIUM

THIS CHAPTER SHOWS how equilibrium can be reached in a capital market and describes the characteristics of such an equilibrium. We present a series of cases, each of which assumes *agreement* among investors concerning the chances of alternative future outcomes. More complex (and realistic) cases are covered in later chapters.

2.1. Trading and Equilibrium

A standard definition of equilibrium is:

> A condition in which all acting influences are canceled by others, resulting in a stable, balanced or unchanging system.*

We will use a much simpler definition: *a financial economy is in equilibrium when no further trades can be made*. But of course in the real world trading seldom stops, and when it does stop, it is typically because low-cost markets are temporarily closed. The implication is that financial markets never really reach a state of equilibrium. Conditions change, there is new information, and people begin to act on the new information before they have fully acted on the old information. In actuality, people make trades to move toward an equilibrium target but the target is constantly changing.

Despite this completely valid observation, we need to understand the properties of a condition of equilibrium in financial markets, because markets will usually be headed toward such a position. And the more efficient the financial system, the smaller will be the discrepancies between market conditions and those of full equilibrium. Moreover, we will see that for many purposes the most important aspects of equilibrium for portfolio choice concern the levels of broad market indices, overall consumption, and other macroeconomic variables, which are likely to be closest to their equilibrium levels.

Understanding the nature of a financial market in equilibrium is a crucial step toward understanding real financial markets. The goal of this book is to explore the relationships between investors' characteristics and investment

---

*Source: *The American Heritage® Dictionary of the English Language*, Fourth Edition. Copyright © 2000 by Houghton Mifflin Company. All rights reserved.

opportunities and the key aspects of the situation that would be obtained if trading continued until equilibrium were reached.

2.2. Determinants and Results

Economics is a social science, dealing with the behavior of individuals and the results of their interactions where money is concerned. When trying to understand equilibrium relationships the focus is *descriptive*, concentrating on what actually happens. But much of financial economics is *prescriptive*, attempting to help people make better financial decisions. Such decisions involve buying and selling financial assets at prices determined in markets. Good financial decisions require an understanding of the forces that determine such prices. More specifically, optimal portfolio choice requires an understanding of equilibrium.

Figure 2-1 provides a simplified version of the operation of an *exchange economy* with two investors. Production is taken as given, with productive outputs represented by a set of *securities*. Individuals start with initial security portfolios, then trade securities in financial markets until no further voluntary trades can be made. When this point is reached, each person has a final security portfolio. The terms on which trades were made or, in some circumstances, the terms on

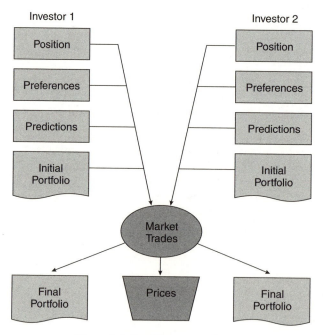

Figure 2-1 Equilibrium simulation.

which additional trades might be made, constitute *security prices* (more broadly, *asset prices*). After equilibrium has been established, time passes and outcomes are determined. Typically, some people do better than others, depending on their portfolio holdings and the nature of events. Then the process begins anew.

In a real economy, and in many of the cases discussed in this book, there will be more than two investors but the essential elements shown in Figure 2-1 remain the same. The trades made by an individual in this process will of course depend on his or her initial holdings of securities (or, more broadly, level of wealth). But other factors will play important roles.

Investors differ in geographic location, home ownership, profession, and so forth. We term these aspects an individual's *position*. If two people have different positions they may wish to hold different portfolios. Similarly, people may have different feelings about risk, present versus future gratification, and so on. We term these an individual's *preferences*. Differences in preferences will lead investors to choose different portfolios.

Finally, investors often assess the chances of alternative future outcomes differently. One investor's *predictions* may differ from those of another, leading to choices of different portfolios.

Taking production as given, the future will provide one of many alternative outcomes. Financial markets allow people to share those outcomes in ways that can take into account their different positions, preferences, and predictions. When thinking about portfolio choice it is important to keep in mind that if one person chooses less than his or her share of some security, someone else must choose more than his or her share. This implies that individuals should be able to justify their investment decisions on the basis of differences among their positions, preferences, and/or predictions. Prices are not determined by random number machines. They come from recent or prospective trades by real people. Investors who fail to fully take this into account do so at their peril.

In this book, we analyze *exchange economies* in which investors build portfolios from existing securities. But those who create such securities to finance productive opportunities base their decisions in part on the prices of current securities. Asset prices, like other prices, are determined by the joint forces of supply and demand. In the short run, supply and demand come from individuals and institutions trading existing securities or new purely financial instruments. In the long run, however, some old securities will expire or become worthless as firms cease production; moreover, new securities will be created to finance new production. We concentrate here on the determination of asset prices and portfolio choice in the short run—a key part of the long-run picture.

Figure 2-1 allows for financial intermediaries that can help markets function. But it includes no financial planners, banks, mutual funds, or other institutional investors, even though such financial services firms are an essential part of any modern financial system. In our examples, such firms will be at best shadowy, helping individuals make better decisions, providing some types of new securities, and so on. We do this primarily to keep things simple. But there is another reason. There are typically many ways that financial institutions can facilitate efficient sharing of investment outcomes. Ultimately, the particular institutional structure found in an economy will depend on relative costs, skill in marketing, and a certain amount of chance. It is extremely difficult to predict the precise nature of financial services; hence we concentrate on the more fundamental aspects of asset prices and the ultimate payoffs from chosen portfolios.

2.3. Time, Outcomes, Securities, and Predictions

Financial economics deals with time, risk, options, and information. Individuals allocate resources over time by borrowing, lending, investing in stocks, and so on. Many of these investments have *risk*—their future values are uncertain. Some allow the *option* of taking an action or not—for example, one may purchase a contract giving the right but not the obligation to buy 100 shares of Hewlett Packard stock a year hence for a price fixed in advance. Finally, *information* is used by investors to make predictions that affect both asset prices and portfolio choices.

We use a simple but powerful structure to incorporate these aspects. First, we divide time into discrete dates and intervals. We examine cases in which there are two dates ("now" and "later") and one time period between them. More realistic cases could involve many dates and periods. We will not deal with such situations explicitly but will indicate some of the ways that long-run considerations can affect short-term asset pricing.

Second, we assume that at each future date there are two or more alternative outcomes, or states of the world (*states* for short). One and only one of these states will actually occur, and there is generally uncertainty about the actual outcome.

Uncertainty is expressed by assigning *probabilities* to the alternative states. Thus if the possible states are that (1) it will rain tomorrow or (2) the sun will shine, investors will agree on the definition of the states, but may have different views about the chances of those states. One investor may think there is a 40 percent chance of rain, while another may think that there is a 60 percent chance. An investor's predictions are stated in the form of a set of probabilities for the different states.

The vehicles that people use for trades are *assets* or *securities*. We will use both terms more or less interchangeably but favor the latter for our cases. A *security* provides payoffs in different states. Thus the stock of an umbrella company might pay $5 if it rains and $3 if it shines. We assume that everyone agrees on the set of payoffs for a given security (here: $5 if rain, $3 if shine). As indicated earlier, however, there may be substantial disagreement about the probabilities of different states.

This approach is sometimes termed *state/preference* theory. Importantly, it allows for considerable generality without making excessive demands on one's mathematical skills. The key objection (often made) is that to reflect even an approximation to reality one must consider cases with thousands, millions, or billions of states and time periods. Some argue that for this reason alternative approaches that rely on smooth probability distributions and/or continuous concepts of time are superior. This argument has some merit, but many key economic relationships can best be understood using a discrete-time, discrete-state approach with a limited number of states and time periods. The resulting qualitative conclusions can then form the basis for building other types of systems for empirical applications. One of the goals of this book is to show that the state/preference approach offers an excellent basis for thinking about asset prices and portfolio choice.

2.4. The Market Risk/Reward Theorem and Corollary

A staple of textbook discussions of asset pricing and portfolio choice is the *market portfolio*. By definition, it includes all securities available in a market. An individual with a budget equal to *x* percent of the value of the overall market portfolio can choose a portfolio with the same composition by holding *x* percent of the outstanding units of each available security.

The simplest mean/variance asset pricing theory (the original Capital Asset Pricing Model [CAPM]) concluded that in equilibrium, investors will choose combinations of the market portfolio and borrowing or lending, with the proportions determined by their willingness to bear risk to obtain higher expected return. Such investors face only one source of uncertainty—the performance of the market as a whole; that is, they bear only *market risk*. An investor who chooses a less diversified portfolio will generally bear both market risk and *non-market risk*—uncertainty that would remain even if the market outcome were known.

In the setting of the original CAPM the expected return of a security or portfolio is greater, the greater its market risk. Non-market risk is not rewarded with higher expected return.

This principle can be stated more generally in a form that we will call the Market Risk/Reward Theorem (MRRT):

Only market risk is rewarded with higher expected return.

This purports to describe actual capital markets, and is hence part of a positive economic theory. Under some circumstances there may follow normative advice that we will call the Market Risk/Reward Corollary (MRRC):

Don't take non-market risk.

The original CAPM leads to an interesting and perhaps correct statement about expected returns and risks (the MRRT) but also to the prediction that all investors will use a market-like index fund for all but their riskless investments. In fact, only a minority of investors do this, so this implication of the model is inconsistent with observed behavior. Nonetheless, the standard presentation of the CAPM concludes that most investors should put most (if not all) of their at-risk money in a broadly diversified market-like portfolio—that is, obey the MRRC.

2.5. Cases

In this book we consider a number of possible *cases*, each of which describes a miniature version of a stylized capital market. In some cases the MRRT holds exactly; in others it holds only approximately (i.e., market risk is a source of expected return but not the only one). In some cases the MRRC represents sound investment advice; in others it must be modified (i.e., some investors should take non-market risk). In some cases market risk can be measured in the manner specified in the original CAPM; in others a different measure is appropriate. And so on.

In an important sense, each case represents a *view* of the nature of the capital market and the best approach to adopt when determining the most appropriate saving and investment strategy for an investor. As indicated earlier, anyone making such decisions or advising others concerning such decisions should have some such view.

Those unfamiliar with the theoretical and empirical work in finance might expect there to be solid evidence in favor of one of these views. Unfortunately this is not the case. Investment decisions are about the future. The relevant aspects are the *probabilities* of possible future events. Investment theory and practice are concerned with *expected future* returns and the associated *future risks*. Information on the frequencies of past events, historic average returns, and variabilities of historic returns may be useful in assessing future prospects, but conditions change and with them future prospects, security prices, and capital market opportunities. At the very least, empirical evidence needs to be combined with the results of experiments in which human beings make decisions concerning uncertain future prospects before a particular view about the capital markets is adopted.

Most of the figures and tables in the book are taken directly from workbooks prepared for cases processed using the APSIM program. This makes it possible for others to replicate the experiments.

2.6. Agreement

This chapter follows in the tradition of the original CAPM by assuming that investors agree on the probabilities of alternative future outcomes. To obtain more general results, however, we do not use standard mean/variance assumptions for the cases in this chapter. In later chapters we show that the specific conclusions of the CAPM can be obtained if special assumptions are made.

2.7. Case 1: Mario, Hue, and the Fish

We now turn to a case designed to include many of the factors in Figure 2-1 and yet be as simple as possible. While economists often choose forestry metaphors ("trees"), we adopt a nautical setting to reflect the author's location on the California coast.

The protagonists are Mario, who lives in Monterey and works at the Monterey Fishing Company, and Hue (rhymes with "whey"), who lives in Half Moon Bay and works at the Half Moon Bay Fishing Company. The investors start out with shares of company stock, with ticker symbols MFC and HFC. Only two dates are of interest—now and later. Mario and Hue consume only fish, and the securities pay off in fish as well. Both players have fish now and must rely on the payoffs from their portfolios for fish later.

The fishing companies will provide the owners of their securities with all the fish that will be caught at the future date. However, the catch will depend on the whims of nature. Two aspects are important. First, how many fish come to the California coast? Second, do these fish favor the north (Half Moon Bay) or the south (Monterey)? There are four different future states. Mario and Hue agree on the sizes of the catches in each of these states and make predictions about the chances of the alternative outcomes. Their goal is to trade with one another until the fish—present and alternative future amounts—are shared voluntarily in the best possible way.

In this case, Mario and Hue have the same opinions about the chances of next year's catch. We use the term *agreement* to connote such a situation. Much of the literature on asset pricing explicitly or implicitly makes this assumption. For example, many books and articles analyze the expected returns on assets. But expected returns are computed using probabilities (as are standard deviations, correlations, and other such measures). If individuals differ concerning

FIGURE 2-2
Case 1: Securities Table

Securities:	Consume	Bond	MFC	HFC
Now	1	0	0	0
BadS	0	1	5	3
BadN	0	1	3	5
GoodS	0	1	8	4
GoodN	0	1	4	8

probabilities, that is, if there is *disagreement*, whose probabilities are to be used? We devote considerable attention to this issue in Chapter 6. For now, we follow common practice.

In this case, markets are *incomplete*. We use this term to mean that there are some trades that cannot be made using available securities. Some of the cases in later chapters involve *complete* markets, which represent the ultimate in security availability, albeit at the cost of some lack of realism.

Here, as in subsequent cases, we show inputs and outputs from the APSIM program. *Securities* provide payments at one or more dates and states. For generality, we specify the amount each security pays in each state, including the present.

The payoffs provided by each of the securities in each possible state of the world are shown in a *securities table* (Figure 2-2). For Case 1, each row in the table represents one of the five states. The first is the present ("Now"). The others are named to indicate the size of the total catch ("Bad" or "Good") and whether more fish go south ("S") or north ("N"). The last two columns show the payoffs (fish per share) for each of the two stocks. Neither stock provides any fish today, as the entries in the first row indicate. As we will see, each company has 10 shares outstanding. Thus the total catch is 80 fish in states BadS and BadN, with Monterey doing better in the former and Half Moon Bay doing better in the latter. The total catch is also the same (120) in both the GoodS and GoodN states, with the two areas dividing the catch differently, as before. As will be seen, these features are highly relevant.

The first column, labeled "Consume," represents a security that pays one fish now and none at any other time or circumstance. It is included so that current consumption can be represented as being provided by securities in an individual's portfolio. This makes it possible to represent decisions to consume less (or more) now in order to consume more (or less) in the future as matters of portfolio choice. Crucial decisions concerning how much to save and invest are thus integrated with more traditional decisions about the allocation of savings among traditional securities. Savings and investment decisions thus are simply parts of the overall portfolio choice decision.

There are no units of the second security ("Bond") in existence when this story begins. This security pays one fish at the future date, no matter what happens. Whatever one thinks the probabilities of the four future states may be, one bond will pay one fish, so that it is truly *riskless*. It is included so that Mario and Hue can make deals in which one of them "issues" a bond to the other, in return for a present payment. Formally, the issuer will have a negative number of bonds while the buyer will have a positive number. In more conventional terms, the issuer will have *borrowed* money and the other party will have *lent* money. In practice, such activities are usually conducted through financial institutions. Thus Hue might deposit money (fish) in a bank so that Mario could obtain a loan (take the current fish in return for promising to pay that amount back with interest). Here such arrangements are made directly, with the bond payoffs providing a template.

In this case, and throughout this book, we consider only securities with payoffs that are represented in the securities table by positive numbers or zeros. Traditional securities such as stocks, bonds, and options provide this type of *limited liability*. More complex securities, such as swaps and futures contracts, require the holder to make payments in some states of the world and require frequent monitoring of credit and/or payments made prior to the future date. We do allow negative holdings of limited liability securities, subject to a credit check, as will be seen.

In this case there are four securities and five states. Formally, if there are fewer securities than states, a market is said to be *incomplete*. If there are as many or more securities than states it can be *complete* in the sense that any desired combination of consumption across states can be obtained by choosing appropriate positions in the available securities. In an incomplete market such as this, some ways of sharing outcomes between the two investors cannot be attained by trading available securities. This may or may not preclude mutually desirable financial arrangements. We explore this matter in detail in later chapters.

Initially Mario has 10 shares of MFC and Hue has 10 shares of HFC. Neither has any bonds. Finally, each has 49 fish at present. The portfolios table for Case 1 is shown in Figure 2-3.

FIGURE 2-3
Case 1: Portfolios Table

Portfolios:	Consume	Bond	MFC	HFC
Mario	49	0	10	0
Hue	49	0	0	10

FIGURE 2-4

Case 1: Probabilities Table

Probabilities:	Now	BadS	BadN	GoodS	GoodN
Probability	1	0.15	0.25	0.25	0.35

The probabilities of the states are shown in Figure 2-4. Each entry indicates the probability that the indicated state will occur. The entries in a row that pertain to the same date sum to 1, because one and only one of the alternatives will occur. The probability that the present state will occur is, of course, 1. In this example, good times are more likely than bad times. Moreover, whether the overall catch is good or bad, the fish are more likely to go north than they are to go south.

In this case, the investors agree on the probabilities of the alternative states and their assessments of the probabilities are correct. This is a characteristic of all the cases in this chapter. In subsequent chapters we consider cases in which an investor can make predictions resulting in probability estimates that differ from those of other investors and/or from the actual probabilities shown in the probabilities table.

We come now to the matter of each player's *preferences*. Two aspects are important. The first concerns attitudes toward consumption at alternative *times*, other things equal. We represent this by a *time preference*, or *discount*. By convention, current consumption serves as a numeraire, with the time preference indicating the desirability of a unit of consumption at a future time, expressed relative to present consumption. In this case, both Mario and Hue consider a unit of consumption in the future as good as 0.96 units now, as shown in the first column of Figure 2-5.

In some cases people will have different views about the desirability of consumption in alternative future states. Thus Mario may consider consumption in south states more desirable than in north states if the fish tend to go south in cold winters in which sufficient nutrition is more valuable. Later we explore the implications of such cases, which involve *state-dependent preferences*. In the

FIGURE 2-5

Case 1: Preferences Table

Preferences:	Time	Risk Aversion
Mario	0.96	1.5
Hue	0.96	2.5

cases in this chapter, however, the desirability of consumption in a state depends only on the amount consumed in that state and the date (now or later).

The other aspect of preferences concerns attitudes toward *risk*. Few people are comfortable with risk, especially when it can lead to a serious reduction in standard of living. In the settings in this book a thoughtful investor will take on risk only in order to achieve higher expected return. But investors differ in their willingness to accept risk in pursuit of higher expected return. As will be seen, the concept of *marginal utility* is helpful for characterizing investors' attitudes toward risk. We discuss this in detail in Chapter 3. For now it suffices to characterize the entries in the last column of the preferences table as numeric measures of *risk aversion*. Hue is more averse to taking on risk in the pursuit of return than is Mario. Not surprisingly, this will lead them to hold different portfolios.

Figures 2-2 to 2-5 constitute the inputs for Case 1. Subsequent cases will include many more features.

2.8. Trading

To improve their situations, Mario and Hue need to trade with one another. They have to consider the terms on which they might be willing to make trades, then reach mutually agreeable arrangements.

Interpreting the setting literally, we might expect Mario and Hue to negotiate with one another using bluffing, feigned disinterest in desirable trades, concealed information about current holdings, and so on. But our interest is not in small markets with personal hand-to-hand combat. Mario and Hue are simply vehicles for understanding larger economies. Thus we will assume that they use a trading mechanism more appropriate for markets with large numbers of participants.

2.8.1. The Role of the Market Maker

In particular, we invoke the services of a *market maker* who gathers information and facilitates trades. Because we are interested more in the properties of equilibrium in capital markets than in the manner in which equilibrium is established, we adopt a trading process that at best only approximates the ways in which actual financial markets operate.

Our market maker's job is to conduct markets for each of the securities, executing trades among the investors. A set of such markets, one for each security, constitutes a *round* of trading. If no trades are made in a round, the process is complete and equilibrium has been attained. If some trades are made in a round, additional rounds are conducted, as needed. Each security market is

---

Do a *round* of trades.

For each security from 2 through *n*:
      Conduct price discovery.
      Select a trade price.
      Obtain bid and offered quantities from investors.
      Make trades for the smaller of amounts bid and offered.

If any trades were made in the last round, do another round.

Figure 2-6 The market maker's procedures.

conducted in four phases. First, the market maker polls investors to obtain information on the prices at which they would enter into trades and possibly on the amounts that they would trade at various prices. This is generally termed the process of *price discovery.* In the second phase, based on the information obtained in the first phase, the market maker announces a price at which orders for trades may be submitted. In the third phase, given the announced price, each individual submits an offer to buy a number of shares, an offer to sell a number of shares, or no offer at all. In the fourth and final phase, the market maker executes the orders. If there is a disparity between the total number of shares offered for sale and the total amount investors would like to buy, some orders are only partially filled. If the quantity demanded exceeds the quantity supplied, all sell orders are executed in full and each buyer is allocated a pro-portionate amount of his or her order, with the proportion given by the ratio of the total amount offered for sale divided by the total amount bid. If the total number of shares buyers wish to purchase is less than the total amount sellers wish to sell, all purchase orders are executed in full, with the corresponding portion of each of the seller's orders filled. Figure 2-6 summarizes the process.

A key function of a market is to establish a price at which substantial num-bers of shares will be traded. In the process of price discovery, a skilled market maker will gather enough information to obtain a good estimate of such a price, often by polling a representative subset of likely buyers and sellers. In our sim-ulations, the market maker gathers information from all the investors. A key aspect is each investor's *reservation price* for a security. The concept is straight-forward: an investor will not buy shares at any price above his or her reserva-tion price and will not sell shares for any price below the reservation price. In our setting, the reservation price for an investor will be unique. Later we show why this is the case.

In the simplest version of our trading process, the market maker chooses a trade price based solely on investors' reservation prices. More specifically, the market maker (1) averages the reservation prices for all potential buyers, (2) averages the reservation prices for all potential sellers, and then (3) sets the trade price halfway between the two amounts. An investor is a potential buyer at a price if no constraints would preclude the purchase of at least some shares. Correspondingly, an investor is a potential seller at a price if no constraints would preclude the sale of at least some shares. In the typical case in which no constraints are binding, the resulting trade price will simply be the average of the investors' reservation prices.

For the cases in this book, the market maker takes this relatively simple approach. In cases with great disparities among investors' situations, however, this may result in markets in which there are considerable differences between the amounts demanded and those supplied at the announced price. To better handle such cases the simulation program allows for a more information-intensive procedure. In this approach the market maker polls investors to find out how many shares they would purchase or sell at various possible prices, then chooses the price that will maximize the number of shares actually traded (i.e., the smaller of the quantity demanded or supplied). The first price tried is the same as in the simpler procedure. If there is excess demand at that price, the next price chosen is halfway between it and the highest unconstrained reservation price (at which there is excess supply). If there is excess supply at the first price, the next price chosen is halfway between it and the lowest unconstrained reservation price (at which there is excess demand). The process can be repeated as many times as desired, always choosing a price halfway between the most recent price with excess demand and that with excess supply.

Real markets are far more complex than our simulations. Market makers and/or traders work hard to estimate the levels of demand and supply at various prices but must eventually act on less than perfect information about investors' likely choices. On the other hand, conditions rarely change radically overnight; thus recent prices convey substantial amounts of information concerning prices that will balance current supply and demand.

While the simulated market mechanisms are far from realistic, they lead to plausible equilibria and thus serve our purposes.

2.8.2. Investor Demand and Supply

How does an investor determine the amount to buy or sell at a given trade price? If the trade price is below the investor's reservation price for the security, he or she will wish to purchase shares. In our simulations, investors' *demand curves* are downward-sloping—the larger the number of shares purchased, the lower is the resulting new reservation price. Given this, it is best for the investor to purchase shares until the reservation price for an additional share equals the trade price. If this is feasible, the investor will submit a purchase order for that number of shares. If only a smaller amount may be purchased, the investor will submit an order for the largest quantity allowed.

If the trade price is above the investor's reservation price for the security, he or she will wish to sell shares. In our simulations, investors' *supply curves* are upward-sloping—the larger the number of shares sold, the higher is the resulting new reservation price. Given this, it is best for the investor to sell shares until the reservation price for an additional share equals the trade price. If this is feasible, the investor will submit a sell order for that number of shares. If only a smaller amount may be sold, the investor will submit an order for the largest quantity allowed.

If an investor's reservation price equals the trade price, he or she will submit neither a sell order nor a buy order.

When stating reservation prices and determining orders, it is assumed investors avoid "playing games." In large markets, this is likely to be sensible behavior. But in a market with few investors, an individual might well decide to engage in tactical behavior, providing less than truthful answers to the market maker's inquiries. Thus Mario might claim that he would buy HFC shares only if the price were very low, hoping thereby to be able to buy shares at a low price. Hue might alter her offer to sell HFC shares in one round in the hope that she could thereby obtain a better outcome in a subsequent round, and so on. We rule out such behavior, assuming that each of the players provides truthful information to the market maker and does not try to take into account possible side effects on other players or on subsequent markets. We do so because our goal is to simulate a relatively simple trading process that can mirror at least some of the characteristics of the larger markets for which our cases serve as proxies.

2.8.3. An Example of a Market for One Stock

Figure 2-7 illustrates the process of making a market for one security. The graph shows the relationship between price per share (in present fish) and the number of shares demanded or supplied if the first security traded were HFC stock. Rounding slightly, Mario's reservation price is 7, while Hue's is 5. This reflects that fact that initially Mario has no HFC stock and Hue has only HFC stock. In a sense, he wants it more than she does.

At prices above 5, Hue would like to sell HFC shares. Her supply curve shows that the higher the price, the more shares she will be willing to sell. Mario is willing to buy shares as long as the price is less than 7. His demand curve shows that the lower the price, the more shares he would like to buy. At any price between 5 and 7 the two will be willing to trade HFC shares.

In this case, the market maker can concentrate on the range between the two investors' reservation prices (5 and 7). The quantity demanded will equal the quantity supplied at a price close to 6, the average of Mario and Hue's reservation prices. At this price Mario would like to buy 0.68 shares and Hue would like to sell him 0.68 shares. The market maker thus announces the trade price is 6, takes orders, and executes the trades.

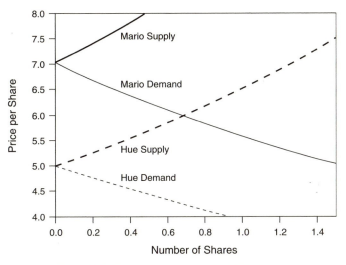

Figure 2-7 Demand and supply for HFC shares.

2.8.4. Purchase and Sale Constraints

It might seem that there would be no reason to constrain investors from buying or selling any number of shares they might desire. Neither Mario nor Hue would voluntarily choose to make a trade that would result in negative consumption in any state as starvation is not an attractive alternative. But some investors might be happy to take positions that would require net payments to creditors in at least some states of the world. Why? Because most countries provide both welfare payments and the possibility of escaping debts by declaring bankruptcy. To avoid this possibility the simulated market maker does not allow any investor to submit a bid or ask offer that would, if executed in full, result in consumption in any future state below a minimum level. This is set at the larger of (1) a very low subsistence level and (2) the investor's *salary* in that state. The first constraint is provided to reduce processing time, and the second to avoid the possibility that an investor will make a promise that can be abrogated by declaring bankruptcy.

2.8.5. Simulation Precision

In practice, markets and investors do not squeeze every last benefit from the trading process, in part because trading uses up resources. In our simulations, no expenses are associated with the market making function, but we stop somewhat short of perfection in order to reduce processing time. Our market maker will not open a market for a security if the highest bid price is only slightly above the lowest ask price. Similarly, an investor may submit a buy or sell order that would still leave a small gap between his or her reservation price and the trade price. The required degree of precision for a simulation can be altered, if desired. As is typical with numeric processing, greater precision increases processing time. For most of the cases in this book, the precision level was set at the APSIM program's default level to provide a balance between processing time and precision.

2.8.6. The Impact of Trading on Equilibrium Conditions

While our trading procedures enable investors to reach equilibrium, the final equilibrium conditions depend to an extent on both the initial conditions and the way in which trading is conducted. This is undoubtedly true in the real world as well. As indicated earlier, no claim is made that the way in which we simulate the trading process is either representative or superior to other possible approaches. We are interested in the general properties of equilibrium in capital markets, not the specific manner in which such an equilibrium may be reached.

2.9. Equilibrium

Many aspects of the equilibrium reached by Mario and Hue are of interest, both in their own right and as illustrations of more general principles.

2.9.1. Portfolios

Figure 2-8 shows the equilibrium portfolios for Mario and Hue, along with the sum of all individuals' holdings, that is, the *market portfolio*. Since we assume no transactions costs, the market portfolio is always the same; trading only changes the division of its components among investors.

As can be seen, both Mario and Hue have *diversified*. Each holds a replica of the market portfolio of stocks. In aggregate, there are equal numbers of shares

FIGURE 2-8
Case 1: Equilibrium Portfolios Table

Portfolios:	Consume	Bond	MFC	HFC
Market	98.00	0.00	10.00	10.00
Mario	48.77	–12.16	6.24	6.24
Hue	49.23	12.16	3.76	3.76

of MFC and HFC stock, and each of the investors chooses to hold equal numbers of shares of the two stocks. To be sure, Mario has 62.4 percent of each company's shares (6.24/10.0) while Hue has 37.6 percent (3.76/10.0). But as long as an investor holds the same percentage of the outstanding shares of available securities, we say that he or she "holds a market portfolio."

2.9.2. Consumption

It is straightforward to determine an individual's consumption in each state, given portfolio holdings and the security payoffs in the states. In Figure 2-9 we show the amounts of consumption in each state for each of our actors and for the aggregate (which we term the market consumption).

Not surprisingly, the total amount available for consumption in each state is fixed; the trades only change the allocation among individuals.

Four aspects of the equilibrium situation deserve comment.

First, Mario has arranged to have the same consumption in each of the bad states, as has Hue. This is also the case for the good states. Each of them has thus diversified away any risk associated with the eventual division of the total catch between north and south. Neither investor has chosen to take any *non-market risk* because such risk is diversifiable. It is always possible for investors to allocate assets so that no one is subject to non-market risk. In this case, since our investors agreed on the probabilities of alternative future states, it was in their mutual interest to do so.

Second, both Mario and Hue remain vulnerable to the risk arising from uncertainty about the total catch, although to different extents. Thus they both bear *market risk* that cannot be diversified away. Ultimately someone must bear this fundamental societal risk. This is of great importance. Asset pricing theory focuses on the distinction between the risk associated with the *size* of the economic pie (market risk) and the risk associated with the *division* of the pie among securities (non-market risk). We will see that the two types of risk are associated with very different expected returns.

Third, Mario has chosen to take more market risk than has Hue. This is not surprising because he is less averse to risk. The equilibrium portfolios show how

FIGURE 2-9
Case 1: Consumptions Table

Consumptions:	Now	BadS	BadN	GoodS	GoodN
Market	98.0	80.0	80.0	120.0	120.0
Mario	48.8	37.8	37.8	62.7	62.7
Hue	49.2	42.2	42.2	57.3	57.3

this happened. Hue ended up holding 12.16 bonds, each of which will pay her one fish no matter what the future state may be. Thus she knows with complete certainty that her bond holdings will provide her with 12.16 fish in the future. Mario created those bonds for Hue, so he will have to pay her 12.16 fish in the future. Of course, Hue paid Mario something to effect this transaction, which is why Mario ended up with 6.24 shares of both MFC and HFC stock and Hue with only 3.76 shares of each. They chose to take different amounts of market risk.

Finally, the actual outcome will have a major impact on the welfare of the investors. This can be seen in the consumptions table. If times are bad, Mario will be worse off than Hue, with 37.8 fish instead of her 42.2. On the other hand, if times are good, Mario will be better off, with 62.7 fish, compared to Hue's 57.3. This highlights an important point about gains through trade under conditions of risk. After each trade, all parties consider themselves better off. But when the future arrives and the actual state of the world is determined, some investors will be worse off than if they had not traded at all. For example, if the state is BadS, Mario will have 37.8 fish, compared with the 50 he would have had without trading. On the other hand, Hue will be better off, with 42.2 fish, compared to her initial amount of 30. A portfolio choice that is desirable before the fact (*ex ante*) can turn out to be undesirable after the fact (*ex post*). Such is the nature of risk.

2.9.3. Gains through Trade

In this case, two factors contributed to Mario and Hue's *ex ante* gains through trade—diversification and the division of market risk between them.

Here, as in many cases in the real world, large gains from sensible portfolio choice may come from achieving adequate diversification. Among financial economists, a standard mantra is "diversify, diversify, diversify." But many investors follow a different path. For example, many people invest substantial portions of their retirement savings in stocks of the companies that employ them. This may provide an incentive to work harder but it leaves much to be desired from an investment standpoint. Concentration of a portfolio in the stock of a single company exposes the owner to substantial non-market risk, which can be avoided through diversification. Mario and Hue know this.

Another drawback associated with investing in company stock is not present in this case, since Mario and Hue do not rely on their employer for any income other than that from their stocks. But many who hold company stock in retirement plans are subject to some risk that their employer will not provide raises or might lay off employees if profits decline or vanish. An employee who holds company stock runs the risk of receiving two concurrent sets of bad news: (1) you are out of work and (2) your retirement savings have suffered a large decline. Absent a compelling argument to the contrary, it is wise to avoid excessive holdings of stock in the company for which one works.

In this case, neither Mario nor Hue takes any non-market risk. But Mario takes more market risk than does Hue. This is not surprising because Hue is more averse to risk than is Mario. But why does Mario choose to take more than his share of market risk? The answer is that while his portfolio has more risk than the market portfolio (which is bad), it also has more expected return (which is good). On the other hand, Hue's portfolio has less risk and expected return than the market portfolio. Both achieve *ex ante* gains through trade by taking different levels of market risk.

For some investors, the *ex ante* gains through trade may not be highly sensitive to small variations in the amount of market risk taken. One sometimes sees aspects of this in the real world. When presented with the consequences of alternative efficient investment strategies, some people find it difficult to make a choice, finding it hard to decide on the amount of risk to be taken in the pursuit of higher expected return. Of course, while differences in *ex ante* gains through trade associated with different efficient portfolios may be small, differences in *ex post* results can be very large.

2.9.4. Asset Prices

Thus far we have focused on Mario and Hue's portfolio choices. It is time to turn to asset prices.

Security prices are used for many purposes, including portfolio valuation. For example, a mutual fund may calculate its net asset value at the end of the day using reported closing prices for the component securities. Typically, the closing price is the price at which the last transaction took place prior to an official "closing time" (4 p.m. EST for U.S. securities). Famously, the transaction in question might have taken place just before the close or considerably earlier (a phenomenon that has led some investment managers to attempt to profit at the expense of other shareholders).

Some bond funds value their holdings using the highest available bid price for each security, in an attempt to determine the value for which the portfolio could be sold. When closing prices are likely to be too stale, equity funds may use a "fair value," which is often estimated by averaging the highest bid and lowest ask price.

For most purposes, one is really interested in the *next* price, not the last. At what price could current holdings of a security be sold? At what price could additional shares be purchased? Answers to these questions require information on current ask and bid prices, respectively.

We follow this approach, using the reservation prices of the investors for each of the securities after trading has ceased. The results for this case are shown in Figure 2-10.

In this equilibrium, both Mario and Hue were able to purchase or sell shares of the securities if they desired. For each security, their reservation prices were

FIGURE 2-10
Case 1: Security Prices Table

Security Prices:	Consume	Bond	MFC	HFC
Market	1.00	0.96	4.35	4.89
Mario	1.00	0.96	4.35	4.89
Hue	1.00	0.96	4.35	4.89

the same (to two decimal places) and hence there was no basis for further gains through trade. This is not surprising. If there were a significant difference between Mario's reservation price for a security and Hue's reservation price, each could gain through further trading. Absent constraints on trading, investors will adjust their portfolios until their reservation prices for a security differ by less than the threshold amount required to make a market.

The top line in the security prices table shows the *market price* for each security. This is the price at which an additional round of trade would take place if a market were to be conducted following the simulated trading procedure. For all the cases in this book, the market price for a security is calculated by (1) averaging the reservation prices of all investors who could purchase shares, (2) averaging the reservation prices of all investors who could sell shares, and then (3) finding the average of the first two amounts. In most cases, no investors are bound by constraints on trading so the market price is simply the average of all the investors' reservation prices.

2.9.5. Security Returns

The *return* on a security depends on its price and its payoff at a future date, and the payoff depends on the future state. It is straightforward to compute the return on a security in each state. For example, MFC stock costs 4.35 and pays 5.00 in state BadS. Thus an investment of 1 fish returns 1.149 fish in that state. This is often reported as a percentage change—here, 14.9 percent. For convenience, throughout we will use *total returns*, calculated by dividing future payoffs by the current price. The returns on the securities for this case are shown in Figure 2-11.

2.9.6. Portfolio Returns

We can also compute the returns on *investment portfolios*, which exclude the first security (present consumption). To do so we compute the value of all the other investment securities (by multiplying the price of each security by the number

FIGURE 2-11
Case 1: Security Returns Table

Security Returns:	BadS	BadN	GoodS	GoodN
Market	0.865	0.865	1.298	1.298
Bond	1.044	1.044	1.044	1.044
MFC	1.149	0.690	1.839	0.920
HFC	0.613	1.022	0.817	1.634

of shares held and summing the products), then divide the total amount received from the portfolio in each state by the initial value of the portfolio. Figure 2-12 shows the returns in each state for Mario and Hue's portfolios and for the market portfolio, which includes the holdings of all investors.

2.9.7. Portfolio and Market Returns

The information in Figure 2-12 is graphed in Figure 2-13. Each point represents a state and a portfolio, with the market return plotted on the horizontal axis and the portfolio return on the vertical axis. For convenience, points for the same portfolio are connected with lines. In this case, the steepest line shows Mario's returns, the least steep shows Hue's returns, and the line in the middle shows the returns on the market portfolio.

In Figure 2-13 there appear to be only two points for each portfolio. In fact, there are four. But for each portfolio the return is the same in each of the two bad market states and the return is the same in each of the two good market states. The result is that each portfolio's points fall on a curve (here a line). This is a result of great relevance. The only source of uncertainty for either Mario or Hue is the overall return on the market. Each takes only *market risk*. *Non-market risk* can be diversified away and neither Mario nor Hue has chosen to take any of it. Thus each of the investors is following the advice of the MRRC.

FIGURE 2-12
Case 1: Portfolio Returns Table

Portfolio Returns:	BadS	BadN	GoodS	GoodN
Market	0.865	0.865	1.298	1.298
Mario	0.820	0.820	1.362	1.362
Hue	0.910	0.910	1.234	1.234

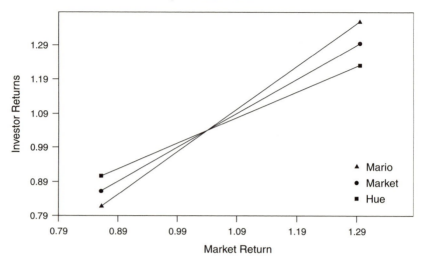

Figure 2-13 Case 1: Investor and market returns.

Graphs of this type will prove central in this book. Any individual for whom portfolio outcomes plot on a single curve in such a diagram can be said to follow a *market-based strategy* and to take only market risk. The curve does not have to be a straight line for this to be the case, but the portfolio must provide the same return in all states of the world with a given market return. For a given investor any scatter of *y* values for a given *x* value in such a *return graph* shows that the investor is taking non-market risk.

2.9.8. Expected Returns

In Case 1 there is complete agreement among the investors about the probabilities of alternative states, so we can unambiguously compute the *expected return* for any security or portfolio. This is simply a weighted average of the returns in the alternative future states, using the probabilities of the states as weights.

Expected returns occupy center stage in much of finance theory. Later we cover cases in which people view expected returns differently. But this cannot happen when there is agreement on probabilities. The expected returns for our securities are shown in Figure 2-14.

The expected return for the bond is, of course, its actual return in all states. Thus the riskless rate of interest is 4.4 percent. Both stocks provide higher expected returns (12.6 percent and 12.4 percent). This is not surprising, because their returns are risky. As we will see, the relevant risk in this regard is the portion related to uncertainty about the overall market, but this discus-

FIGURE 2-14
Security Expected Returns

Security Characteristics:	Exp Return
Market	1.125
Bond	1.044
MFC	1.126
HFC	1.124

sion must await a richer example. The portfolio expected returns are shown in Figure 2-15.

Mario's expected return is considerably greater than that of the market; Hue's is the smallest of the three. Mario expects to beat the market by 2.1 percent and Hue expects to underperform it by 2.0 percent. Of course, if things go badly, Mario will have fewer fish than Hue, as we have seen. This is a standard property of equilibrium—with good news (higher expected return) there is bad news (the possibility of worse results). Mario takes on greater risk and has a higher expected return. Because he has more tolerance for risk, he has chosen a higher combination of risk and expected return.

2.9.9. Risk Premia

For many purposes it is useful to focus on the difference between a return and the riskless rate of interest. This is usually termed an *excess return*. The difference between an expected return and the riskless rate is thus equal to the *expected excess return*. More commonly, it is termed a *risk premium*. Much of financial theory and practice is devoted to the estimation of risk premia and their determinants. The security and portfolio risk premia for this case are shown in Figures 2-16 and 2-17.

The market risk premium in this case is 8.1 percent per year. Mario's expected excess return is greater because he has chosen to be more exposed to

FIGURE 2-15
Portfolio Expected Returns

Portfolio Characteristics:	Exp Return
Market	1.125
Mario	1.146
Hue	1.105

FIGURE 2-16
Security Expected Excess Returns

Security Characteristics:	Exp Return	Exp ER
Market	1.125	0.081
Bond	1.044	0.000
MFC	1.126	0.083
HFC	1.124	0.080

market uncertainty. Hue's is less because she has chosen to be less exposed to market uncertainty.

We can now succinctly characterize key aspects of the equilibrium:

The *reward for waiting* is 4.4 percent.
The *reward for taking market risk* is 8.1 percent.

These are plausible results. Of course they depend on both demand and supply conditions. The key drivers of demand are investors' preferences and positions, while supply is represented by security payoffs, the total available numbers of shares of those securities, and probabilities of the alternative states. In this book we consider only exchange economies, in which supply is fixed, with prices and investors' holdings determined by the terms on which investors trade available securities. To obtain plausible results thus requires plausible inputs. For most of the cases we experimented with different amounts for the total amount of consumption now (security 1) until a plausible expected bond return (reward for waiting) was obtained. For example, in Case 1 the expected future consumption is 104. In a typical economy, expected future consumption is greater than current consumption. To reflect such a condition we thus set the current consumption to be lower than 104. A level of 100 gave an equilibrium with a very small riskless rate of interest. This led to our choice of a total initial consumption of 98.

FIGURE 2-17
Portfolio Expected Excess Returns

Portfolio Characteristics:	Exp Return	Exp ER
Market	1.125	0.081
Mario	1.146	0.102
Hue	1.105	0.061

It may seem strange that the characteristics of equilibrium in this type of exchange economy are so sensitive to the inputs. But this should not be a surprise. If available productive investments lead to a very low interest rate, firms will raise new funds to undertake productive investments offering greater returns. This will lower the total amount available for current consumption and raise the amounts to be received in various future states of the world, leading to a higher interest rate. Our goal is to create cases that reflect plausible prospects for security payoffs. This often leads to the choice of an amount of current consumption designed to accord with a longer run equilibrium process.

2.10. Summary

Case 1 describes an extremely simple economy, yet produces an equilibrium with many features of standard asset pricing models. In particular, our actors, trading with no ultimate social goal in mind, end with positions for which the MRRT holds. Moreover, each adopts a portfolio consistent with the MRRC, as neither chose to take non-market risk. To see why they make these choices we need to go deeper. Such is the task of the next two chapters.

THREE

PREFERENCES

THE TRADING PROCESS used in Case 1 involved a number of markets. In each, the market maker asked Mario and Hue to indicate their reservation prices for a specific security, and then to denote the number of shares they would be willing to buy or sell at an announced price based on those reservation prices. We characterized Mario and Hue's behavior as consistent with downward-sloping demand curves and upward-sloping supply curves. We also represented each of them as having a *time preference* and a *risk aversion*. This was, at best, an opaque description of their preferences. In this chapter, we aim to remove most of the mystery. We provide the details of the types of preferences exhibited by Mario and Hue and introduce some alternative types of investor behavior.

Though trading with fish served us well in Chapter 2, it is time to drop that particular conceit. Henceforth we will refer to payoffs as either units of consumption or *real dollars* (dollars adjusted for changes in purchasing power).

3.1. Expected Utility

It is not unreasonable to assume that an individual will enter into a trade only if he or she would prefer the result to the status quo. Another way to put this is to say that the goal of an investor is to maximize the expected happiness associated with his or her investments. For decades, economists have operationalized this concept by assuming that an investor seeks to maximize *expected utility*. As we will see, this is not an innocuous assumption. On the other hand, it need not be as unrealistic as some believe.

In general, a person's expected utility will depend on the consumptions to be obtained in the states $(X_1, X_2, \ldots)$ and his or her assessment of the probabilities of the states $(\pi_1, \pi_2, \ldots)$:

$$EU = f(X_1, X_2, \ldots, \pi_1, \pi_2, \ldots)$$

Other things equal, for a state with positive consumption and probability, the higher the consumption the greater its contribution to expected utility; and the higher the probability of the state, the greater its contribution to expected utility.

To actually simulate an equilibrium process we need more specificity. To keep things simple, we assume that each level of consumption in a state provides an amount of *utility* (u) and that the utility of consumption in a state is greater the larger the amount of consumption in that state. The expected utility of consumption in a state is simply the utility of consumption in that state times the probability that the state will occur. The overall expected utility is then the sum of the expected utilities for the states:

$$EU = \sum \pi_s u_s(X_s)$$

Assuming that the components of expected utility can be separated into the amounts associated with each state (and time) and then combined can imply actions inconsistent with some people's actual behavior. Substantial research has been devoted to formulations in which a person's utility of consumption in one period can depend on the amounts consumed in prior periods. Though it is possible to simulate such behavior, we will not do so, choosing instead to concentrate on the implications of different types of utility functions.

The equation we have written allows for an investor's utility function to be different in one state than in another. This is an important aspect of some investors' preferences, but we limit our analyses to cases in which an investor's utility function for one state is equal to that for another times a constant. Thus each investor is characterized by a single utility function and a *discount factor* (d_s) for each state, giving an expected utility of

$$EU = \sum \pi_s d_s u(X_s)$$

3.2. Marginal Utility

Thus far we have argued only that the utility of consumption should increase with the amount consumed. This may or may not be true for eating fish but is almost certainly the case for the generalized consumption that can be purchased with money. But what about the rate at which utility increases with consumption? In most of economic theory, consumers are assumed to experience *diminishing marginal utility*, so that the rate of increase in utility is smaller the greater the amount of consumption.

We assumed as much in Case 1. Figure 3-1 shows Mario's utility and Figure 3-2 his marginal utility, both as functions of his consumption. Utility increases with consumption at a decreasing rate, and thus marginal utility decreases with consumption.

Note that the rate at which Mario's marginal utility falls decreases as consumption increases. The curve is downward-sloping but gets flatter as one moves to the right. This could be a complex function with many parameters. But it is not, as can be seen in Figure 3-3, which plots the relationship between the *logarithm* of Mario's consumption and the *logarithm* of marginal utility (i.e., with "log/log" scales).

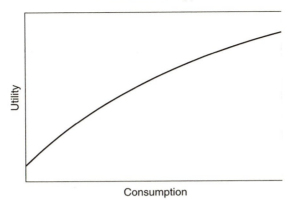

Figure 3-1 Mario's utility function.

Mario's utility curve plots as a straight line in Figure 3-3. Such a line can be described via two parameters—an intercept (a) and a slope (b). Letting m stand for marginal utility:

$$\ln(m) = a - b\ln(X)$$

In terms of the original variables:

$$m = aX^{-b}$$

For Mario, the slope of the curve is -1.5. But recall that we specified that Mario's *risk aversion* was 1.5. We now see what that meant: Mario was assumed to have a marginal utility function that plotted as a downward-sloping line in a diagram such as Figure 3-3 and had a slope of -1.5.

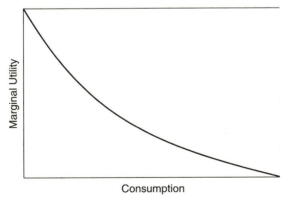

Figure 3-2 Mario's marginal utility function.

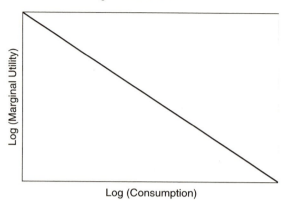

Figure 3-3 Mario's marginal utility function with log/log scales.

To be more precise, the absolute value of the slope of a person's marginal utility curve in a diagram with the log of marginal utility on the vertical axis and the log of consumption on the horizontal axis is his or her *relative risk aversion* at that point. Mario thus exhibits *constant relative risk aversion* (CRRA). So, for that matter, does Hue, but her curve is steeper, with a slope of –2.5. Later we will see some implications of marginal utility functions of this type.

Economists have a term for the slope of a curve when both variables are plotted on logarithmic scales: "In economics, *elasticity* is the ratio of the incremental percentage change in one variable with respect to an incremental percentage change in another variable. Elasticity is usually expressed as a positive number (i.e. an absolute value) when the sign is already clear from context" (Wikipedia).

Thus risk aversion is the elasticity of marginal utility with respect to consumption. For investors with CRRA utility functions, this elasticity is the same for all levels of consumption. Mario's marginal utility decreases by approximately 1.5 percent for every 1 percent increase in consumption, while Hue's decreases by approximately 2.5 percent. (The actual numbers will be slightly different, since we measure elasticity as the slope of the curve at a point rather than the slope of a line connecting two points.)

In a very broad sense, investors with CRRA utility think in terms of percentage rather than absolute changes. Such behavior has been found in other contexts. For example, Stevens (1957) describes psychological experiments in which the amount of sensation is related to the intensity of a stimulus by a formula that exhibits constant elasticity of marginal sensation with respect to stimulus.

We will meet investors with different types of marginal utility curves later in this chapter. Before doing so we turn to relationships between marginal utility and trading behavior. And central to these relationships are securities that we term *state claims*.

3.3. State Claims

In the state/preference approach, a security is viewed as a set of payoffs in different states of the world. Corporations issue securities that can be held directly by individuals. But in modern financial markets, many types of *financial institutions* hold one or more preexisting securities and issue one or more claims on the resulting portfolio. Such activities can either reduce or enlarge the range of possible consumption patterns that investors can obtain. The polar case is one in which institutions or original issuers provide investors with a complete range of choices.

Imagine a financial institution (Carmel Bank) that makes the following offer to anyone holding a share of MFC stock: "Bring us one share of MFC; we will put it in our vault and give you in return the following shares issued by us:

five shares of $BadS,
three shares of $BadN,
eight shares of $GoodS, and
four shares of $GoodN."

These new securities are called *state claims*. For example, to return briefly to our fish example, a share of $BadS states: This share entitles the holder to receive from Carmel Bank one fish if and only if the catch is bad and the fish go south; otherwise the holder gets nothing. The other shares are similar, differing only with respect to the state on which the payment is contingent.

Clearly Carmel Bank can fulfill its obligations. No matter which state occurs, the share of MFC held in its vault will pay precisely the number of fish required for it to discharge its outstanding obligations.

More generally, a state claim pays 1 unit of consumption if and only if a specified state of the world occurs. Since a state has both a time dimension and an outcome dimension, there can be many alternative states and associated state claims. The closest analogy in everyday life is a term life insurance contract. Thus a one-year policy might pay $100,000 in the state "insured is dead at the end of the year" and nothing otherwise. This is equivalent to 100,000 shares, each of which pays $1 in the "dead" state. State claims are often given other names, such as *contingent claims*, *pure securities*, or *Arrow/Debreu securities*.

State claims are the simplest possible type of security. In a sense, they are the *atoms* out of which security matter is constructed. A share of MFC stock can thus be considered to be composed of five shares of $BadS, three shares of $BadN, and so on.

3.4. State Reservation Prices

Imagine that the market maker in Case 1 began by asking each investor for his or her reservation price for 1 unit of $BadS. What would Mario think about before answering the question?

In effect the question concerns the rate at which Mario is willing to substitute a small amount of consumption in state 2 (BadS) for consumption in state 1 (Now). This, in turn, depends on the marginal utilities of consumption in the two states, the discount factors, and the probabilities of the states. A small change in the amount consumed in state 2 will change Mario's expected utility at the rate:

$$\pi_2 d_2 m(X_2)$$

while a small change in the amount consumed in state 1 will change his expected utility at the rate:

$$\pi_1 d_1 m(X_1)$$

Mario's *marginal rate of substitution* is the rate at which he is willing to trade the two claims:

$$\frac{\pi_2 d_2 m(X_2)}{\pi_1 d_1 m(X_1)}$$

For example, if the numerator were half as large as the denominator, Mario would be willing to give up 0.50 units of consumption today to get one additional unit of consumption if (and only if) state 2 occurs.

Since we are concerned with trades in which state 1 (Now) serves as the numeraire, we can simplify the expression for the marginal rate of substitution by recalling that the probability of state 1 is 1 and, by convention, so is the discount factor. Thus an investor's marginal rate of substitution for any future state j will be:

$$r_j = \frac{\pi_j d_j m(X_j)}{m(X_1)}$$

If the price of a claim for state j were greater than this, the investor would offer to sell some units of the claim. If the price were less, he or she would wish to buy some units. The marginal rate of substitution is thus the investor's *reservation price* for state claim j—hence the notation r_j. Other things equal, an investor's reservation price for a state claim will be greater the higher the probability of the state, the greater the discount factor (i.e., the more desirable the consumption in the state), and the greater the marginal utility of the amount currently planned to be consumed in the state. The reservation price for a claim will also be greater the smaller the marginal utility of the amount currently planned to be consumed in the present.

3.5. Characteristics of Marginal Utility Curves

Mario and Hue's marginal utility curves have two important characteristics. First, they are *continuous*—that is, they can be drawn by hand without removing pen from paper. Second, they are *downward-sloping*—that is, marginal utility decreases as consumption increases. These quite plausible assumptions about investor preferences are similar to those made in many non-financial types of economic analysis. Throughout this book, we limit our focus to investors with such preferences. Simply put, we assume that an investor can assess the desirability of an additional unit at any possible current level and that the more he or she has of a good, the less desirable is an additional unit.

It is convenient to use a formal description for this relationship. We will say that for every investor, marginal utility is a *decreasing function* of consumption in each state. The term "function" indicates that there is a one-to-one relationship between the variables, using the dictionary definition (for mathematics):

a. A variable so related to another that for each value assumed by one there is a value determined for the other.

b. A rule of correspondence between two sets such that there is a unique element in the second set assigned to each element in the first set. (*The American Heritage® Dictionary of the English Language*, Fourth Edition)

The term "decreasing" means simply that when one value in a pair is greater, the other is smaller. We will use the term "decreasing function" in other contexts. We will also encounter increasing functions, where the term "increasing" means that when one value in a pair is greater, so is the other.

We have seen that an investor's reservation price for a state claim depends on the characteristics of his or her marginal utility curves. But the key ingredient is the ratio of the marginal utility of consumption in the future state to the marginal utility of consumption at present. If every marginal utility were multiplied by a positive constant, no reservation prices would change. For example, recall the formula for an investor with constant relative risk aversion:

$$m = aX^{-b}$$

Clearly, the value of parameter a will have no effect on reservation prices or, for that matter, demand and supply. It can thus be set to any arbitrary positive constant. For an investor with CRRA preferences, only the degree of relative risk aversion (b) matters.

It is not difficult to show that investors with downward-sloping and continuous marginal utility functions will have downward-sloping demand curves and upward-sloping supply curves for state claims. Assume, for example, that the price for a claim is below Hue's reservation price. She will consider it desirable to buy a small amount—say, 1 unit, leading to a larger planned consumption in the future state. This will decrease the marginal utility of consumption in that state. Of course, she will have to pay for the state claim, decreasing the amount to be consumed at present. This, in turn, will increase the marginal utility of present consumption. The net result is that the marginal rate of substitution for the state claim will decrease, making purchase of an additional quantity less desirable. If the resulting reservation price still exceeds the market price, she will consider purchasing more; if not, she will stop.

Given this line of reasoning, it is clear that for prices lower than an investor's initial reservation price, the lower the market price of a state claim, the more will be demanded by an investor with a downward-sloping continuous marginal utility function. Similar reasoning leads to the conclusion that for prices higher than an investor's initial reservation price, the greater the market price of the claim the more will be supplied.

3.6. Security Reservation Prices

Thus far we have established characteristics of an investor's demand and supply for state claims. But no such claims were traded in Case 1. Nonetheless, investors demanded and supplied the existing securities, and equilibrium was attained. Moreover, they did so using only their assessments of probabilities, discount factors, and marginal utility functions. How did they do it?

The answer is not complicated. Consider Hue contemplating the result of purchasing one share of MFC stock. She notes that a share would provide 5 units of consumption in state 2, each unit of which is worth r_2 to her at the margin. Thus she would be willing to pay approximately $5r_2$ for the additional consumption provided in state 2 by an additional unit of the security. Correspondingly, she would be willing to pay approximately an additional $3r_3$ for the additional consumption provided in state 3 by an additional unit of the security, and so on. In general, if security i provides X_{ij} units of consumption in state j, the reservation price for the security (R_i) will be:

$$R_i = \sum X_{ij} r_j$$

This is consistent with the view that a standard security is composed of atoms (consumption in different future states), leading to the conclusion that the security value equals the sum of the values of the atoms that it contains.

In this book, we deal only with securities that provide a positive or zero payoff in each future state. Such securities are often said to have *limited liability* since there are no circumstances in which the holder may be required to make a future payment to someone else. One who sells such a security need not perform a credit check on the buyer as long as the price is received at the outset. Nor need the seller monitor the buyer's solvency after the sale is consummated.

We do, however, allow investors to take negative (short) positions in securities, but only subject to associated credit checks to ensure that no one enters into any trade that promises future payments that might not be made.

It is easy to see that our investors' demand curves for limited-liability securities will be downward-sloping and that their supply curves will be upward-sloping. As more of a security is purchased, the reservation prices for each of the future states in which there is a payoff will fall. But then so will the reservation price for the security. Similar reasoning shows that supply curves for securities will be upward-sloping. An investor with a decreasing marginal utility function will consider an addition unit of a limited-liability security worth less the more he or she already has.

3.7. Bids and Offers

We have shown how an investor determines a reservation price for a security, given the current amounts of consumption in each of the states. But how does the investor determine the amount to be offered for sale or the amount desired to be purchased at the price announced by the market maker?

The procedure incorporated in the simulator is quite simple. Recall Mario's situation if the first security traded had been HFC shares. His reservation price was 7.00. Hue's was 5.00, and the market maker announced that bids and offers would be taken at a price of 6.00. Clearly Mario will submit a bid to purchase shares, but how many?

To answer the question, the investor begins by considering purchasing as many shares as he can, up to the point at which his present consumption would reach the minimum allowed (1 unit in most cases). Call this quantity Q_H. He then calculates his reservation price for the security if he were to make that change. If it is below the market price he knows that this would be too large an offer, for were he to make such a change he would subsequently want to reenter the market as a seller. In Case 1 this is Mario's situation. He now knows the reservation prices for two possible bids: 0 (which we will call Q_L) and Q_H. For the smaller quantity, the reservation price is above the market price; for the latter quantity the reservation price is below the market price. Clearly, the optimal quantity lies between them.

Mario's next step is also simple. He has two possible quantities, one that is too small (with a reservation price above the market price) and one that is too big (with a reservation price below the market price). He splits the difference, obtaining a new quantity Q_M, halfway between them. Then he calculates the reservation price were he to purchase Q_M shares. If it is greater than the market price, this is not a large enough bid and he should focus on the range between it and Q_H. He thus makes Q_M the new Q_L. If, on the other hand, the reservation price for Q_M shares is above the market price, this is too large a bid and he should focus on the range between Q_L and it. He thus makes Q_M the new Q_H. Either way, Mario has narrowed the range within which the right quantity lies.

Mario continues in this manner, narrowing the range within which the optimal bid lies until the smaller of the two quantities has a reservation price closer to the market price than the precision required for the simulation.

A similar procedure is used to determine the amount supplied if the market price is above the initial reservation price. In cases in which constraints on purchases or sales are binding it may be necessary to stop when a constraint is reached even though the resulting reservation price is above the market price (for bids to purchase) or below it (for offers to sell). We will encounter cases of this sort later, when we consider the influence of investors' positions on prices.

3.8. Expected Utility Maximization

We have revealed the secrets of our investors' decision-making processes. They are rigorous, highly rational, and efficient calculators. Many critics of standard financial economic analysis find the view that capital markets are populated exclusively by such "rational economic persons" too much to bear. They argue that human beings are not perfect computational engines. Instead, they contend, real investors use simple heuristic approaches when dealing with uncertainty, making both logical and calculation errors, resulting in at best clumsy attempts to increase their overall welfare.

There is much merit in such arguments and it would be foolish to defend our characterization of the decision-making process as consistent with the behavior of every investor. However, it is entirely possible that our approach represents a central tendency and that collectively, investors' actions lead to asset prices similar to those that would be obtained in a market populated by such rational actors.

In later chapters, we will meet investors who make erroneous predictions and will see that such errors may tend to cancel one another, leaving asset prices relatively unaffected. It is entirely possible that a similar result would hold if we were to incorporate human foibles in our investors' decision-making processes, but to keep things simple we will not do so. Fortunately, our assumptions are not as extreme as some have argued. The choices made by our investors derive solely from their marginal utility functions. As we have shown, it is possible to multiply any investor's marginal utility function by a constant without affecting his or her choices. Thus no importance should be attached to the absolute magnitude of such a function. This applies, *a fortiori*, to any notion of utility or expected utility. For example, whatever function one might write down for a utility function, the same choices would be obtained if the original function were multiplied by a positive constant and/or a constant added to it.

In a sense, an investor's marginal utility function can be viewed as a representation of some of the characteristics of his or her demand and supply curves for consumption in alternative states of the world. Recall the formula for a state reservation price:

$$r_j = \frac{\pi_j d_j m(X_j)}{m(X_1)}$$

Now consider a situation in which an investor is asked for the reservation price for state j, given the current amounts of consumption in each state. Arbitrarily, we can set $m(X_1)$ equal to 1. This determines $d_j m(X_j)$. Now ask the investor to consider a situation with the same amounts of consumption in every other state but with X_j' in state j and then to indicate the reservation price for state j in that case. The answer will determine $d_j m(X_j')$. In principle, one could use a series of such questions to specify a complete marginal utility function that would "predict" the investor's choices as long as reservation prices are related to marginal utilities in the manner we have assumed.

This is not the only approach that can be used to reveal an investor's marginal utility function from choices that he or she makes in hypothetical situations. In Chapter 7 we describe an experiment that used a promising method with real people to provide empirical evidence about marginal utility functions.

For better or worse, we will soldier on, assuming that investors maximize expected utility with the key assumption that investors consider additional units of consumption worth less, the more they already have.

3.9. Case 2: Mario, Hue, and Their Rich Siblings

Mario and Hue's marginal utility functions had a constant slope when plotted against consumption using log/log scales. We defined the slope in such a diagram as the investor's relative risk aversion. Hence, by definition, both Mario and Hue exhibited constant relative risk aversion. Indeed, the simple default in our simulation program is to give every investor a CRRA marginal utility function, with investors differing only in their degrees of relative risk aversion. But why name the slope in such a diagram relative risk aversion? The reason is that there is an important relationship between this slope and the amount of risk that an investor will take. We illustrate this first with a new case, then examine the formulas for reservation prices to explain the results.

Case 2 is like Case 1 in several respects. The securities are the same, with the same payoffs. Mario and Hue are back, with the same portfolios and preferences. However, they are joined by their rich siblings. At the outset, Mario's sister Marie has twice as much of everything as Mario and Hue's brother Hugo has twice as much of everything as she does. However, preferences appear to be hereditary, since both Mario and Marie have constant relative risk aversions

FIGURE 3-4
Case 2: Portfolios Table

Portfolios:	Consume	Bond	MFC	HFC
Mario	49	0	10	0
Marie	98	0	20	0
Hue	49	0	0	10
Hugo	98	0	0	20

of 1.5, while Hue and Hugo have constant relative risk aversions of 2.5. Figures 3-4 and 3-5 show the new inputs for this case.

As usual, we turn all the investors loose with the assistance of the market maker. When the trading has stopped, they have the equilibrium portfolios shown in Figure 3-6. Not surprisingly, the less risk averse Mario and Marie end up with riskier portfolios, obtained by leveraging portfolios containing market proportions of stocks, while the more risk averse Hue and Hugo hold bonds and smaller positions in portfolios containing market proportions of the stocks.

It is not surprising that Marie has larger positions than Mario, since she is richer. But notice that her positions are all twice as large as Mario's. In terms of proportions of value, Marie and Mario have the same portfolio. This can be seen in the portfolio returns table in Figure 3-7. Despite the disparity in their wealth, Mario and Marie take the same amount of risk. As the tables in Figures 3-6 and 3-7 show, this is also true for Hue and Hugo.

The result is quite general. Absent binding constraints, no matter what their wealth, two investors with the same degree of constant risk aversion who agree on probabilities and have no outside positions will hold the same portfolio measured in terms of relative security values. Equivalently, an investor with constant relative risk aversion will hold the same portfolio proportions by value as he or she gets richer or poorer.

FIGURE 3-5
Case 2: Preferences Table

Preferences:	Time	Risk Aversion
Mario	0.96	1.5
Marie	0.96	1.5
Hue	0.96	2.5
Hugo	0.96	2.5

FIGURE 3-6
Case 2: Equilibrium Portfolios Table

Portfolios:	Consume	Bond	MFC	HFC
Market	294.00	0.00	30.00	30.00
Mario	48.77	−12.16	6.24	6.24
Marie	97.55	−24.32	12.48	12.48
Hue	49.23	12.16	3.76	3.76
Hugo	98.45	24.32	7.52	7.52

It is not difficult to see why this is the case. Consider Mario's reservation prices for the states when he has obtained his equilibrium portfolio. Recall that the reservation price for state j is:

$$r_j = \frac{\pi_j d_j m(X_j)}{m(X_1)}$$

Given the formula for a constant risk aversion marginal utility function, this becomes:

$$r_j = \frac{\pi_j d_j a X_j^{-b}}{a X_1^{-b}}$$

or:

$$r_j = \pi_j d_j (X_j/X_1)^{-b}$$

Now assume that Marie has a portfolio with the same composition but twice as many shares of each security. Since her reservation price for a state depends only on the ratio of consumption in that state to consumption now, she will

FIGURE 3-7
Case 2: Portfolio Returns Table

Portfolio Returns:	BadS	BadN	GoodS	GoodN
Market	0.865	0.865	1.298	1.298
Mario	0.820	0.820	1.362	1.362
Marie	0.820	0.820	1.362	1.362
Hue	0.910	0.910	1.234	1.234
Hugo	0.910	0.910	1.234	1.234

have the same reservation price for that state as does Mario. This will be true for every state. Recall that the reservation price for a security is obtained from its payoffs across states and the reservation prices for states. Thus Marie will have the same reservation price for each security as does Mario. But we know that Mario is happy with his portfolio, given the equilibrium prices of securities. Therefore Marie must be too. In short, Marie will want a portfolio in which each security position is the same multiple of Mario's position. Hence they will take the same risk.

We have created these four investors such that they have constant relative risk aversion and will take the same amount of portfolio return risk whether they are rich or poor. Do many real investors act this way? Introspection and observation suggest that many people are likely to wish to take more portfolio risk as they become wealthier. If so, they must have marginal utility functions with *decreasing relative risk aversion*. We will deal with this possibility later. But first we need to consider the less likely cases in which investors display *increasing relative risk aversion*—choosing to take less portfolio risk as they become wealthier.

3.10. Quadratic Utility Functions

In Cases 1 and 2, all our investors exhibited constant relative risk aversion. For each one, marginal utility was related to consumption by the formula:

$$m = aX^{-b}$$

where a and b are both positive. In addition to the property of constant relative risk aversion, such a function has two other properties, each of which seems consistent with most people's preferences. First, no matter how large consumption (X) may be, the marginal utility of additional consumption is positive. Simply put: more consumption is always preferred to less. Second, marginal utility is infinite if consumption is zero. This is consistent with the unsurprising observation that consumption is highly prized if starvation is the alternative. An investor with this type of utility function will never voluntarily choose to take a chance on starving to death.

While CRRA utility functions are used in many applications in financial economics, there are major exceptions. An alternative assumption, widely used, is that an investor's utility function can be approximated with a quadratic equation:

$$u(X_s) = a + bX_s - cX_s^2$$

and thus the associated marginal utility is linearly related to consumption:

$$m(X_s) = b - 2cX_s$$

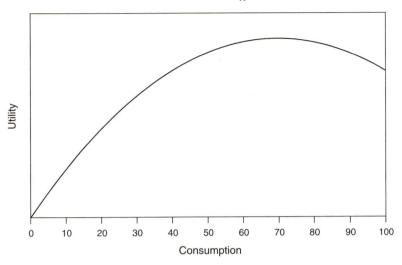

Figure 3-8 A quadratic utility function.

Figures 3-8 and 3-9 show both utility and marginal utility functions for a particular quadratic utility function. Note that, inconsistent with most observed behavior, utility actually peaks at a satiation point (75 in this case), then declines. Correspondingly, the marginal utility of consumption becomes negative after this "satiation point" is reached. Worse yet, marginal utility is still finite when consumption is zero. An individual with such a function might well choose to take a chance on starvation.

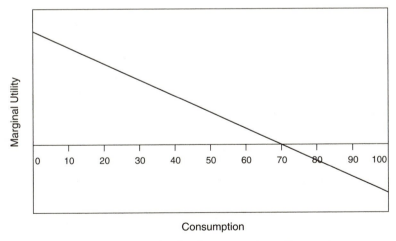

Consumption

Figure 3-9 A marginal utility function with quadratic utility.

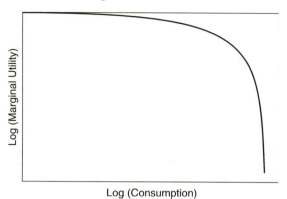

Figure 3-10 A marginal utility function with quadratic utility on log/log scales.

Figure 3-10 plots this investor's marginal utility function on log/log scales. As can be seen, the slope (relative risk aversion) increases as consumption increases. Such an investor becomes more risk averse as his or her wealth increases.

3.10.1. Case 3: Quentin and His Rich Sister Querida

To show the implications of quadratic utility functions we introduce Quentin and his sister Querida. Each starts out with diversified stock portfolios but Querida has twice as much of every security as does Quentin, as shown in Figure 3-11.

Since both investors have quadratic utility we need to specify their utility function types and parameters explicitly, along with the rates at which they discount future consumption. The associated input tables are shown in Figures 3-12 and 3-13.

In the simulator, quadratic utility is denoted type 1 (CRRA is type 2). Only one parameter is required since the ability to multiply marginal utility by a positive constant makes it possible to utilize a function of the form:

$$m = 1 - (1/S)X$$

FIGURE 3-11
Case 3: Portfolios Table

Portfolios:	Consume	Bond	MFC	HFC
Quentin	49	0	5	5
Querida	98	0	10	10

FIGURE 3-12
Case 3: Discounts Table

Discounts:	Future
Quentin	0.96
Querida	0.96

The value of S indicates the satiation level of consumption, at which marginal utility reaches zero. In Figure 3-13 this is 200 for both Quentin and Querida, so their marginal utility functions are the same.

As a practical matter, of course, marginal utility should never be zero (or, *a fortiori*, negative). We handle this awkward aspect in simulations by switching from the quadratic utility function to a CRRA function for values of consumption greater than 99 percent of S. We also impose a requirement that no one's consumption is allowed to be less than a small positive amount, ensuring that only levels of consumption with positive marginal utility will be considered. In Case 3 all chosen levels of consumption are within the range in which the utility function is quadratic, so these precautions have no effect on the results.

Figure 3-14 shows the portfolios chosen by our investors. The results are dramatic, to say the least. Querida, the richer of the two, takes far less risk than Quentin. In fact, she holds fewer shares of each of the stocks than he does. This reflects a lower level of a property termed *absolute risk aversion*. Not only is her relative risk aversion less, so is her absolute risk aversion. This seems an improbable result. However, it follows from the extreme curvature of the marginal utility function in Figure 3-10. A simple way to see this is to think about approximating the curve with a straight line in the range of consumption that an investor will be able to afford. Quentin will be toward the top left part of the diagram where the curve is relatively flat. Thus he will make choices similar to those of a CRRA investor with a low degree of relative risk aversion. Querida will be toward the bottom right part of the diagram and will make choices similar to those of a CRRA investor with a high degree of relative risk aversion.

It is unlikely that very many people truly have quadratic utility functions that apply over the full range of possible levels of consumption. However, over

FIGURE 3-13
Case 3: Utilities Table

Utilities:	Type	Parameter
Quentin	1	200
Querida	1	200

FIGURE 3-14
Case 3: Equilibrium Portfolios Table

Portfolios:	Consume	Bond	MFC	HFC
Market	147.00	0.00	15.00	15.00
Quentin	48.33	−39.52	8.97	8.96
Querida	98.67	39.52	6.03	6.04

a relevant range of consumption an investor's true marginal utility could be well approximated by the linear marginal utility function implied by quadratic utility. This possibility should not be dismissed out of hand, since a great deal of modern investment theory and practice is based on behavior that is consistent with quadratic utility functions.

3.10.2. Mean/Variance Preferences

Despite its possible drawbacks, the assumption that people have quadratic utility over a relevant range of consumption is extremely useful. Absent state-dependent preferences or outside positions, an investor with quadratic utility will care only about the mean (expected return) and variance of return of his or her portfolio. Among a set of portfolios with equal expected return, such an investor will choose the one with the smallest variance, no matter how the shapes of their underlying probability distributions may differ. Portfolios with minimum variance for given expected return are *efficient portfolios* in mean/variance theory. Investors with quadratic utility can approach the selection of a portfolio in two stages: (1) find the set of mean/variance efficient portfolios, then (2) select the one that provides the greatest expected utility, given the investor's attitude toward risk.

To see why mean and variance are *sufficient statistics* for an investor with quadratic utility to use when choosing among alternative portfolios, note that for such an investor the expected utility of a set of consumption values (X) will be:

$$EU = a + bE(X) - cE(X^2)$$

Variance is simply the expected value of the squared difference between a set of values and their means. This implies that:

$$V(X) = E(X^2) - E(X)^2$$

Combining the two equations shows that expected utility can be determined solely from the expected return and variance of a portfolio's outcomes:

$$EU = a + bE(X) - cE(X)^2 - cV(X)$$

As we have shown, the parameter values (a, b, and c) can be summarized with one number, for example, the satiation level (S). A more common approach is to summarize such an investor's preferences in terms of the amount of added expected return he or she requires to take on an additional unit of variance.

While the assumption of quadratic utility leads to the conclusion that investors care only about mean and variance of portfolio returns, this is not the only basis that can be used to assume that investors have such preferences. Such a conclusion can be justified by assuming that all investment portfolios provide return probability distributions that have the same shape and thus can be fully described by two parameters such as the mean and variance. If so, among portfolios with the same variance, the one with the greatest mean (expected return) will be clearly superior (this is the other part of Markowitz's definition of efficient portfolios).

Unfortunately, this line of argument is less than compelling. Even if the total returns from corporations' activities have the same type of probability distribution, this will generally not be true for the securities they issue, nor of options and other derivative products. Thus it seems best to regard mean/variance preferences and the investment methods and equilibrium results derived from assuming such preferences as approximations that will be closer to reality the closer are investors' marginal utility curves to straight lines over the relevant ranges of consumption. Over short periods of time, when returns are unlikely to cover a very wide range of possibilities, mean/variance results may be very useful. But for the analysis of decisions covering extended time periods, when returns can vary substantially, more plausible assumptions about investors' preferences are likely to prove superior.

3.11. Decreasing Relative Risk Aversion

Do rich people take more risk than poor people, the same, or less? We have presented two alternative types of preferences. People with quadratic utility take less risk when they become richer. Those with CRRA utility take the same amount of risk as they become richer. We need at least one type of function that describes investors who are willing to take more risk when their wealth increases. In short, we need a marginal utility curve that plots in a diagram with log/log scales as a curve with a slope that decreases as consumption increases.

There are many ways this can be accomplished. We describe the use of piecewise curves in the next section. Here we present an alternative procedure that involves a single curve. Key is the notion of a minimum consumption level that the investor considers absolutely essential. If he or she were to have only that consumption in any state, the marginal utility of additional consumption would be infinite. Letting M represent this minimum level, we write the investor's marginal utility as:

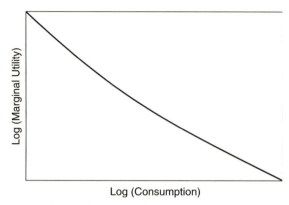

Figure 3-15 A marginal utility function with decreasing relative risk aversion on log/log scales.

$$m = (X - M)^{-b}$$

Figure 3-15 shows the relationship between the logarithm of marginal utility and the logarithm of consumption for a case in which $M = 20$ and $b = 1$. All the amounts of consumption shown are well above 20. The degree of curvature is small, but risk aversion does decrease as consumption increases.

3.11.1. Case 4: David and Danielle

Case 4 introduces two new investors, David and Danielle. Both have decreasing relative risk aversion (type 4 in the simulator) but the parameters for their utility curves are identical. However, Danielle is richer.

The securities and probabilities are the same as in Case 1 and there is agreement. The investors' initial portfolios, discounts, and utilities are shown in Figures 3-16, 3-17, and 3-18, respectively. As shown in Figure 3-18, both David and Danielle have utility functions of type 4 with a minimum consumption of 20 and a risk aversion of 1.

Figure 3-19 shows David and Danielle's portfolios after equilibrium is reached and Figure 3-20 their consumptions in each state. As predicted, Danielle takes

FIGURE 3-16
Case 4: Portfolios Table

Portfolios:	Consume	Bond	MFC	HFC
David	49	0	5	5
Danielle	98	0	10	10

FIGURE 3-17

Case 4: Discounts Table

Discounts:	Future
David	0.96
Danielle	0.96

FIGURE 3-18

Case 4: Utilities Table

Utilities:	Type	MinCons	Risk Aversion
David	4	20.00	1.00
Danielle	4	20.00	1.00

FIGURE 3-19

Case 4: Equilibrium Portfolios Table

Portfolios:	Consume	Bond	MFC	HFC
Market	147.00	0.00	15.00	15.00
David	49.01	9.14	4.07	4.07
Danielle	97.99	−9.14	10.93	10.93

FIGURE 3-20

Case 4: Consumptions Table

Consumptions:	Now	BadS	BadN	GoodS	GoodN
Market	147.0	120.0	120.0	180.0	180.0
David	49.0	41.7	41.7	58.0	58.0
Danielle	98.0	78.3	78.3	122.0	122.0

more risk than David, as indicated by her decision to borrow money from David. Moreover, because she is wealthier, she is able to live better than David, no matter what happens.

But there is more to be learned from this case. The first two rows in Figure 3-21 show the excess amounts each consumes over the minimum consumption and the last row the ratio of Danielle's "excess consumption" to David's.

Note that all the ratios are the same. In effect, each investor has chosen to "lock in" an amount of consumption in each state equal to his or her minimum (20, in this case). Then, with the remaining wealth, each has purchased the same relative amounts of consumption in each of the states. This is not too surprising. After ensuring the minimum amount of consumption, each investor exhibits constant relative risk aversion with his or her remaining resources. Overall, however, relative risk aversion declines as the portion of wealth at risk increases.

Before proceeding, it is useful to note that the function we have used for these examples:

$$m = (X - M)^{-b}$$

is in fact quite versatile. As we have seen, with a positive value of M, interpreted as minimum consumption, it exhibits decreasing relative risk aversion. If M is set to zero it becomes a constant relative risk aversion function. And if M is set to a negative number, it exhibits increasing relative risk aversion. The generic term for all these manifestations is to say that this function exhibits *hyperbolic absolute risk aversion* (HARA), but the reasons for the title need not concern us.

While the simulation program allows for zero or negative values of M, the most interesting cases are those with positive values of M exhibiting decreasing relative risk aversion, with M interpreted as a minimum or subsistence level of consumption. This may characterize the approach that some investors take toward investment when they make statements such as: "I have to get at least M from my investments; after that, I'm willing to take some risk." A HARA utility function with M greater than zero can capture such preferences.

FIGURE 3-21
Case 4: Consumptions in Excess of Minimum Consumptions

Consumptions:	Now	BadS	BadN	GoodS	GoodN
David	29.0	21.7	21.7	38.0	38.0
Danielle	78.0	58.3	58.3	102.0	102.0
Ratio	2.7	2.7	2.7	2.7	2.7

3.12. Kinked Marginal Utility Functions

In experiments conducted by cognitive psychologists, individuals presented with simple decisions under uncertainty tend to make choices that reveal asymmetric views of small gains and losses from some sort of *reference point*. For example, assume that an investor's reference point for next year's consumption is X_r. Someone proposes flipping a coin. If it comes up tails, next year's consumption will be $X_r - \$1$. If it comes up heads, next year's consumption will be $X_r + \$z$. How big does z have to be to get the investor to take the bet? When asked such questions, many people indicate z must be equal to or greater than $2, even though the amounts to be won or lost are small.

Results from numerous cognitive experiments are summarized in variations of the famous *Prospect Theory* of Daniel Kahneman and Amos Tversky (Tversky and Kahneman 1992). This theory posits a model of behavior that differs in several ways from the approach to investment choice that we have used thus far. We will not attempt to examine all of its aspects, choosing instead to concentrate on the characteristic asymmetric views of gains and losses near a reference point.

The most direct way to reflect such an attitude would be to represent an investor as having a discontinuous marginal utility curve, with the marginal utility just to the left of the reference point two or more times greater than the marginal utility just to the right of the reference point. But this would violate our assumption that all investors have downward sloping and continuous marginal utility functions. Fortunately, it is possible to retain our prior assumption but nonetheless capture the essence of this aspect of the behavior implied by prospect theory. The solution is to replace a hard reference point with a slightly soft one. We continue to require marginal utility functions to be continuous and downward-sloping but allow them to have "kinks."

A useful example is provided by a marginal utility function that has three or more segments, each of which exhibits constant relative risk aversion. Consider Kevin, who regards a future consumption close to 50 to be very important. For levels of consumption below 50 he has a constant relative risk aversion of 2. For levels above 50.5 (101 percent of 50) he also has a constant relative risk aversion of 2. But his marginal utility of consumption at 50 is roughly twice as great as his marginal utility at 50.5. We represent this with a segment having a constant relative risk aversion of 70, since for such a function an increase in consumption of 1 percent will reduce marginal utility by slightly more than half (more precisely, $1.01^{-70} = 0.4983$).

Figure 3-22 shows Kevin's marginal utility as a function of consumption while Figure 3-23 shows the relationship using log/log scales. Not surprisingly, the function plots as a piecewise linear curve when the logarithms of the values are utilized. For simplicity we will say that such a function exhibits piecewise constant relative risk aversion.

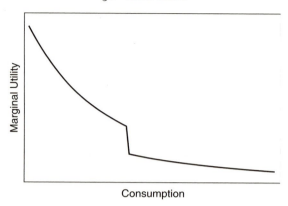

Figure 3-22 A marginal utility function with piecewise constant relative risk aversion.

3.12.1. Case 5: Kevin and Warren

To see an investor with a kinked marginal utility curve in action we utilize a case in which Kevin shares the market with Warren, who is much richer. The securities are once more those of Case 1, as are the probabilities of the states. And, as in all the cases thus far, the investors agree on state probabilities and have no outside positions. Their initial portfolios are shown in Figure 3-24.

Figure 3-25 shows the investors' discounts and Figure 3-26 the parameters of their marginal utility functions. Warren is a constant relative risk aversion investor (type 2) with a risk aversion of 2. Kevin's marginal utility function is of type 4, with the segments we have previously described.

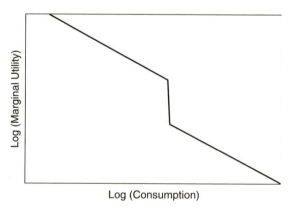

Figure 3-23 A marginal utility function with piecewise constant relative risk aversion on log/log scales.

FIGURE 3-24
Case 5: Initial Portfolios Table

Portfolios:	Consume	Bond	MFC	HFC
Warren	4900	0	500	500
Kevin	49	0	5	5

Despite Kevin's fondness for a consumption of 50, it turns out that both he and Warren can achieve some gains by trading. After the market maker has performed her job, the situation is that shown in Figures 3-27, 3-28, and 3-29.

As the portfolios table in Figure 3-27 shows, Kevin has chosen to take some risk by holding MFC and HFC shares. And, as in all the previous cases, both investors hold market portfolios of risky assets, conforming to the advice of the Market Risk/Reward Corollary. The consumptions table in Figure 3-28 shows that Kevin has decided to take a chance that he will consume less than 50 and to be in a position such that he might be able to consume more than 50. But he still chooses to stay close to his favored comfort zone.

Despite his small show of bravado, Kevin has chosen a quite conservative portfolio, as the returns graph in Figure 3-29 shows. His fortunes are far less related to the market's performance than are Warren's. Although Warren has accommodated Kevin by taking a bit of extra market risk, his returns graph is nonetheless indistinguishable from that of the market as a whole since his portfolio constitutes such a large part of the overall market.

FIGURE 3-25
Case 5: Discounts Table

Discounts:	Time
Warren	0.96
Kevin	0.96

FIGURE 3-26
Case 5: Utilities Table

Utilities:	Type	RiskPref	RefLow	RiskPref	RefHigh	RiskPref
Warren	2	2.00				
Kevin	3	2.00	50.00	70.00	50.50	2.00

FIGURE 3-27
Case 5: Portfolios Table

Portfolios:	Consume	Bond	MFC	HFC
Market	4949.00	0.00	505.00	505.00
Warren	4898.93	−27.70	503.11	503.11
Kevin	50.07	27.70	1.89	1.89

FIGURE 3-28
Case 5: Consumptions Table

Consumptions:	Now	BadS	BadN	GoodS	GoodN
Market	4949.0	4040.0	4040.0	6060.0	6060.0
Warren	4898.9	3997.2	3997.2	6009.6	6009.6
Kevin	50.1	42.8	42.8	50.4	50.4

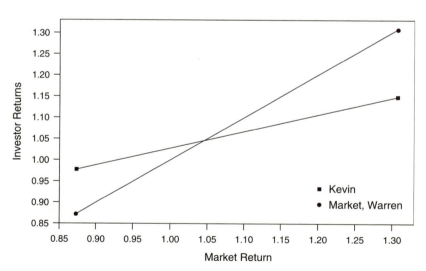

Figure 3-29 Case 5: Returns graph.

3.13. Summary

We have introduced four types (or families) of investor preferences. There is no reason to believe that every investor's preferences can be described via one of the four types, although it may well be possible to approximate any investor's preferences with a piecewise CRRA function if enough pieces are utilized. At the very least, it must be admitted that investors have diverse types of preferences and that real capital markets reflect such diversity.

It is tempting to trumpet the advantage that our simulation approach has over traditional closed-form models, since we can accommodate investors with different types of preferences. Traditional models are often forced to assume that all investors are of one type or, at the least that the market acts as if there were only one investor, whose preferences are "representative" of those of the entire population of investors. But, as we have indicated, simulation has its disadvantages, in particular the difficulty of easily understanding the relationships between inputs and outputs. Nonetheless there are general lessons to be learned from cases such as those we have presented thus far, as subsequent chapters will show.

FOUR

PRICES

THIS CHAPTER FOCUSES on prices—the prices of both securities and the state claims introduced in Chapter 3. Of particular interest are the relationships among expected returns, various measures of risk, and measures of responsiveness to changes in market-wide variables. We introduce alternative versions of the Market Risk/Reward Theorem (MRRT) and investigate the conditions under which one or more version may hold. As in previous chapters, we assume that investors agree on the probabilities of future states, have no outside positions, and discount the utilities from all states at a given time in the same way, leaving for future chapters the investigation of the characteristics of equilibrium when some or all of these assumptions are violated.

4.1. Complete Markets

We have defined a state claim as a security that pays 1 unit if and only if a specific state occurs. We have also argued that such state claims can be considered the atoms of which actual securities are made. While some such claims may be traded explicitly, this is rare. Nonetheless it is extremely useful to consider the characteristics of a world in which all possible state claims can be traded. Such a world is defined as a *complete market*.

If financial institutions and markets operated without cost, everyone could trade their standard securities for state claims in the manner described in Chapter 3. However, it might be more efficient if a market maker simply opened a market for trades in one or more state claims, with sellers able to create them and buyers able to purchase them. In such a case, each state claim, like the bond in our previous cases, would be in zero net supply. And, as with other such instruments, buyers would have to make certain that issuers (sellers) could deliver on their promises.

To simulate a complete market we adopt a sequential approach. We let investors reach an equilibrium using available standard securities; we then open a market for trading state claims. The possible trading procedures used by the market maker for state claims are the same as those used for standard securities. In all the cases in this book, we use the simple type of price discovery in which trades are made in each market using a price halfway between the average of the reservation prices of investors who are able to buy and the average of the reservation prices of those who are able to sell.

In the real world, of course, there are costs of all types, financial and otherwise, so a complete market is at best an approximation to reality. In some cases it may be a good approximation; in others a poor one. We explore these issues in detail later in this chapter. First we examine the characteristics of prices, risks, and expected returns in a complete market.

4.2. Case 6: Quade, Dagmar, and the Index Funds

Case 6 involves only two investors, Quade and Dagmar, but they operate in a considerably richer environment than encountered in earlier examples. There are now ten future states of the world and six standard securities. Figure 4-1 shows the securities table and Figure 4-2 the initial portfolios table.

Those with backgrounds in investments may be familiar with the names of most of these securities. The first is, of course, our usual representation of present consumption. The second is a riskless security representing borrowing and lending—in this case it is called "STBond" to indicate that it is a short-term bond. Each of the remaining securities is an *index fund*—that is, a portfolio that includes proportionate holdings of all the securities of a given type. In this case, it is assumed that every individual security is included in one and only one of the five index funds, which represent, respectively, government bonds, nongovernment bonds, large value stocks, large growth stocks, and small stocks.

FIGURE 4-1
Case 6: Securities Table

Securities:	Consume	STBond	GovBds	NonGvBds	ValueStx	GthStx	SmlStx
Now	1.0000	0.0000	0.0000	0.0000	0.0000	0.0000	0.0000
Depression1	0.0000	1.0000	0.9594	0.8897	0.8772	0.7789	0.8560
Depression2	0.0000	1.0000	1.0672	1.0470	0.7436	0.7164	0.8062
Recession1	0.0000	1.0000	0.8968	0.9038	0.9229	0.9605	0.8989
Recession2	0.0000	1.0000	0.9135	0.9289	0.9297	0.9579	0.8207
Normality1	0.0000	1.0000	1.0692	1.0543	1.1506	0.9814	1.1135
Normality2	0.0000	1.0000	0.9636	0.9940	1.1849	1.0584	1.1672
Prosperity1	0.0000	1.0000	1.1931	1.3131	1.1086	1.1186	1.1186
Prosperity2	0.0000	1.0000	1.0434	1.0377	1.2397	1.3053	1.1915
Boom1	0.0000	1.0000	1.1063	1.1220	1.1793	1.3374	1.4193
Boom2	0.0000	1.0000	1.1085	1.1141	1.2947	1.3060	1.2611

FIGURE 4-2
Case 6: Initial Portfolios Table

Portfolios:	Consume	STBond	GovBds	NonGvBds	ValueStx	GthStx	SmlStx
Quade	515	0	100	100	120	120	60
Dagmar	515	0	100	100	120	120	60

The latter three funds are typical of equity index funds created by financial firms, with each individual stock included in a specific index fund based on the market capitalization of its company's shares and the relationship between its market price and the characteristics of one or more of its accounting measures (e.g., per share book value or earnings).

The index fund returns and initial holdings shown in Figures 4-1 and 4-2 are designed to be reasonably representative of the total returns per dollar invested that might be obtained with different types of economic conditions.

As the state names indicate, there are different overall levels of the economy and total returns from the market portfolio (e.g., depression, recession) and, for each overall level, a different allocation of the total market return across the available investments. Before trading begins, both investors hold market portfolios and avoid non-market risk. Thus Quade will have the same ending value in state Depression1 as in state Depression2, as will Dagmar. This will also be the case for every other pair of states with the same level of the economy. Finally, to lend more credibility, the total numbers of outstanding shares of the index funds have been designed to roughly reflect the size of each sector.

Figure 4-3 shows the probabilities table. The least likely states are associated with depression and boom times. Recession and prosperity states are more likely, and the most likely outcomes are those associated with normal economic times. Finally, for each possible level of overall economic outcome, there are two equally likely divisions of the overall output of the economy.

The investors' names provide a clue to their preferences. Quade has the somewhat improbable preferences represented by a quadratic utility function; thus his risk aversion increases with consumption. Dagmar's preferences are less surprising; her relative risk aversion decreases with consumption. Figure 4-4 shows their discounts and utility parameters, using the conventions described in Chapter 3.

4.2.1. Equilibrium with Conventional Securities

To examine the characteristics of a market with conventional securities we let Quade and Dagmar trade using the short-term bond and the five index funds. When trading stops we find that our investors have chosen to hold very

FIGURE 4-3

Case 6: Probabilities Table

Probabilities:	Now	Depression1	Depression2	Recession1	Recession2	Normality1	Normality2	Prosperity1	Prosperity2	Boom1	Boom2
Probability	1	0.05	0.05	0.10	0.10	0.20	0.20	0.10	0.10	0.05	0.05

FIGURE 4-4
Case 6: Discounts and Utilities Tables

Discounts:		Future	
Quade		0.96	
Dagmar		0.96	

Utilities:	Type	Param1	Param2
Quade	1	600	
Dagmar	4	100	2.00

different portfolios, as shown in Figure 4-5. Quade is more conservative, choosing to lend $211.4 to Dagmar. But otherwise it is hard to discern a pattern. Quade holds more than his proportionate share of nongovernment bonds and value stocks and less than his proportionate share of government bonds, growth stocks, and small stocks. This is not because they disagree about the future prospects of the securities. Nor are they adjusting their portfolios to better fit with other sources of income because there are no outside positions. What is going on here?

The returns graph shown in Figure 4-6 sheds considerable light on this question. Note that both investors have chosen to take non-market risk, as shown by the fact that neither portfolio has returns that plot as a strictly increasing function of the return on the overall market. For example, Dagmar, the more aggressive investor, will have different returns in the two boom states (shown at the right of the graph), as will Quade. This is the case for other levels of market return as well. Neither investor obeys the Market Risk/Reward Corollary (MRRC).

There is more. Neither investor's returns fall near a straight line relating portfolio returns to market returns. Dagmar's returns fall closer to a curve that becomes steeper, going from left to right, while Quade's returns fall closer to a curve that becomes flatter as one proceeds in that direction. Why? Because they

FIGURE 4-5
Case 6: Portfolios Table

Portfolios:	Consume	STBond	GovBds	NonGvBds	ValueStx	GthStx	SmlStx
Market	1030.00	0.00	200.00	200.00	240.00	240.00	120.00
Quade	516.05	211.44	−19.68	111.79	132.14	32.95	28.71
Dagmar	513.95	−211.44	219.68	88.21	107.86	207.05	91.29

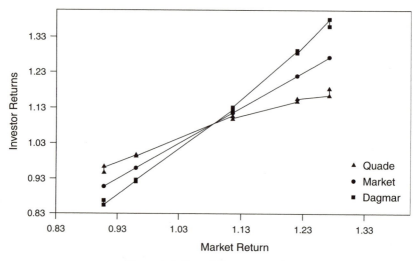

Figure 4-6 Case 6: Returns graph.

have very different marginal utility functions. Dagmar becomes less risk averse as she grows richer while Quade becomes more risk averse. More specifically, in better times Dagmar's risk aversion increases relative to the average of all investors while Quade's decreases relative to the average. They can each gain in expected utility by arranging for their portfolio returns to reflect this, as they do in Figure 4-6. But they cannot do this with combinations of the market portfolio and borrowing and lending, so they resort to doing the best that they can with the existing securities. As a result, they take on non-market risk.

Figure 4-7 shows the security prices and our two investors' reservation prices for the securities (to three decimal places). Not surprisingly, there are no further gains to be made by trading in conventional securities.

Despite the calm exterior of this equilibrium, our investors are nonetheless frustrated, as can be seen in the state prices table shown in Figure 4-8. Dagmar would be willing to pay up to 0.085 to buy a claim for 1 unit of consumption if

FIGURE 4-7
Case 6: Security Prices

Security Prices:	Consume	STBond	GovBds	NonGvBds	ValueStx	GthStx	SmlStx
Market	1.000	0.951	0.952	0.958	0.989	0.947	0.967
Quade	1.000	0.951	0.952	0.958	0.989	0.947	0.967
Dagmar	1.000	0.951	0.952	0.958	0.989	0.947	0.967

FIGURE 4-8

Case 6: State Prices

State Prices:	Now	Depression1	Depression2	Recession1	Recession2	Normality1	Normality2	Prosperity1	Prosperity2	Boom1	Boom2
Market	1.000	0.082	0.082	0.139	0.139	0.170	0.167	0.060	0.061	0.026	0.024
Quade	1.000	0.079	0.082	0.141	0.139	0.174	0.165	0.060	0.062	0.027	0.022
Dagmar	1.000	0.085	0.082	0.138	0.138	0.166	0.169	0.061	0.060	0.026	0.027

the Depression1 state occurs, while Quade would be willing to sell one for any price above 0.079. Both could gain by trading at any price between these amounts. There are also disparities in their reservations prices for other state claims.

Such situations are seldom ignored by financial services firms. If new securities can attract enough buyers and sellers to more than offset the costs of trading, there is seldom a dearth of firms seeking to profit from the introduction of such securities and/or the creation of markets for trading them.

In this case, there are no markets for trading state claims. But we can determine the prices at which such claims might start trading. The entries in the top row in Figure 4-8 show the prices that would be chosen by a market maker using the simplest form of our price discovery process. Each price is halfway between the average reservation price for those able to purchase the claim and the average reservation price for those able to sell the claim. In this case, the "market prices" are simply the averages of the two investors' reservation prices.

4.3. Case 7: Quade and Dagmar in a Complete Market

In Case 7 we show compassion for Quade and Dagmar by letting them trade state claims, but only after they have reached an equilibrium using conventional securities. The trading process is the same as that used for the conventional securities, with each state claim traded in turn and rounds of trading conducted until no trades have been made in a complete round. As with Case 6, the simple type of price discovery based on the reservation prices is utilized, using the same required level of precision chosen for trading conventional securities. As always in our simulations, market makers work for nothing.

In every other respect, Case 7 is the same as Case 6. The only differences arise from the trading in state claims conducted after the conventional security trading is finished (in fact, Case 7 was produced by using the inputs for Case 6 and changing one control variable). Not surprisingly, the equilibrium portfolios of conventional securities are the same as in Case 6 (previously shown in Figure 4-5). But in addition, there are now holdings in state claims, as shown in Figure 4-9.

This provides further evidence that our investors were not satisfied with their ability to adequately divide economic outcomes using only available conventional securities. Since they chose to trade state claims, each believed that he or she was better off as a result.

Figure 4-10 shows what Quade and Dagmar accomplished by making these trades. They take no non-market risk, and obtain returns that fall nicely on curves that reflect the disparate ways in which their risk aversions change as they become richer. Were there more states of the world this would be even

FIGURE 4-9

Case 7: State Claims

Claims:	Now	Depression1	Depression2	Recession1	Recession2	Normality1	Normality2	Prosperity1	Prosperity2	Boom1	Boom2
Market	0.000	0.000	0.000	0.000	0.000	0.000	0.000	0.000	0.000	0.000	0.000
Quade	−0.018	−5.398	0.273	1.599	0.547	2.736	−1.219	−1.020	1.252	1.595	−7.146
Dagmar	0.018	5.398	−0.273	−1.599	−0.547	−2.736	1.219	1.020	−1.252	−1.595	7.146

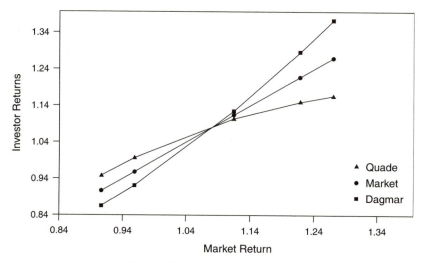

Figure 4-10 Case 7: Returns graph.

more evident, since the lines we use to connect points visually would fall closer to the true underlying curves.

In this complete market, the MRRC is not dead. Since Quade and Dagmar are both risk averse it makes sense for them to avoid non-market risk. Given a rich enough investment environment they can do so and still take on appropriate amounts of market risk for different levels of market return. A complete market allows them to do just this.

4.3.1. State and Security Prices

Figure 4-11 shows the state prices after the trading in state claims has concluded. As expected, for each state claim the investors' reservations prices are the same (to three decimal places) and equal to the market price. Note also that the price for a claim to $1 in state Depression1 is $0.082, as is the price for a claim to $1 in state Depression2. As we will see, this reflects the facts that total consumption is the same in each state and that the two states are equally probable. Similar relationships apply for each of the other pairs of states representing different divisions of a pie of the same size.

While the ability to trade all state claims precludes any need for our investors to return to trading conventional securities, it is important to recognize that if such trades were contemplated, the equilibrium prices for the securities could differ from those in Case 6. However, the differences are small in this case. Figure 4-12 shows the security prices based on investors' reservation prices after they have changed their consumption amounts using both

FIGURE 4-11

Case 7: State Prices

State Prices::	Now	Depression1	Depression2	Recession1	Recession2	Normality1	Normality2	Prosperity1	Prosperity2	Boom1	Boom2
Market	1.000	0.082	0.082	0.139	0.139	0.168	0.168	0.061	0.061	0.026	0.026
Quade	1.000	0.082	0.082	0.139	0.139	0.168	0.168	0.061	0.061	0.026	0.026
Dagmar	1.000	0.082	0.082	0.139	0.139	0.168	0.168	0.061	0.061	0.026	0.026

FIGURE 4-12
Case 7: Security Prices

Security Prices:	Consume	STBond	GovBds	NonGvBds	ValueStx	GthStx	SmlStx
Market	1.000	0.950	0.952	0.957	0.989	0.947	0.967
Quade	1.000	0.950	0.952	0.957	0.989	0.947	0.967
Dagmar	1.000	0.950	0.952	0.957	0.989	0.947	0.967

conventional securities and state claims. Some of the entries differ from those in Figure 4-7, but only slightly.

4.4. Price per Chance

What are the determinants of the state prices shown in Figure 4-11? Certainly probabilities must be relevant. Other things equal, one would expect to pay more for a security that provides a given payment in a more likely state. But other things are not equal in this case. Note, for example, that it costs $0.082 to obtain $1 in state Depression1 and only $0.061 to obtain $1 in state Prosperity1, despite the fact that the latter state is twice as likely to occur.

To help explain this phenomenon and to provide a foundation for much that is to come, we introduce a well-known concept using a somewhat novel name. We define the *price per chance* (PPC) for a state claim as its price divided by the probability that the state will occur. In a complete market, state prices are observable. And when investors agree on probabilities, so are probabilities (just ask anyone). The net result is that PPCs are unique and observable. As we will see later, this is not always so. For now, however, we focus on cases involving agreement and complete markets, where PPCs are knowable by all.

A state's PPC provides a better indication than the state price alone of the extent to which a state claim is cheap or expensive. To see why, imagine a situation in which an agent offers you an insurance policy that will pay $1,000 if your computer is stolen this year. The policy costs $60, or 6 cents (0.06) per dollar of coverage. Should you buy the policy? The answer depends on your assessment of the chance that the computer will be stolen. If you believe that there is an 8 percent chance, you are more likely to buy the policy than if you think that the chance is 4 percent. In the former case, the PPC is 0.06/0.08, or 0.75; in the latter it is 0.06/0.04, or 1.50. The lower the PPC, the more attractive the offer.

We can compute PPC values for investors, using their reservation prices for state claims. We can also do so for the market, using the market prices for the claims. Figure 4-13 shows the results for Case 7.

FIGURE 4-13

Case 7: PPCs Table

PPCs:	Now	Depression1	Depression2	Recession1	Recession2	Normality1	Normality2	Prosperity1	Prosperity2	Boom1	Boom2
Market	1.000	1.635	1.635	1.389	1.389	0.840	0.840	0.607	0.607	0.520	0.520
Quade	1.000	1.635	1.635	1.389	1.389	0.840	0.840	0.607	0.607	0.520	0.520
Dagmar	1.000	1.635	1.635	1.389	1.389	0.840	0.840	0.607	0.607	0.520	0.520

Two features are notable. First, it is cheaper to obtain a given chance of consumption in a good (high aggregate output) state of the world than in a bad one. Second, it costs the same for a given chance of consumption in states that have the same aggregate output. This is not an artifact of the particular numeric values in this case. Instead, it follows from the quite reasonable assumptions about investor choice that we have made and that underlie much of asset pricing theory.

4.5. PPCs and Consumption

Equilibrium is established when people stop trading. In a complete market, state prices are determined and, given agreement on probabilities, PPC values are known to all. The causation runs from portfolio choice to asset prices.

But we can view equilibrium in a different manner. After it is established, imagine telling Dagmar that she can buy and sell any desired amount of each state claim at its equilibrium state price. After giving the matter some thought she would choose precisely her current portfolio and pattern of consumption over states. If Quade were given the same opportunities, he would choose his current portfolio and pattern of consumption. The situation is the same as if the prices caused the investors to choose their current portfolios and consumption levels.

We have argued that in choosing how to respond to these questions, investors look not at state prices, but at PPC values. Figure 4-14 shows the results, allowing comparisons of the PPC values for the future states with the amounts consumed.

Note that if two states cost the same (have the same PPC), Quade chooses to consume the same amount in each state. But if one state is cheaper (has a lower PPC) than another, he chooses to consume more in the cheaper state. Dagmar exhibits similar behavior. Why do our investors act this way? The reason is that each feels that "other things equal, the more consumption that I have, the less valuable is one unit more or less." More formally, as we showed in Chapter 3, each has a marginal utility curve that is downward-sloping when plotted against consumption.

Recall the ingredients of an investor's reservation price for a claim to receive one unit in state j:

$$r_j = \frac{\pi_j d_j m(X_j)}{m(X_1)}$$

Absent constraints on holdings, in a complete market equilibrium an investor will trade until his or her reservation price equals the market price for the state claim. Thus:

$$\frac{\pi_j d_j m(X_j)}{m(X_1)} = p_j$$

FIGURE 4-14

Case 7: PPCs and Consumption for Future States

	Depression1	Depression2	Recession1	Recession2	Normality1	Normality2	Prosperity1	Prosperity2	Boom1	Boom2
Market PPC	1.635	1.635	1.389	1.389	0.840	0.840	0.607	0.607	0.520	0.520
Market Cons.	870	870	920	920	1070	1070	1170	1170	1220	1220
Quade Cons.	453	453	476	476	527	527	549	549	557	557
Dagmar Cons.	417	417	444	444	543	543	621	621	663	663

Dividing both sides by the probability of the state gives:

$$\frac{d_j m(X_j)}{m(X_1)} = \frac{p_j}{\pi_j}$$

Importantly, the expression to the right of the equal sign is the PPC for the state.

Consider two states with the same PPC. To maximize expected utility, an investor will choose a portfolio with the same consumption in each state in the same time period; otherwise, there will be a discrepancy between his or her reservation price and the market price in one or both states.

Consider next two states, j and k, with state j having a higher PPC than state k. An investor will choose a portfolio that provides a higher reservation price per chance in state j. This requires consumption that leads to a higher marginal utility of consumption, that is, to less consumption. Thus the investor will choose to have less consumption in state j than in state k.

In the setting of Case 7, we reach the highly reasonable conclusion that each investor will choose the same consumption in states that cost the same (have equal PPCs) and each will choose less consumption in states that are more expensive (have higher PPCs).

4.6. The Pricing Kernel

As we have seen, once there is equilibrium in a complete market with agreement we can talk meaningfully about *market PPCs*. Conventionally, the set of market PPCs is called the *pricing kernel*.

A key aspect of such an equilibrium is that shown in Figure 4-15, which plots the relationship between the market PPCs (on the vertical axis) and total market consumptions (on the horizontal axis) from Case 7. For convenience, the points representing the states are connected with lines; however, only the points themselves are relevant.

While there are ten future states of the world in Case 7, only five separate points are visible in the graph because each point includes two states, since states with the same aggregate consumption have the same PPC. When the points representing future states are connected, the resulting curve is downward-sloping. These are characteristics of complete market equilibrium when investors' marginal utilities decrease with consumption and the other conditions of this case hold (agreement, state-independent utilities, no outside positions, and the absence of binding constraints).

4.7. Market-Based Strategies

We now have the pieces in place to show that in this type of market, every investor will choose to take only market risk and hence will abide by the

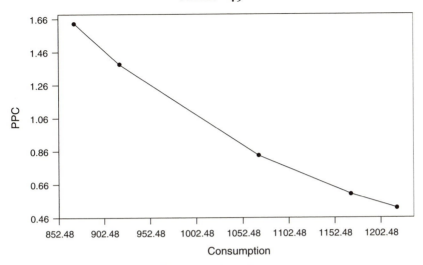

Figure 4-15 Case 7: The pricing kernel and total consumption.

MRRC. We know that in such a setting each investor will choose more consumption in cheaper (lower PPC) states and the same amount in equally expensive (PPC) states. But total consumption is simply the sum of the amounts consumed by all investors. Thus total consumption will be the same in states with the same PPC values and lower in states with lower PPC values. More formally:

Each investor's consumption will be inversely related (only) to PPC.

Thus:

Aggregate consumption will be inversely related (only) to PPC.

But then it follows immediately that:

Each investor's consumption will be directly related (only) to aggregate consumption.

In short, each investor will follow a market-based strategy.

4.8. Expected Return and Aggregate Consumption

Only a few steps remain to reach a general version of the MRRT that states that only market risk is rewarded with higher expected return. To start, we need to compute the expected return in each state. This is simple enough. A state's PPC is its price divided by its probability. The reciprocal is the probability divided by the price. Since a state claim pays $1 if the state in question occurs, the probability of the state (times 1) is the expected payment. Dividing this by the price gives the expected total return for the claim. At the risk of belaboring the obvious, Figure 4-16 repeats the information in Figure 4-14, with an extra row for the expected total return in each future state.

We know that in this setting PPCs are the same for states with the same market return and lower for states with higher market return. It follows that expected returns must be the same for states with the same market return and higher for states with higher market return.

An investor who takes non-market risk chooses a portfolio that provides different payoffs in states with the same market return. But in this setting such states have the same expected return. Thus there is no reward in higher expected return associated with non-market risk. This establishes part of the MRRT: there is no reward in higher expected return associated with non-market risk.

It remains to show that there is a reward in higher expected return associated with taking at least some type of market risk. To do so it is useful to introduce the concept of market states.

4.8.1. Market States

In all our cases, we have arranged the states in increasing order of aggregate consumption. This may have seemed arbitrary, but the reason should now be clear. By doing so, all states with the same aggregate consumption are adjacent in a single group, with the groups in increasing order of consumption. Figure 4-17 shows new *market states* for Case 7 called, not surprisingly, Depression, Recession, Normality, Prosperity, and Boom. Each market state combines all the states with the same market return, has a probability equal to the sum of the probabilities of its substates and a state price equal to the sum of the state prices of its substates. Since each of the states within such a group has the same PPC, the market state has the same PPC as its substates. This is also true for the expected returns.

4.8.2. Market Risk and Reward

Our next goal is to show that it is possible to obtain a higher expected return by taking *market risk*. To start, consider the individual's decision concerning allocation of investment across market states. Assume that his or her budget is just enough to purchase a riskless security that pays 1.00 in every state.

FIGURE 4-16

Case 7: PPCs, Expected Returns, and Consumption for Future States

	Depression1	Depression2	Recession1	Recession2	Normality1	Normality2	Prosperity1	Prosperity2	Boom1	Boom2
Market PPC	1.635	1.635	1.389	1.389	0.840	0.840	0.607	0.607	0.520	0.520
Expected return	0.612	0.612	0.720	0.720	1.191	1.191	1.649	1.649	1.924	1.924
Market cons.	870	870	920	920	1070	1070	1170	1170	1220	1220
Quade cons.	453	453	476	476	527	527	549	549	557	557
Dagmar cons.	417	417	444	444	543	543	621	621	663	663

FIGURE 4-17

Case 7: PPCs, Expected Returns, and Consumption for Market States

	Depression	Recession	Normality	Prosperity	Boom
Market PPC	1.635	1.389	0.840	0.607	0.520
Expected return	0.612	0.720	1.191	1.649	1.924
Market cons.	870	920	1070	1170	1220
Quade cons.	453	476	527	549	557
Dagmar cons.	417	444	543	621	663

Figure 4-18 shows the relevant calculations. Importantly, the expected return for the portfolio is a weighted average of the expected returns of its components, with the proportions of value used as weights.

Now consider reducing the payment in the Depression market state enough to lower the associated value by 1 cent (0.010), and using the proceeds to increase the payment in the Boom market state as much as possible. The results are shown in Figure 4-19.

The expected return for the portfolio is considerably higher. Why? Because money was taken from a market state with a lower expected return and put in a market state with a higher expected return. As a result, the portfolio expected return, which is a value-weighted average of the component expected returns, increased. The greater the amount of money reallocated in this manner, the larger will be the portfolio's expected return.

This shows that taking market risk can increase expected return, but only if it is done intelligently. For example, we could have started with the riskless security, then taken money from a high expected return state and used it to buy more consumption in a lower expected return state. This would have reduced

FIGURE 4-18

Case 7: Expected Return for a Riskless Portfolio

	Depression	Recession	Normality	Prosperity	Boom	Portfolio
Payment	1.000	1.000	1.000	1.000	1.000	
State price	0.163	0.278	0.336	0.121	0.052	
Value	0.163	0.278	0.336	0.121	0.052	0.950
Proportion of value	0.172	0.292	0.353	0.128	0.055	1.000
Expected return	0.612	0.720	1.191	1.649	1.924	1.052

FIGURE 4-19
Case 7: Expected Return for a Portfolio with Market Risk

	Depression	Recession	Normality	Prosperity	Boom	Portfolio
Payment	0.939	1.000	1.000	1.000	1.192	
State price	0.163	0.278	0.336	0.121	0.052	
Value	0.153	0.278	0.336	0.121	0.062	0.950
Proportion of value	0.161	0.292	0.353	0.128	0.065	1.000
Expected return	0.612	0.720	1.191	1.649	1.924	1.066

expected return to a level below the riskless rate! Clearly, not all types of market risk are rewarded.

This issue is easily dismissed. Our investors will choose more consumption in cheaper (lower PPC) states. But these are higher expected return states. Thus the only market risk they will (and should) take will be associated with upward-sloping portfolio return curves such as the ones shown earlier in Figure 4-10.

In this case, Dagmar's return curve is steeper than Quade's. She takes more market risk, but is rewarded with a higher expected return, as shown in Figure 4-20.

We still need a formal measure of market risk to give specific meaning to the MRRT. We will do so in stages, obtaining a series of *asset pricing formulas* of increasing specificity.

4.9. Asset Pricing Formulas

Cases with agreement, complete markets, investors with decreasing marginal utility, state-independent utility, and no outside positions have a number of properties, each of which figures importantly in asset pricing theory. We present

FIGURE 4-20
Case 7: Portfolio Expected Returns

Portfolio Characteristics:	Exp Return
Market	1.096
Quade	1.080
Dagmar	1.113

them here in sequence without caveats. In subsequent chapters we will consider the extent to which each may or may not hold in more general settings.

4.9.1. The Law of One Price

Anyone able to buy and sell state claims at market prices can construct any desired type of security. Now, imagine that a security is trading for a price that differs from the price of such a *replicating portfolio* of state claims. Any clever investor could then make money by purchasing the cheaper alternative and selling the more expensive one. No matter what the future state of the world, the purchased asset would generate enough money to make the payment required for the asset that was sold. The difference between the lower purchase price and higher sales price could be spent today, providing truly "something for nothing." Opportunities for this kind of *arbitrage* are few and fleeting. In the vast majority of markets at almost all times, they are unavailable. In a complete market, the price of an asset will equal the price of a replicating portfolio of state claims.

The *Law of One Price* (LOP) states this relationship succinctly:

(LOP) $$P_i = \sum p_s X_{is}$$

Here, i represents a security and P_i its price. One unit of the security pays X_{is} in state s; p_s is the state price for state s. Each state's payment is *priced* by multiplying it by the price per unit, and the results are then summed to obtain the price or *present value* of the security. A variant of the LOP is widely used in financial engineering. It is simply a transformation that adds nothing to our version and sometimes conceals the underlying economics. For completeness we will describe it briefly.

In our version, p_s is the price that must be paid today to receive 1 unit at the future date if and only if state s occurs. The sum of all these state prices is the amount that must be paid today to receive 1 unit at the future date with certainty, since one of the states will occur. Thus if the sum of the state prices is 0.96, a dollar at the future date costs $0.96 today. Denote this d. Now, imagine that you wish to receive $1 at the future date if and only if state s occurs. You can borrow p_s dollars to buy the state claim, which will require you to pay p_s/d at the future date, whether state s occurs or not. This amount is known as the *forward price* (f_s) of a claim for a dollar in state s. One could contract directly to pay f_s for each payment X_{is}; the sum of these amounts would be the *forward cost* of security i. Multiplying this by the discount factor would give the current price. Thus the LOP can be stated as follows. Multiply each payment by the forward price of a claim in the corresponding state, then discount the sum using the riskless rate of interest. Many financial engineers use this approach, calling each forward price a "risk-neutral probability," although this obscures the underlying economics. While the forward prices will sum to 1

(since a dollar should cost a dollar), they will typically differ from true probabilities. Moreover, the world is not one in which people are neutral to risk.
Nonetheless the procedure is harmless enough, and those who use this version
share our goal of understanding the determinants of state prices.

4.9.2. The Law of One Price in an Incomplete Market

In a complete market with no arbitrage opportunities the LOP must hold and
the price of any security (P_i) can be determined by "pricing" its payoffs $(X_{is}$ values) using observable state prices $(p_s$ values).

But what about an incomplete market, when only the prices of traded securities can be observed? Can one construct a set of state claim prices that will
correctly price all traded securities in the sense that the LOP equation will hold
for each one? As shown in Rubinstein (1976) and Ross (1977), the answer is
generally yes, assuming that no arbitrage opportunities exist.

To provide a simple illustration we return to Case 1 in which Mario and Hue
could only trade shares of the two fishing companies and a riskless bond. Figure 4-21 shows key information from the case. The market state prices provided
by the simulator are shown in the top left table, the security payoffs in the top
right table, and the actual prices from the equilibrium in the first row of the
bottom right table. Each entry in the bottom row of the latter table is computed by multiplying the state prices by the payoffs for the security in question.
In this case, each such *implied price* is equal to the actual price. Thus the state
prices in Figure 4-21 do in fact price each of the available securities. We will

FIGURE 4-21
Case 1: Equilibrium State Prices

State Prices:	Price	Securities:	Consume	Bond	MFC	HFC
Now	1.000	Now	1	0	0	0
BadS	0.211	BadS	0	1	5	3
BadN	0.352	BadN	0	1	3	5
GoodS	0.164	GoodS	0	1	8	4
GoodN	0.230	GoodN	0	1	4	8
StdDev	0.080	Security Prices:	Consume	Bond	MFC	HFC
		Actual	1.000	0.958	4.350	4.895
		Implied	1.000	0.958	4.350	4.895

FIGURE 4-22
Case 1: Alternative State Prices #1

State Prices:	Price	Securities:	Consume	Bond	MFC	HFC
Now	1.000	Now	1	0	0	0
BadS	0.254	BadS	0	1	5	3
BadN	0.309	BadN	0	1	3	5
GoodS	0.143	GoodS	0	1	8	4
GoodN	0.252	GoodN	0	1	4	8

StdDev	0.070	Security Prices:	Consume	Bond	MFC	HFC
		Actual	1.000	0.958	4.350	4.895
		Implied	1.000	0.958	4.350	4.895

see shortly why this is the case. First, however, it is important to understand that other sets of state prices may also suffice.

Any set of state prices that produces implied security prices equal to the actual prices will satisfy the LOP. To show that other such prices exist we perform two optimization analyses, each of which focuses (arbitrarily) on the standard deviation of the prices for the future states, shown below the set of state prices. Figure 4-22 shows the results for the first optimization, in which the goal was to find a set of state prices that (1) produce an implied price for each security equal to its actual price and (2) provide the smallest possible standard deviation of future state prices.

As can be seen, these state prices also price the securities, but they differ significantly from those in Figure 4-21. To provide an even more dramatic example, Figure 4-23 shows the results obtained when an optimization analysis was performed to select a set of future state prices that would (1) each be greater than or equal to 0.01, (2) price the available securities, and (3) maximize the standard deviation of the state prices.

Here, too, the state prices conform to the LOP. But they differ very significantly from those in the previous examples. By construction, any set of state prices that makes each of the differences between actual and implied security prices equal to zero will price all existing securities correctly. Absent arbitrage, such a set of state prices will also price any security with payoffs that can be replicated using some combination of existing securities. Any of the three sets of prices shown in Figures 4-21, 4-22, and 4-23 could do the job and other combinations of state prices could work as well.

FIGURE 4-23
Case 1: Alternative State Prices #2

State Prices:	Price	Securities:	Consume	Bond	MFC	HFC
Now	1.000	Now	1	0	0	0
BadS	0.010	BadS	0	1	5	3
BadN	0.553	BadN	0	1	3	5
GoodS	0.265	GoodS	0	1	8	4
GoodN	0.130	GoodN	0	1	4	8

		Security Prices:	Consume	Bond	MFC	HFC
StdDev	0.234	Actual	1.000	0.958	4.350	4.895
		Implied	1.000	0.958	4.350	4.895

These examples show both the good news and the bad news about the LOP in an incomplete market. The good news is that one can find a set of state prices that will correctly price any security that can be replicated with existing securities. The bad news is that in most cases a set of such state prices will not be unique. Additional bad news is that the state prices chosen may not provide any useful information about the price for which one could buy or sell a "new" security—that is, one with payments that cannot be replicated using currently available securities.

But all is not lost. Figure 4-21 showed that the market state prices computed in the simulation analysis for Case 1 satisfied the LOP. And those prices do contain information about the prices at which state claims could be traded, at least initially, if such trades were possible. The state prices in Figure 4-21 are thus of more economic relevance than those in Figures 4-22 and 4-23 which were obtained by minimizing or maximizing an arbitrary function of the state prices.

It is not difficult to see why this is the case. In Case 1, and for that matter, all the cases that we have analyzed thus far, no investor is subject to a constraint concerning the purchase or sale of any security or state claim when equilibrium is obtained. Thus Mario's reservation prices for the state claims will "price out" each of the available securities, as will Hue's. We compute the market price for each state claim by averaging (1) the average of the reservation prices for all investors who would be able to purchase the claim and (2) the average of the reservation prices for all investors who would be able to sell the claim. As long as all investors are able to purchase or sell all claims, the set of market state claim prices will thus be an average of all investors' reservation prices. But if each investor's reservation prices conform to the LOP, so will an average of all investors' reservation prices.

In an incomplete market, any unconstrained investor's state reservation prices will price any security that is currently available or that can be replicated using available securities. Averaging the reservation prices of unconstrained investors will also give a set of state prices that will price any such security.

If one is interested only in the prices of securities that exist or that can be replicated by combining currently traded securities, there is no need to even compute a set of state prices that conforms to the LOP. If, on the other hand, one would like to estimate the prices at which truly new securities might trade, it is desirable to utilize a set of state prices that not only prices currently available securities but also contains information about investors' reservation prices. Ultimately, the only way to determine the price at which a new security will trade is to open a market in which it can be traded. But the "market state prices" that we compute provide useful estimates of such prices.

4.10. Sufficiently Complete Markets

Thus far we have described two broad types of markets. In *complete markets* investors can trade both existing securities and state claims. Formally, many of the concepts of asset pricing theory are based on the existence of a complete market in this sense. But in actual markets few state claims are traded explicitly. In actuality, *incomplete markets* are the rule, not the exception.

Case 6 provided a good example of an incomplete market. Quade and Dagmar were prime candidates for new securities that could enable them to achieve additional gains through trade. This was evident in Figure 4-8, which showed significant disparities in their reservation prices for several state claims. In Case 7, when trading in such claims was made available, substantial amounts were traded.

This need not be the case in every incomplete market. Case 1 provided an example of a different situation. Figure 4-24 shows Mario and Hue's reservation state prices and the market prices computed by averaging their reservation prices from the equilibrium.

While no trading in state claims was allowed in Case 1 and the existing securities did not allow replication of the payments for any such claim, this situation was not fertile ground for an ambitious investment banker. Indeed, if a market maker were to open markets in all the state claims at the prices shown in the top row in Figure 4-24, little if anything would change. While the market was incomplete, the equilibrium was consistent with a complete market with state prices similar to those shown in the simulation output.

FIGURE 4-24
Case 1: State Prices

State Prices:	Now	BadS	BadN	GoodS	GoodN
Market	1.000	0.211	0.352	0.164	0.230
Mario	1.000	0.211	0.352	0.164	0.230
Hue	1.000	0.211	0.352	0.164	0.230

When an equilibrium is reached with such characteristics we will say that the market is *sufficiently complete*. Either of two definitions can be used for this purpose: (1) for each state claim investors' reservation prices are the same or (2) if markets were opened for trading state claims, no trades would be made. More broadly, in a sufficiently complete market, investors can accomplish their goals with existing securities.

In the real world and in our simulations, incomplete markets are unlikely to strictly conform to this definition. Actual capital markets have transactions costs and our simulations stop when a desired level of precision is reached. But many markets, real and simulated, can be almost sufficiently complete and thus conform closely to the results of asset pricing theories that assume markets are in fact complete.

4.11. The Basic Pricing Equation

The LOP equation does not incorporate probabilities. It thus can be applied whether or not people agree on the probabilities of future states of the world. But much of financial economics is concerned with expected values and other measures that are based on estimates of state probabilities. This is evident in the equation that Cochrane, in his *Asset Pricing* text (Cochrane 2001, p. 8), calls the basic pricing equation (BPE). He writes it as:

$$P = E(mX)$$

In this notation $E(\ )$ represents the expected value of the enclosed expression. In our discrete world, the equivalent expression is:

$$P_i = \sum \pi_s m_s X_{is}$$

Here P_i and the X_{is} values are the price of security i and its payoffs in the various states, as before. The symbol π_s is the probability of state s and m_s is the so-called *stochastic discount factor* for the state. Much of the asset pricing literature assumes that there is agreement on the probabilities of various states, so only the m values need to be determined. Cochrane emphasizes this: "my organizing principle is that everything can be traced back to specializations of the basic pricing equation" (Cochrane 2001, p. xvii).

When the LOP holds, the BPE follows immediately when the stochastic discount factor for a state is defined as:

$$m_s \equiv p_s / \pi_s$$

Substituting this into the BPE gives:

$$P_i = \sum_s \pi_s (p_s / \pi_s) X_{is}$$

which simplifies to the LOP.

Of course, the stochastic discount factor for a state is the value that we have termed its price per chance (PPC). In a complete market with agreement both the price for a state and its probability are known so there is no ambiguity about the associated value of m. And, as in Figure 4-15, PPCs will be a decreasing function of aggregate consumption.

4.11.1. The Basic Pricing Equation in an Insufficiently Complete Market

The BPE will also hold in a sufficiently complete market with agreement, no outside positions, and state-independent utilities, since for the variables in question equilibrium in such a market is equivalent to an equilibrium in a complete market. However, in a market that is *insufficiently complete* the BPE may not hold precisely if the state prices are based on investors' reservation prices, as in our simulation results. Nonetheless, it may still provide a good approximation.

Figure 4-25 is a plot of the relationship between the pricing kernel based on our computed market prices and total consumption for Case 6, in which Quade and Dagmar were not sufficiently served by the available securities. As can be seen, the relationship does not represent a true function. At the far right in the diagram are two states with the same aggregate consumption and different PPC values. This is also the case, although to a lesser extent, for other levels of aggregate consumption. Nonetheless, the graph is very close to one in which PPC is a decreasing function of aggregate consumption.

4.12. The Kernel Beta Equation

The BPE can be manipulated to produce an extremely valuable relationship that can help provide needed specificity for the MRRT. The derivation will be sketched here; the curious can easily fill in the blanks.

Start with the simpler form of the BPE for asset i:

$$P_i = E(mX_i)$$

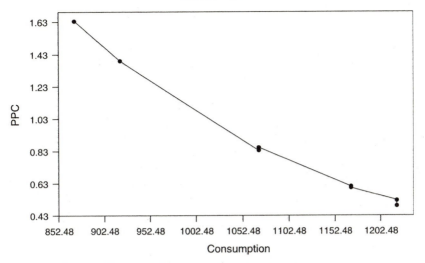

Figure 4-25 Case 6: The pricing kernel and total consumption.

Dividing both sides by the security price gives a version stated in terms of total return (X_i/P_i):

$$1 = E(mR_i)$$

Statisticians frequently use a measure called *covariance*. As the name suggests, it measures the extent to which two variables vary with one another. Formally, it is the expected product of the deviation of one variable from its mean times the deviation of the other variable from its mean. This implies a relationship that, in our case, can be written as:

$$E(mR_i) = \text{cov}(m, R_i) + E(m)E(R_i)$$

But we know from the BPE that the term on the left equals 1. Moreover, $E(m)$ must equal the discount factor (d), since it is the sum of the product of terms, each of which equals a state probability times the ratio of the state price to the probability. This gives:

$$E(R_i) = (1/d) - (\text{cov}(m, R_i)/d)$$

Of course $1/d$ is the total return on a riskless asset, which we can write as r. We use this and the fact that the covariance of two variables is the same no matter which is listed first, to obtain:

$$E(R_i) - r = -\text{cov}(R_i, m)/d$$

One of the many useful properties of covariances is that they are additive. In our context this implies that the covariance of a portfolio with m will be a weighted average of the covariances of its securities with m, using the market values in the portfolio as weights. This means that the equation above will hold for any security or portfolio. Of particular interest here, it will hold for the market portfolio, so that:

$$E(R_M) - r = -\text{cov}(R_M, m)/d$$

Dividing the equation for security i by that for the market portfolio gives:

$$\frac{E(R_i) - r}{E(R_M) - r} = \frac{\text{cov}(R_i, m)}{\text{cov}(R_M, m)}$$

The term on the right is a measure of relative covariance. To avoid confusion with the more common term described later, we call it security i's *kernel beta:*

$$\beta_i^k \equiv \frac{\text{cov}(R_i, m)}{\text{cov}(R_M, m)}$$

Combining the last two equations gives the *kernel beta equation:*

(KBE) $\qquad\qquad E(R_i) = r + \beta_i^k(E(R_M) - r)$

This shows that differences in the expected returns of securities or portfolios will arise only from differences in their covariances with the pricing kernel (m), since all the other terms in the KBE equation are the same for every security or portfolio.

4.13. The Market Beta Equation

In a complete market with agreement, the kernel beta equation follows directly from the LOP, which must hold if there are no arbitrage opportunities. This is tantalizingly close to providing a definition for "market risk" that can be used for the MRRT. But in the KBE equation the market portfolio plays only an arbitrary role, since we could have chosen any other portfolio when deriving the relationship. To obtain the MRRT we need to add a crucial ingredient.

In all the cases that we have considered thus far, investors obtained all their future consumption from returns on the securities in their portfolios. Thus we have been able to use the terms "aggregate consumption" and "market portfolio return" interchangeably. In Chapter 5 we will confront cases in which these measures may differ. For now, however, we follow tradition, assuming that there are no sources of consumption outside the security markets.

The key relationship is the one shown in the graphs of the pricing kernel and aggregate consumption. If PPC is a decreasing function of aggregate consumption, and if the return on the market is equal to aggregate consumption, then in a complete or sufficiently complete market PPC will be a decreasing function of the return on the market. Using the current notation, we represent the relationship between the pricing kernel and total market return as:

$$m = f(R_M)$$

Substituting this into the definition for a kernel beta gives a definition for a security or portfolio *market beta*:

$$\frac{\mathrm{cov}(R_i, f(R_M))}{\mathrm{cov}(R_M, f(R_M))} \equiv \beta_i^{f(R_M)}$$

Thus the market beta for a security or portfolio is a scaled measure of the co-variance of its return with a function of the return on the market portfolio.

We are finally in a position to give precision to the MRRT by defining market risk as an investment's market beta. To be explicit, the MRRT is:

(MRRT) $$E(R_i) = r + \beta_i^{f(R_M)}(E(R_M) - r)$$

where $f(R_M)$ is a function relating the pricing kernel to total market return. As long as the pricing kernel is a decreasing function of market return the MRRT will hold. The APSIM program computes market state prices for both complete and incomplete markets, uses such prices and actual probabilities to compute PPC values, and then provides a graph with both the resulting PPC values and total market return. If there is a one-to-one relationship between the two variables, with larger values of one associated with smaller values of the other, the MRRT holds. Of the seven cases we have examined thus far, only Case 6 provided an exception, and a relatively small one at that.

The MRRT is on solid ground in cases in which there is agreement, markets are complete, investments are the sole sources of consumption, and each investor has the same discount and marginal utility function for all the states in a given time period. In other cases it may or may not hold exactly, and, if the latter, be a good approximation or a poor one.

As stated, the MRRT is relatively general since $f(R_M)$ is restricted only to be decreasing in R_M. This is both good news and bad news: good news because the theorem can cover any case in which the pricing kernel is a decreasing function of market return, and bad news for the same reason. To obtain a more specific theorem one must specify at least some of the characteristics of $f(R_M)$. We will do so shortly. First we consider the implications of the general form of the MRRT for portfolio choice.

4.14. Preferences, the Pricing Kernel, and Portfolio Choice

The graphs in Figure 4-26 show key features of an equilibrium with two investors and many possible states of the world. The investors agree on probabilities, have

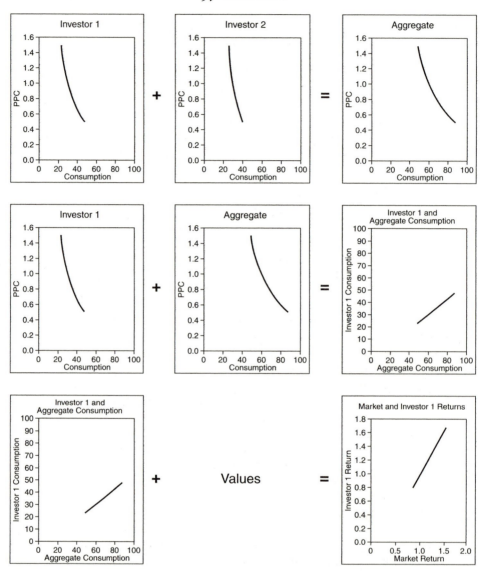

Figure 4-26 Equilibrium prices and portfolio choice.

state-independent utilities, no outside positions, and marginal utilities that decrease with consumption. Moreover, the market is either complete or sufficiently complete.

The first two graphs in the top row of Figure 4-26 show each investor's consumption as a function of the equilibrium PPC values. Note that each graph is downward-sloping. This follows from the assumption that every investor's marginal utility decreases with consumption. Recall that in equilibrium, any investor not subject to constraints will choose a portfolio for which the reservation price of each state claim equals its market price, which implies that:

$$\frac{d_j m(X_j)}{m(X_1)} = \frac{p_j}{\pi_j}$$

Since the term on the right is the PPC for the state, we can rewrite this as:

$$m(X_j) = \frac{m(X_1)}{d_j} PPC_j$$

For investors with state-independent utility, d_j will be the same for states at the same time period. Since this is the case for all future states in our examples, for a given investor the ratio on the right-hand side of the equation will be a positive constant for all such states. It follows that $m(X_j)$ will be an increasing function of PPC_j. But for any investor for whom marginal utility decreases with consumption, $m(X_j)$ will be a decreasing function of X_j. Hence for every such investor, consumption will be a decreasing function of PPC, as shown in the first two graphs in the top row of Figure 4-26.

The aggregate consumption in any state will, of course, equal the sum of the amounts consumed by all investors, as shown in the right-hand graph in the top row of Figure 4-26. This, too, is downward-sloping, a property that follows directly from the fact that each investors' graph is downward-sloping.

The second row in Figure 4-26 repeats the first and last graphs from the top row, then combines them to show the relationship between aggregate consumption and the amount consumed by investor 1 in each state. Since each of the first graphs plots a downward-sloping function, the final graph in the row shows that investor 1's consumption increases with aggregate consumption. This is a key property of equilibrium under the assumed conditions. The final row in Figure 4-26 repeats the final graph from the second row, then rescales the amounts by dividing the amounts consumed by the present values of the portfolios. The total return on the market is equal to aggregate consumption divided by the present value of the amounts of consumption provided in various states by the market portfolio. Similarly, the total return for investor 1 is equal to his or her aggregate consumption divided by the present value of the amounts provided in various states by his or her portfolio. Since the final graph is obtained by dividing the amounts in the graph to its left by constants, it is also an upward-sloping function.

The graph in the lower right corner of Figure 4-26 shows that investor 1 follows the MRRC (takes no non-market risk). His or her portfolio return is an increasing function of the return on the overall market portfolio. The resulting return graph is upward-sloping with no "fuzz." As previously discussed, we say that such a portfolio reflects a *market-based strategy*.

Importantly, Figure 4-26 made no assumptions about preferences other than that each investor's marginal utility declined with consumption and that each investor's marginal utility for consumption in a state depended only on the amount consumed in that state and the time at which the state occurred.

In settings in which these conditions are met and in which investors agree on probabilities of future states and markets are complete or sufficiently complete, the MRRC will hold. In such a world each investor should adopt a market-based strategy (that is, take only market risk). Each investor's return graph will be upward-sloping but investors' choices will differ owing to differences in preferences. Some curves will lie above the 45-degree line that represents the return on the market portfolio, others below it. But for any given level of market return, it must of course be true that the value-weighted average of all investors' portfolio returns must equal the market return—a point to which we will return more than once.

4.15. The Capital Asset Pricing Model

The curve in the final graph in Figure 4-26 appears to be almost linear but does have some curvature. In general, investors with sufficient investment choices may adopt strategies that do not plot as straight lines in a return graph. This was clearly so in Case 7, as shown in Figure 4-10. But there are conditions in which every investor will choose a *linear market-based strategy*—a portfolio that provides returns linearly related to the returns on the market portfolio.

Assume that every investor has quadratic utility. As shown in Chapter 3, an investor with such a utility function will care only about the mean and variance of portfolio return. Moreover, his or her marginal utility will be a linear function of consumption at least over a wide range of outcomes.

Figure 4-27 shows the same set of graphs as Figure 4-26 with a key exception. Each of the two investors has quadratic utility that applies over the range of consumption chosen in equilibrium. As a result, each investor's consumption is a linear function of PPC. But then, so is aggregate consumption. And, since all the graphs in the top row are linear, so are all the rest. This is the world of the original version of the Capital Asset Pricing Model (CAPM) of Sharpe (1964), Lintner (1965), Mossin (1966), and Treynor (1999). Investors care only about portfolio mean and variance, agree on probabilities, have no outside positions, and are subject to no binding constraints on holdings. The implications are dramatic.

Every investor will choose a linear market-based strategy. This in turn implies that every investor will choose a combination of the market portfolio and the riskless asset. The reason is not hard to see. The market portfolio plots as a 45-degree line in a return graph and the riskless portfolio plots as a horizontal line. Any combination of the two will thus plot as a straight line pass-

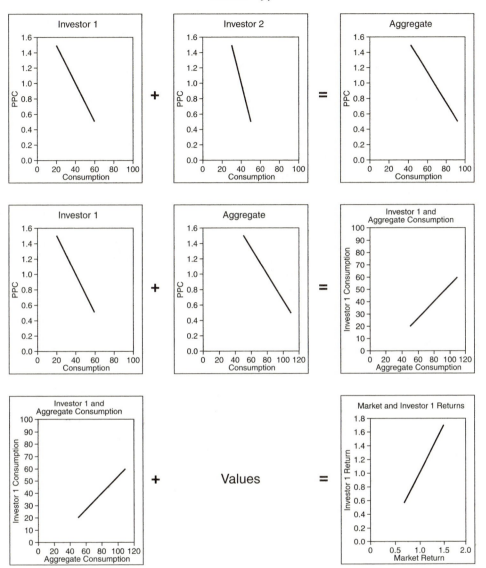

Figure 4-27 Equilibrium prices and portfolio choice with quadratic utility.

ing through their intersection. But in equilibrium there cannot be any strategy that plots as any other straight line. Why? Imagine that such a strategy existed. Consider a combination of the riskless security and the market portfolio that plots as a parallel straight line. Each strategy has the same cost. But one gives a higher return in every possible future state of the world. Clearly one could sell short the inferior strategy and use the proceeds to buy the superior one. This would have zero cost but provide a net payment in every possible state. One would thus obtain a riskless arbitrage and get something for nothing, a possibility that is highly unlikely in a modern capital market.

The analysis in Figure 4-27 assumed that a complete market is available. But in a world of mean/variance investors such a market is not needed. At the end of the day each investor chooses to hold a combination of the market port-folio and the riskless asset. As long as borrowing and lending are available, only standard securities are required. A market populated only by investors with quad-ratic utility will be sufficiently complete.

Another important implication of a market populated solely with mean/variance investors concerns the pricing kernel. As shown in the top right-hand graph in Figure 4-27, the pricing kernel will be a linear function of con-sumption. This leads to a much simpler form of the MRRT, as we show next.

4.16. The Security Market Line

The general version of the MRRT asserts that expected returns are linearly re-lated to beta values based on covariances with a function of the return on the market portfolio:

(MRRT) $$E(R_i) = r + \beta_i^{f(R_M)}(E(R_M) - r)$$

In turn, the function $f(R_M)$ represents the relationship between the pricing kernel and the return on the market portfolio.

In the world of the CAPM this function is linear, that is:

$$m = a - bR_M$$

From the properties of covariance it follows that:

$$\text{cov}(R_i, m) = -b\,\text{cov}(R_i, R_M)$$

and:

$$\text{cov}(R_M, m) = -b\,\text{cov}(R_M, R_M)$$

Of course the covariance of the market return with itself is simply the variance of the market return. Thus the beta of the MRRT can be simplified to give:

$$\beta_i \equiv \frac{\text{cov}(R_i, R_M)}{\text{var}(R_M)}$$

This measure is almost universally termed *beta*, a convention that we will follow.

In this special case the MRRT implies that the expected return of a security or portfolio is a linear function of its market risk as measured by its beta value.

Following tradition, as in Sharpe (1970) we call this the *security market line* relationship:

(SML) $$E(R_i) = r + \beta_i(E(R_M) - r)$$

This result is familiar to generations of students and practitioners, most of whom reached it via a different path.

4.17. The Power Security Market Line

The SML relation is easy to apply since no parameters are required for $f(R_M)$. However, it rests on the assumption that the pricing kernel is a linear function of the return on the market portfolio. This requires that on average investors' absolute risk aversion decreases with increases in consumption, an assumption that seems somewhat implausible.

This said, for short periods over which the range of possible market returns is relatively small it may be reasonable to approximate the pricing kernel with a linear function of the return on the market portfolio. In such circumstances, the SML may hold approximately. But there may be better approximations.

For longer periods with greater ranges of possible outcomes, it may be preferable to use a function in which the logarithm of PPC is a linear function of the logarithm of the total return on the market portfolio. In effect, this represents a market in which the average investor's preferences reflect constant relative risk aversion.

In such a market, the logarithm of the pricing kernel will be a linear function of the logarithm of the market return:

$$\ln(m) = a - b\ln(R_M)$$

Equivalently:

$$m = AR_M^{-b}$$

In this case the MRRT relationship becomes:

$$\frac{E(R_i) - r}{E(R_M) - r} = \frac{A\operatorname{cov}(R_i, R_M^{-b})}{A\operatorname{cov}(R_M, R_M^{-b})}$$

Canceling the constant that appears in both numerator and denominator and choosing a name that reflects the fact that the chosen function utilizes a power of the total return on the market, we define a security or portfolios' *power beta* as:

$$\beta_i^p \equiv \frac{\operatorname{cov}(R_i, R_M^{-b})}{\operatorname{cov}(R_M, R_M^{-b})}$$

This gives a special version of the MRRT that we will call the *Power Security Market Line* equation:

(PSML) $$E(R_i) = r + \beta_i^p(E(R_m) - r)$$

This version requires one parameter (b): the elasticity of the pricing kernel with respect to the return on the market portfolio. In our simulations we calculate this by performing a standard regression analysis, with the independent variable equal to $\ln(R_m)$ and the dependent variable equal to $\ln(m)$. The slope from the regression equation is then used as the value of b when calculating the power beta values.

4.18. Alpha Values

We have introduced two special cases of the Market Risk/Reward Theorem—the Security Market Line and the Power Security Market Line. If the conditions of the CAPM are met, all security and portfolio expected returns will conform to the SML equation, plotting along a line connecting the market portfolio and the riskless asset in a diagram with expected return on the vertical axis and beta on the horizontal axis. Otherwise, some or all such points may diverge from the line. Figure 4-28 shows results from Case 7.

The difference between the expected return on an asset and the expected return for its beta value implied by the SML equation is termed the asset's *alpha value*, or alpha. In an SML graph such as that in Figure 4-28 this is shown

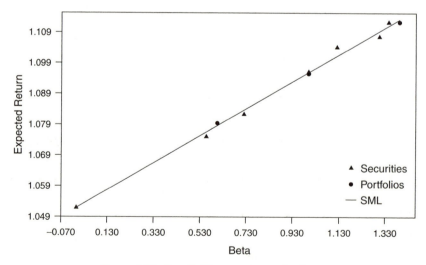

Figure 4-28 Case 7: The security market line.

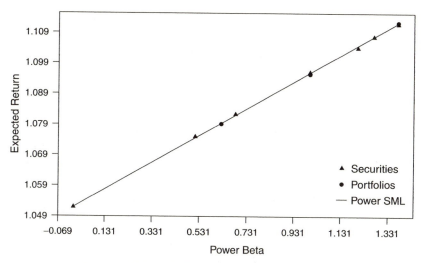

Figure 4-29 Case 7: The power security market line.

by vertical distance between a point and the SML line. As can be seen in the figure, the portfolio alpha values are small in this case, but some of the securities have positive alpha values and others have negative values.

For Case 7 the alpha values are smaller when power betas are utilized, as shown in Figure 4-29. While the fitted Constant Relative Risk Aversion function does not perfectly represent the pricing kernel, it comes very close to doing so.

Note that these positive and negative alpha values do not arise because securities are "mispriced" in the sense that prices reflect errors in investors' assumptions about the probabilities of the states of the world. Rather, they reflect the fact that neither the standard beta values nor the power beta values provide completely appropriate measures of market risk. However, in both cases, the approximations are quite good.

4.19. Sharpe Ratios

If investors care only about the mean and variance of portfolio return and it is possible to borrow or lend at the riskless rate of interest, the desirability of a portfolio can be assessed by computing its *Sharpe Ratio:* the ratio obtained by dividing (1) the portfolio's expected excess return over the riskless rate of interest by (2) the standard deviation of its excess return. In the world of the CAPM the market portfolio will have the highest possible Sharpe Ratio. The reason is relatively straightforward. If an investor can borrow or lend as desired, any portfolio can be levered up or down. A combination with a proportion k

invested in a risky portfolio and $1 - k$ in the riskless asset will have an expected excess return of k and a standard deviation equal to k times the standard deviation of the risky portfolio. Importantly, the Sharpe Ratio of the combination will be the same as that of the risky portfolio.

Now, imagine an investor choosing between two alternatives: (1) to invest in portfolio A plus borrowing or lending, as desired or (2) to invest in portfolio B plus borrowing or lending, as desired. If portfolio A has a higher Sharpe Ratio than B, then for any desired standard deviation of return, a combination of A plus borrowing or lending can provide a higher expected return than a combination of B plus borrowing or lending. If the investor cares only about expected return and standard deviation of return, portfolio A will be preferred to B, with borrowing or lending used to obtain the optimal amount of risk.

In the world of the CAPM every investor cares only about expected return and standard deviation of return. As long as it is possible to borrow or lend as desired at the riskless rate of interest, in equilibrium no portfolio will have a higher Sharpe Ratio than the market portfolio. Why? Because if this were the case, every investor would choose it instead of the market portfolio and the market would not clear.

In the world of the CAPM every investor will also hold a portfolio with the market Sharpe Ratio. Thus each investor will adopt a linear market-based strategy, with a return graph that plots as a straight line.

In more complex cases none of these results may hold exactly, although deviations may be relatively small. Figure 4-30 shows the computations for Case 7. Quade has chosen a portfolio with a higher Sharpe Ratio than that of the market as a whole, while Dagmar has chosen one with a lower Sharpe Ratio than that of the market.

Figure 4-31 shows the expected returns and standard deviations of return for both the portfolios and the securities in Case 7. Again following Sharpe (1970) the line drawn through the points for the riskless asset and the market portfolio is termed the *Capital Market Line* (CML). The slope of a line drawn from the riskless asset point to the point representing a portfolio or security equals its Sharpe Ratio. If the CAPM holds, every portfolio or security will plot on or below the CML and the portfolios that investors choose will plot on it. In this case, the securities plot below the CML but at least one possible portfolio

FIGURE 4-30
Case 7: Portfolio Sharpe Ratios

Portfolio Characteristics:	Exp Return	Exp ER	SD Return	SR
Market	1.096	0.044	0.116	0.378
Quade	1.080	0.027	0.071	0.383
Dagmar	1.113	0.060	0.162	0.372

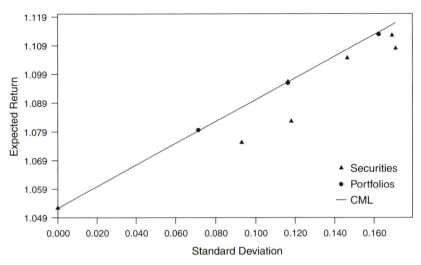

Figure 4-31 Case 7: The Capital Market Line.

(Quade's) plots above it and at least one investor (Dagmar) chooses a portfolio that plots below it.

Why is Dagmar content with a higher standard deviation than she could obtain from a combination of the market portfolio and borrowing or lending with the same expected return? The reason is that her strategy has another desirable property. This can be seen in Figure 4-32, which shows her return graph and that for a combination of the market portfolio and the riskless asset with the same expected return.

While Dagmar's portfolio will underperform the linear market-based strategy in normal times, it will either equal or exceed its performance in other markets. In particular, Dagmar's portfolio will beat the linear market strategy in times of extreme market returns. Given her preferences and the prices of the securities, she considers these characteristics sufficiently desirable to offset a slight increase in the standard deviation of returns.

While the Sharpe Ratios in Case 7 are not completely consistent with the properties of the CML of the CAPM, the differences are quite small. To see how far other situations may depart from the CAPM's characteristics, the simulation program produces a "CML graph" such as that shown in Figure 4-31 for every case.

4.20. Case 8: The Representative Investor

As we have seen, in a complete market with agreement, both state prices and state probabilities are known by all. Thus the pricing kernel is observable and

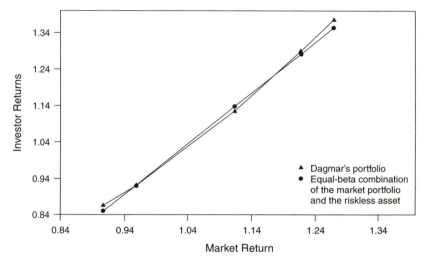

Figure 4-32 Case 7: Dagmar's portfolio and an equal-beta combination of the market portfolio and the riskless asset.

if it can be well approximated by a function of total market return, the general form of the MRRT will hold, with market risk measured by the beta of an asset with respect to the function of the market determined by the pricing kernel.

Now, consider a market with a single investor holding the entire market portfolio. Such an investor will not enter into any trades, hence security prices will be determined solely by his or her reservation prices for state claims. As a result, each PPC value will equal the investor's reservation price for the state in question divided by its probability. Repeating the formula shown earlier:

$$\frac{d_j m(X_j)}{m(X_1)} = \frac{p_j}{\pi_j}$$

Rearranging, as before:

$$m(X_j) = \frac{m(X_1)}{d_j} PPC_j$$

If the marginal utility function is the same for all states at a given time we can use a single discount factor (d) for all the states at time 2. Moreover, as we have seen, the choices an investor makes are unaffected if all his or her marginal utilities are multiplied by a constant. For convenience, we can thus assume that $m(X_1)$ equals 1. After these changes, for all states at time 2 we have:

$$m(X_j) = \frac{1}{d} PPC_j$$

This solves the mystery concerning the notation used for the pricing kernel in the financial economics literature. Each value of the pricing kernel (PPC_j) can be considered equal to a constant (d) times the marginal utility $m(X_j)$ of the representative investor for the associated total amount of consumption X_j.

Given a set of PPC values, we can compute a representative investor's marginal utilities for the amounts of aggregate consumption in each state using the formula above. But this does not provide any new information concerning possible prices for other amounts of aggregate consumption. Further, as we have seen, in an incomplete market more than one set of state prices may be consistent with observed security prices. For these reasons, financial economists have explored the efficacy of approximating observed data by assuming that prices are consistent with those in a market with a representative investor having a particular form of marginal utility function.

The simulation program provides an example of this type of calibration exercise for the case in which the representative investor is required to have constant relative risk aversion. In this case the equation can be written as:

$$X_j^{-b} = \frac{1}{d} PPC_j$$

Taking the logarithms of each side and simplifying gives:

$$\ln(PPC_j) = \ln(d) - b\ln(X_j)$$

But this is the equation that the simulator fits to the data in order to derive the coefficient (b) for the power beta calculations. Standard least-squares regression is used, with each future state constituting an observation, the $\ln(X_j)$ values serving as observations for the independent variable and the $\ln(PPC_j)$ values as observations for the dependent variable. The resulting slope coefficient is b and the intercept is $\ln(d)$. The former serves as the representative investor's risk aversion and the latter is converted to obtain his or her discount factor. The extent to which the equation fits the data is given by the R^2 value for the regression. The output for Case 7 is shown in Figure 4-33. As can be seen, in this case a market with a quadratic utility investor (Quade) and an investor with decreasing relative risk aversion (Dagmar) can be represented quite well by a single investor with a constant relative risk aversion.

To illustrate further, we create Case 8. We now have only one investor, Rex, who holds all the securities from Case 7 and has the preferences shown in Figure 4-33. Figure 4-34 compares the security prices from Cases 7 and 8. While they are not the same, none of the prices from Case 8 differs by more than 1 percent from that of Case 7.

In this instance, Rex has served his function well. The market in Case 8 is similar, if not exactly the same, as the one in Case 7. Rex thus represents the situation in Case 7 rather nicely. More generally, it is tempting to want to compare an investor's characteristics with those of a representative investor,

FIGURE 4-33

Case 7: Kernel Approximation Results

Kernel Approximation:	Parameter
Risk aversion	3.399
Discount	0.936
R^2	0.999

tilting the investor's portfolio away from the market portfolio based on the differences between his or her preferences, predictions, and positions and those of the representative investor. Unfortunately this is not always easily done. First, it should be remembered that in markets that are not sufficiently complete it may be possible to create alternative representative investors, depending on the state prices utilized. Worse yet, with disagreement on probabilities the range of alternatives is likely to be even wider. Differences in investor positions add to the complications. Finally, no standard functional form for the representative investor's preferences may be able to replicate the equilibrium security prices with a great deal of accuracy.

The notion that a single investor with a relatively simple set of preferences can represent a complex market can provide great comfort to those who build models of financial markets. But here, as in most economic applications, it is important to exercise caution before making too many simplifying assumptions.

4.21. *Ex Ante* and *Ex Post* Relationships

This book focuses on the relationships among economic variables before the fact and the implications of those relationships for investors' portfolio choices. More elegantly, we can say that our analyses deal primarily with *ex ante* values. But it is difficult to measure such values. In recent years, financial economists have begun to use survey results and experiments in which human subjects play

FIGURE 4-34

Cases 7 and 8: Security Prices

Security Prices:	STBond	GovBds	NonGvBds	ValueStx	GthStx	SmlStx
Case 7	0.950	0.952	0.957	0.989	0.947	0.967
Case 8	0.944	0.946	0.951	0.981	0.940	0.961
Percentage difference	−0.65	−0.61	−0.63	−0.75	−0.70	−0.71

the roles of financial market participants in order to obtain measures of individual's predictions about the future. Nonetheless, the majority of empirical research in this area relies on the analysis of actual outcomes over many periods. In effect, historic frequencies of experienced outcomes are used as proxies for predicted probabilities of possible alternative future outcomes. The data thus measure actual outcomes in past periods (*ex post* outcomes) rather than predictions of what might happen in the next period (*ex ante* forecasts).

This would be fine if (1) the *ex ante* equilibrium had been the same in each past period and (2) the alternative possible outcomes occurred with frequencies equal to their *ex ante* probabilities. Unfortunately, in the vast majority of cases neither of these two conditions is likely to have been met. Thus one should view many "tests" of proposed models of equilibrium in financial markets with considerable skepticism.

We illustrate the nature of the problem using the equilibrium results from Case 7. In the SML graph in Figure 4-28, the six securities plot very close to the line representing the combinations of expected return and beta that can be obtained with combinations of the market portfolio and borrowing or lending. The differences are small, with the largest alpha value equal to .003 (0.3 percent/year) and the smallest –.002 (–0.2 percent/year). The SML equation is thus a good approximation for the *ex ante* relationship between the securities' expected returns and their beta values.

Now imagine that this equilibrium relationship has held for 25 years. To simulate a possible historical record for this length of time we use a Monte Carlo procedure using a random number generator. In effect, an urn is filled with balls on each of which is printed a state name. Five percent of the balls are labeled "Depression1," another 5 percent are labeled "Depression2," and so on. For each of the 25 years a ball is drawn and the security returns for the associated state entered in the historic record. This record is then used to compute security average returns, the returns on the market portfolio, and security beta values. Figure 4-35 shows the resulting *ex post* relationships, with average returns plotted on the vertical axis and realized beta values on the horizontal axis.

The historic alpha values were much larger in absolute value than were the expected alpha values. The government bond index fund had the best record, with an alpha of .0103 or 1.03 percent per year. The value stocks fund had the best performance among the equity classes, with an alpha of .0091, or 0.91 percent per year. The biggest loser was the growth stock fund, with an alpha of –.0245 or –2.45 percent per year.

This is simply an example. But the numbers in Case 7 were chosen to be reasonably representative of returns that might be obtained from portfolios including the securities in each of these asset classes. And, despite the diversification within each of the portfolios, we obtained an *ex post* record for 25 years that differed substantially from the *ex ante* relationships.

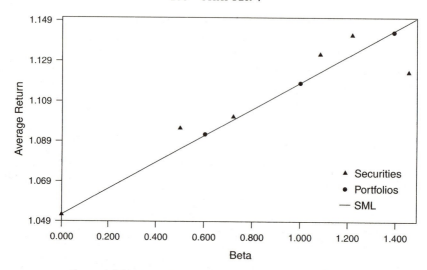

Figure 4-35 Case 7: *Ex post* Security Market Line: 25 years.

The results in Figure 4-35 are based on one possible 25-year record (the first one tried). But this is only one of countless possible 25-year scenarios. To obtain a more thorough view of the possible results over a 25-year period the analysis was repeated, obtaining 1,000 possible 25-year historic records. Figure 4-36 shows the distribution of the resulting 6,000 alpha values for the six securities in the 1,000 simulations. While almost 40 percent were between –0.5 percent per year and +0.5 percent per year, more than 60 percent were outside that range. Most dramatically, there were some possible cases in which an asset class achieved an alpha value more than 10 times its expected value.

These results illustrate the range of possible disparities between *ex ante* and *ex post* values in financial markets. We will return to this issue in Chapter 8. For now, it suffices to quote the advice by the U.S. Securities and Exchange Commission offered to those who invest in mutual funds: "Past performance is not a reliable indicator of future performance." To which we add ". . . nor often of the performance that was expected in the past."

4.22. Summary

This chapter has covered a great deal of ground, focusing on cases involving agreement among investors on the probabilities of future outcomes, the absence of outside sources of consumption, and the lack of state-dependent preferences among outcomes at the same time period. We have examined conditions in which any type of claim on future consumption can be traded or equivalent

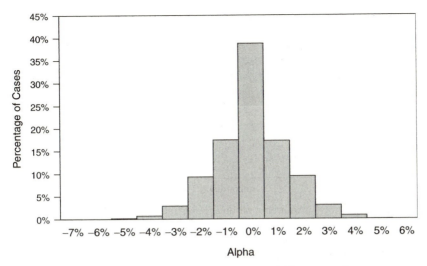

Figure 4-36 Case 7: *Ex post* alpha values: 1,000 25-year simulations.

results can be obtained using available securities—conditions that will be relaxed in subsequent chapters. Nonetheless, the examples in this chapter provide much of the received wisdom of current academic investment theory and advice. At the risk of overkill, we summarize by repeating the results.

In this setting, expected returns on securities or portfolios are solely a function of the relationships between their returns and the returns on the market portfolio as a whole. More specifically, the expected return of a security or portfolio is related to its covariance with a function of the return on the market portfolio. Thus the MRRT holds:

Only market risk is rewarded with higher expected return,

with market risk measured using the function of the market portfolio's return determined by the pricing kernel.

Given this, sensible investors should take only market risk. And in this setting, they all do, primarily because they all agree on the probabilities of future events. Thus the MRRC holds:

Don't take non-market risk.

Equivalently:

Follow a market-based strategy.

In this setting all the investors do just this.

These results follow from the plausible assumption that the less consumption an investor has, the more he or she values additional consumption. Equilibrium asset prices reflect this. The cost of a chance to get consumption in a bad (low aggregate consumption) state will be greater than that of a chance to get consumption in a good (high aggregate consumption) state. From this follows the existence of a risk premium for the market portfolio vis-à-vis the riskless investment, the desirability of more and less aggressive market-based strategies for investors with, respectively, greater and smaller risk tolerance, and many other aspects of standard investment advice.

These are comfortable worlds for the theorist, and lead to advice favored by many financial economists. But they predict that everyone will act in accordance with that advice, which is patently untrue.

Many investors take non-market risk. The points in their portfolio return graphs do not fall neatly on an upward-sloping curve. Why do investors do this? And what sort of advice should one offer investors in a world in which such behavior takes place? To approach these questions we have to leave the comfortable setting of this chapter. Such is the task of Chapters 5 and 6.

FIVE

POSITIONS

5.1. Investor Diversity

IN THE CASES that we have analyzed thus far, investors exhibited substantial diversity. They held different initial portfolios and had different marginal utility functions. On the other hand, they were alike in a number of respects. Most important, they all agreed on the probabilities of future states of the world. Moreover, none had sources of consumption outside the financial markets. Finally, none favored any future state over another—more specifically, for each investor the marginal utilities of consumption in future states with the same consumption were the same.

In this chapter, we investigate cases in which investors are more diverse. First, we consider the impact of outside sources of consumption, which we term investors' *positions*. Then we examine the possible impact of differences in investor's preferences for consumption in different possible states of the world—differences that may also reflect the influence of outside positions, broadly construed. As before, we retain the assumption that all investors agree on the probabilities of future states of the world, leaving for Chapter 6 the analysis of the possible effects of disagreement concerning future prospects.

5.2. Salaries and Collateral

For most people, investments are only one source of consumption. Other sources include wage and salary income and consumption obtained from durable goods and physical assets such as owner-occupied housing. To keep matters simple we will divide all non-investment sources of consumption into two categories: *salary* and *collateral*. Collateral includes items such as houses and cars that can be pledged to borrow money and to take other positions that require payments in some or all future states of the world. Salary cannot be used in this way, primarily because of bankruptcy laws. In many countries if one's debts exceed one's assets it is possible to declare bankruptcy, default on debts that exceed one's asset value, and keep income from subsequent labor services.

Of course there are gray areas. People can take some uncollateralized loans, since bankruptcy may involve social stigma, difficulty in obtaining future credit, and so on. The cost of borrowing may also be greater the greater a person's debt as a percentage of the value of assets posted as collateral. But these aspects can

FIGURE 5-1

Case 9: Portfolios Table

Portfolios:	Consume	Bond	MFC	HFC
Mario	49	0	5	0
Hue	49	0	0	5

be represented reasonably well by allocating consumption arising from actual salary and non-investment assets between our specified categories of salary and collateral.

For purposes of our simulations, salaries and collateral are represented as tables indicating the amount of consumption provided in each state of the world. Bankruptcy laws are taken into account by requiring that in each state an investor must have total consumption from sources slightly greater than the consumption provided by salary alone in that state. The net result is the denial of any trade that would result in a situation in which an investor could file for bankruptcy and fail to make a promised payment in any state. No such procedure is needed for collateral, since the party to whom a payment is due can seize the underlying property if needed.

5.3. Case 9: Positions That Affect Portfolios but Not Prices

To keep matters simple, we return to Mario, Hue, and the fish, modifying Case 1 to illustrate the effects of these new aspects. Case 9 is similar to Case 1 with a few key differences. Mario starts with the same overall benefits from the Monterey Fishing Company except that half is provided as a profit-sharing retirement payment that can be used as collateral, with the remainder in tradable shares. Hue is in a similar position with regard to Half Moon Bay Fishing Company. Figures 5-1 and 5-2 show the new inputs. Everything else is the same as in Case 1.

For realism we assume markets are incomplete so that Mario and Hue trade only their shares of the two stocks and the riskless bond. The resulting port-

FIGURE 5-2

Case 9: Collateral

Collateral:	Now	BadS	BadN	GoodS	GoodN
Mario	0	25	15	40	20
Hue	0	15	25	20	40

FIGURE 5-3
Case 1: Equilibrium Portfolios

Portfolios:	Consume	Bond	MFC	HFC
Market	98.00	0.00	10.00	10.00
Mario	48.77	−12.16	6.24	6.24
Hue	49.23	12.16	3.76	3.76

folios of tradable securities differ from those in Case 1 in predictable ways, as a comparison of Figures 5-3 and 5-4 shows. Mario has adjusted his portfolio to reflect that fact that his outside income is equivalent to five shares of MFC and Hue has adjusted her portfolio to reflect the fact that her outside income is equivalent to five shares of HFC. Their total consumption in each of the future states of the world is thus precisely the same in both Case 1 and Case 9.

Since Mario and Hue have the same consumption patterns across states as they did in Case 1, their marginal utilities of consumption will also be the same in both cases, as will security prices, state prices, security expected returns, and security beta values. But Mario and Hue's portfolios of tradable securities will be very different in the two situations. The changes can be seen by comparing the Capital Market Line (CML) graphs in Figures 5-5 and 5-6.

Both Mario and Hue now choose portfolios of tradable securities with Sharpe Ratios that are much lower than that of the market portfolio. This does not concern them, since each takes into account not only the risk of his or her portfolio, but also the extent to which it fits with other sources of consumption.

In this case the Market Risk/Reward Theorem (MRRT) holds because the market portfolio of investment securities has future payoffs that are proportional to the aggregate amounts of consumption. Hence the returns on the market portfolio are the same as those on the broader portfolio that includes all sources of aggregate consumption. Clearly, however, the Market Risk/Reward Corollary (MRRC) does not hold, as can be seen in the returns graph in Figure 5-7 (shown without connecting lines).

FIGURE 5-4
Case 9: Equilibrium Portfolios

Portfolios:	Consume	Bond	MFC	HFC
Market	98.00	0.00	5.00	5.00
Mario	48.77	−12.16	1.24	6.24
Hue	49.23	12.16	3.76	−1.24

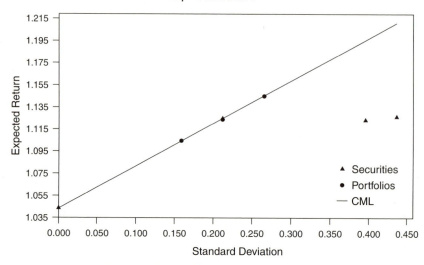

Figure 5-5 Case 1: The Capital Market Line.

Mario (whose returns are shown by the diamonds) takes non-market risk, as does Hue (whose returns are shown by the squares). Each does so, of course, in order to have the same amount of total consumption in each pair of states with the same aggregate consumption. Had we included all consumption when measuring both individual portfolios and the market portfolio the MRRC would have held.

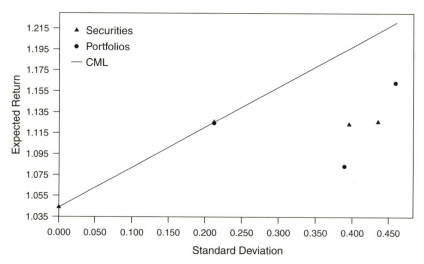

Figure 5-6 Case 9: The Capital Market Line.

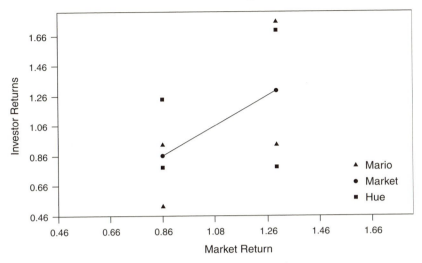

Figure 5-7 Case 9: Returns graph.

Case 9 involved an outside source of consumption that could be used as collateral. However, it turned out that in the equilibrium only Mario incurred any obligation to make payments, and he chose a portfolio that provided sufficient payments to more than cover his obligation in every state of the world. Hence the outside source of consumption could have as well have been salaries. The results would have been precisely the same, since the "no-bankruptcy" constraint would not have been binding.

This emphasizes a point made earlier. From a purely investment viewpoint it is generally unwise to buy stock in one's own company. There is a strong investment argument for holding a portfolio that has less than the market proportion of stock in one's company and more than market proportions of stocks in other companies (including those of competitors!). At least partially offsetting this good investment advice are the concerns of those who run firms. It seems unlikely that the board of a corporation would be pleased to find that the chief executive not only refused to invest in the firm but also had significant amounts of money invested in the stocks of the company's closest competitors. The primary argument for investment in company stock relies on the assumption that the holder will have a greater incentive to further the interests of the company. The argument against such investment is simply that the resulting lack of diversification is bad investment policy.

If company stock is to be held, it is important for an investor to choose a portfolio that complements the payments from that stock. Those who fail to take such holdings into account when making investment decisions will almost certainly obtain inferior portfolios.

5.4. Case 10: Positions That Affect Prices and Portfolios

A key feature of Case 9 is that in states for which the consumption provided by securities is the same (e.g., BadS and BadN) the consumption from salaries and collateral is also the same, and thus so is total consumption from all sources. Since Mario and Hue were concerned with all sources of consumption, this led to asset prices that gave equal PPC values for all such states. If non-investment consumption sources line up with investment consumption sources in this manner as in Case 9, the presence of significant positions may not affect asset prices at all, even though they will almost certainly cause people to take non-market risk in their investment portfolios.

But what if this condition isn't met? Case 10 provides an example. It is similar to Case 9 with one important difference. First, we assume that Mario and Hue have outside income from salaries rather than from collateral. Second, we assume that in addition to the previous amounts, Mario can get extra work that will bring him five additional fish in either of the two states in which the fish go south. The resulting salaries table is shown in Figure 5-8. Neither Mario nor Hue has any collateral. The rest of the inputs are the same as in Case 9.

As before, the total consumption provided by portfolios of tradable securities is the same in the two Bad states. It is also the same in the two Good states. But this is not true for total consumption from salaries nor, therefore, for total consumption.

Figure 5-9 shows the type of pricing kernel graph used in other cases, in which the PPC value for each state is plotted with the total consumption in that state. There is nothing exceptional about this figure: states with greater aggregate consumption are cheaper, in the sense that they have lower prices per chance.

But we can no longer make our usual assumption that the return on the market portfolio is proportional to aggregate consumption. We know that the return on the market portfolio is the same in the two Bad states and that it is the same in the two Good states. Plotting the PPC values with the market portfolio returns gives the decidedly different graph shown in Figure 5-10. As can be seen, the two Bad states, which have the same market return, have different PPC values. Thus they have different expected returns. The same can be

FIGURE 5-8
Case 10: Salaries

Salaries:	Now	BadS	BadN	GoodS	GoodN
Mario	0	30	15	45	20
Hue	0	15	25	20	40

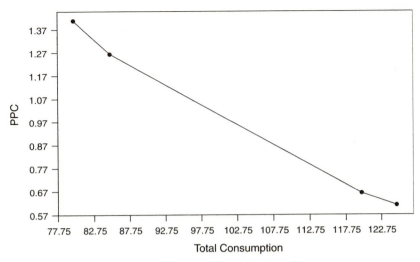

Figure 5-9 Case 10: The pricing kernel and total consumption.

said for the two Good states. Expected return is no longer a function of market return, so the MRRT is violated. Not surprisingly, so is the MRRC.

There is more. The plot of security and portfolio expected return and beta values, shown in Figure 5-11, is unfamiliar. What explains these results? The answer is straightforward. When we look at the capital market, we see only part of the picture. In principle, we should broaden our view to include all forms of

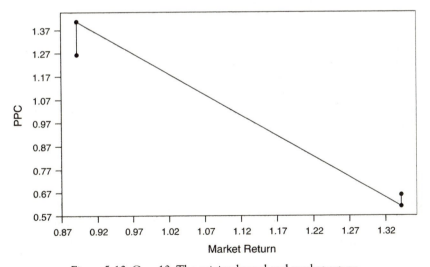

Figure 5-10 Case 10: The pricing kernel and market return.

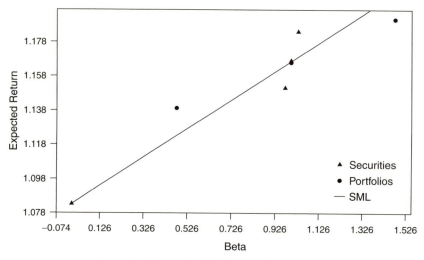

Figure 5-11 Case 10: The Security Market Line.

capital—human, tangible, and financial. The market portfolio would then in-clude all capital, beta values would be measured accordingly, and all would be well with the world and with asset pricing theory.

But it is hard enough to estimate expected returns, beta values, and other values for traded securities, let alone include human and tangible capital. As a result, most analysts hope that the world is closer to Case 9 than to Case 10. If so, expected returns may be similar if not identical for all states in which the return on the market portfolio of traded securities is the same. Then the MRRT will hold, at least approximately. Nonetheless, investors with diverse non-investment sources of consumption should take on non-market risk so that their investment portfolios will complement their other assets. As a result the MRRC will not hold for investment portfolios. This is not all bad, for it gives financial planners and other advisors something to do even in a world in which everyone agrees on the probabilities of possible future outcomes.

5.5. Taxes and Home Bias

We have seen that investors' diverse positions can affect portfolios and may affect asset prices. Two likely causes of such diversity arise from differences in tax status and location. In many countries, different forms of income are taxed differently. Moreover, people pay different tax rates on income from the same source. In the United States, for example, interest from bonds issued by states and municipalities is not subject to certain income taxes that must be paid on interest from other bonds. For people with high marginal tax rates such bonds can be quite attractive. For those with low marginal tax rates they are less so. And for those saving in tax-deferred retirement accounts such bonds offer no tax advantage at all. As a result, municipal bonds are priced to give lower before-tax returns than taxable bonds of similar duration and credit quality. Asset prices reflect this, and people adjust their portfolios accordingly, with many high-tax investors investing in more than their proportionate share of the municipal bond market, many low-tax investors holding few if any such bonds, and, with rare (and often inexplicable) exceptions, municipal bonds are absent from tax-deferred accounts.

Investors' home countries and currencies also affect portfolios. While securities issued in the United States constitute roughly half the outstanding value of the world's marketable securities, more than half of Americans' invested wealth is allocated to American securities. Europeans hold a disproportionate share of their wealth (relative to the world market portfolio) in European securities. Such *home bias* is also present in Japan and other countries. Some of this bias may be based on political concerns or excessive myopia. But some is certainly due to differences in investors' positions. If you live in a country and spend a large part of your budget on goods and services produced in that country and priced in its currency, to some extent you can purchase your future consumption by investing in companies domiciled in your country. Once we drop the convenient assumption of a single good (fish) or generalized purchasing power (money) there well may be a rational basis for at least some home bias.

While home bias certainly does affect portfolios and probably should do so, it is not obvious that it need affect asset prices. As with other aspects of capital markets, one should not jump to the conclusion that diversity that can and should affect portfolios will necessarily affect asset prices.

5.6. Case 11: Senior, Junior, and the Bankruptcy Law

In none of the cases that we have examined thus far has an investor been precluded from purchasing or selling a security, given his or her budget and the prices at which trades could be made. To be sure, each simulation included constraints specifying the minimum consumption allowed each investor in each state, but such constraints were not binding when equilibrium was attained. We now turn to a case in which such a constraint is binding.

The goal of Case 11 is to reflect possible differences between young and old investors, as best possible in a two-date setting. Young investors tend to have limited financial capital but considerable human capital, which can produce future savings from income. Older investors tend to have considerable financial

FIGURE 5-12
Case 11: Inputs

Securities:	Consume	Bills	Bond	Stock
Now	1	0	0	0
Depression	0	1	34	36
Recession	0	1	39	56
Normality	0	1	42	68
Prosperity	0	1	43	72
Boom	0	1	45	80

Portfolios:	Consume	Bills	Bond	Stock
Senior	1000	0	9	9
Junior	1000	0	1	1

Probabilities:	Now	Depression	Recession	Normality	Prosperity	Boom
Probability	1.00	0.10	0.20	0.40	0.20	0.10

Preferences:	Time	Risk
Senior	0.96	4
Junior	0.96	4

Salaries:	Now	Depression	Recession	Normality	Prosperity	Boom
Senior	0.00	100	100	100	100	100
Junior	0.00	900	900	900	900	900

capital and relatively little human capital, since their future income is limited, as is their future savings.

Figure 5-12 shows all the inputs for Case 11. As can be seen, there are two investors, whom we call Senior and Junior. Senior has nine times as many bonds and stocks as Junior, but Junior has nine times as much consumption from salary. Happily, each of them has a totally secure job, with the same income in every state. By design, their overall abilities to consume are similar.

FIGURE 5-13
Case 11: Consumptions with No Bankruptcy Law

Consumptions:	Now	Depression	Recession	Normality	Prosperity	Boom
Total	2000	1700	1950	2100	2150	2250
Senior	1000	850	975	1050	1075	1125
Junior	1000	850	975	1050	1075	1125

Moreover, despite their differences in age, both have precisely the same preferences. And they agree on the probabilities of the states as well.

Despite the substantial differences in Senior and Junior's positions, one would anticipate that they would end up with similar overall consumption patterns in the absence of any limitations on their abilities to take long and short positions in financial securities. To see if this would be the case, we changed the title of the positions table from Salaries to Collateral. The resulting equilibrium consumptions are shown in Figure 5-13. To accomplish this result, Junior borrows heavily from Senior in order to purchase a portfolio of risky securities, as shown in Figure 5-14.

But there is a problem. Both Senior and Junior choose a consumption of 850 in the Depression state. This is fine for Senior. His salary is 100 in that state, so 750 comes from his portfolio. But Junior has a salary of 900 in the Depression state. To achieve consumption of 850 he has taken portfolio positions that require him to pay Senior 50 if there is a depression, an amount that can only come from his salary. In effect, Junior has pledged his income as collateral. This would be fine in the absence of a bankruptcy law. But if there is such a law and a Depression ensues, Junior can simply declare bankruptcy, keep his 900 salary, and tell Senior that he is not going to fulfill his loan obligation. Of course, Senior will anticipate this, refusing to be put in a position in which a state-contingent promise will not be fulfilled. This is why in our simulations no trade is allowed that would leave a trader with total consumption in any state that is smaller than his or her salary in that state.

FIGURE 5-14
Case 11: Portfolios with No Bankruptcy Law

Portfolios:	Consume	Bills	Bond	Stock
Market	2000.00	0.00	10.00	10.00
Senior	1000.03	311.92	8.52	4.12
Junior	999.97	−311.92	1.48	5.88

FIGURE 5-15
Case 11: Portfolios with a Bankruptcy Law

Portfolios:	Consume	Bills	Bond	Stock
Market	2000.00	0.00	10.00	10.00
Senior	1002.06	181.63	8.79	6.07
Junior	997.94	−181.63	1.21	3.93

To see the impact of a bankruptcy law on Case 11, we simply change the title of the positions table back to Salaries and find the resulting equilibrium. The results, shown in Figure 5-15, are as expected. Junior borrows considerably less than before and holds smaller positions in risky securities.

There is a certain frustration in this situation, as can been seen from the reservation prices for securities, shown in Figure 5-16. Junior would be willing to sell a treasury bill to Senior at a price of 0.90 and Senior would be willing to buy it for a price of 0.95. But Senior knows that if the transaction were completed, Junior wouldn't fully deliver on his obligation if there is a Depression. Thus no further trades are made.

If such situations are widespread, capital markets could be affected significantly, as shown in a paper on the subject titled "Junior Can't Borrow: A New Perspective on the Equity Premium" (Constantinides, Donaldson, and Mehra 2002).

On a more general level, this case shows that human capital can have a major impact on optimal portfolio choice. Figure 5-17 shows the returns on our investors' portfolios. Senior's is somewhat less risky than the market portfolio, but Junior's is a great deal riskier. This is not because they have different preferences; as indicated, their risk aversions are precisely the same. Rather it is because much of Junior's wealth is riskless already and he thus seeks to add risk and expected return via his portfolio. Senior has most of his wealth in financial assets and chooses to take somewhat less risk than that of the market portfolio so that Junior can take more. As always, investors' positions average to

FIGURE 5-16
Case 11: Security Reservation Prices with a Bankruptcy Law

Reservation Prices:	Consume	Bills	Bond	Stock
Senior	1.00	0.95	37.65	55.53
Junior	1.00	0.90	36.36	55.53

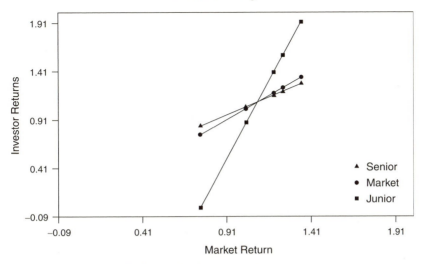

Figure 5-17 Case 11: Investor and market returns.

that of the market, but in this case Junior has a much smaller part of the market of financial assets than does Senior.

These results reflect the fact that both investors had riskless jobs. The situation could have been very different if each of their positions had been dependent on overall economic conditions or if one had a position subject to greater economic risk than that of the other. It may well be that in many corporations, wages and salaries are somewhat less risky than corporate securities. If so, the typical worker in such a firm may well wish to hold a less risky portfolio of financial assets as he or she moves closer to retirement.

More generally, the conclusion to be drawn by investors and financial advisors is simple: take both the nature and the amount of human capital into account when selecting an investment portfolio.

5.7. State-Dependent Preferences

In our previous cases, investors had time preference, discounting expected utility in future states of the world more than that in the present, but all states at the same future date were discounted at the same rate. But what if some investors have reasons to prefer consumption in one future state to consumption in another state at the same date?

As we will see, state-dependent preferences can affect portfolio choice, asset prices, or both.

FIGURE 5-18
Case 12: Discounts

Discounts:	Now	BadS	BadN	GoodS	GoodN
Mario	1	0.99	0.96	0.96	0.96
Hue	1	0.99	0.96	0.96	0.96

5.7.1. Case 12: Common State-Dependent Preferences

To create the next example we revert to Case 1, then make one change. In Case 12 both Mario and Hue prize consumption in state BadS more than that in any other future state, and they do so equally. Here is the story: when there are small numbers of fish that tend to go south, the weather is cold and rainy, making people hungrier. The simulation discounts for this case are given in the detailed table shown in Figure 5-18. All the other inputs are the same as in Case 1. Figure 5-19 shows the PPC values and consumptions when equilibrium is reached. As can be seen, two states with the same aggregate consumption (BadS and BadN) sell for different prices per chance. Thus the MRRT does not hold.

Although two states with the same aggregate consumption have different expected returns, neither investor chooses to take non-market risk, as can be seen in the returns graph in Figure 5-20. Thus the MRRC holds. Asset prices are affected but portfolio choices are not.

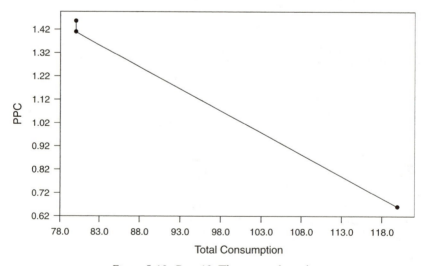

Figure 5-19 Case 12: The pricing kernel.

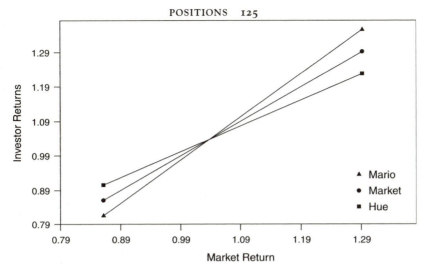

Figure 5-20 Case 12: Investor and market returns.

5.7.2. Case 13: Diverse State-Dependent Preferences

Case 13 involves even stranger preferences. Here Mario and Hue have different preferences over states but one is the mirror image of the other, as shown
in Figure 5-21. In this case the PPC values fall very close to a function solely
of aggregate consumption as shown in Figure 5-22. Thus the MRRT holds,
at least as a good approximation. But as seen in Figure 5-23, investors choose
to take at least some non-market risk and the MRRC is violated, albeit only
slightly.

To be sure, both Cases 12 and 13 are contrived. In more plausible situations,
both asset prices and portfolio choices would likely be affected. But these cases
illustrate once more the fact that prices are affected more by the *average* of
investor's preferences than by their variation, while portfolios are affected more
by the variation in investors' preferences than by their averages.

The impacts of such attitudes on prices will depend on investors' relative
wealth and on their attitudes toward risk. Roughly, the greater an investor's wealth

FIGURE 5-21
Case 13: Discounts

Discounts:	Now	BadS	BadN	GoodS	GoodN
Mario	1.00	0.99	0.96	0.96	0.96
Hue	1.00	0.96	0.99	0.96	0.96

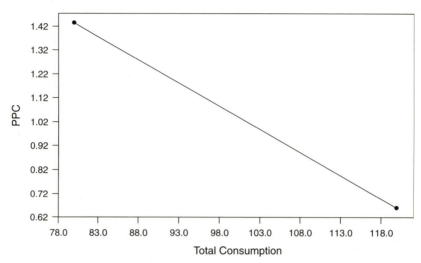

Figure 5-22 Case 13: The pricing kernel.

and the greater his or her willingness to take on risk, the more he or she is likely to affect asset prices. Unfortunately except in special cases, no simple formula can capture the relationship exactly. But the intuition is clear. Rich people have more votes in capital markets, and less risk-averse investors cast more of their votes for risky securities.

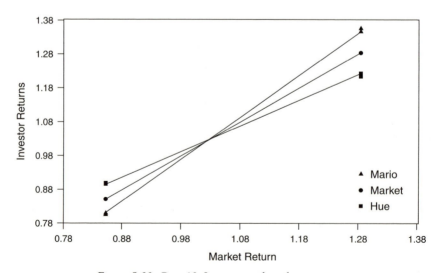

Figure 5-23 Case 13: Investor and market returns.

5.7.3. Horizons

In this book we cover only cases involving two dates: "now" and "the future," with one period between. In the real world, of course, most investors' *horizons* extend well beyond the next month or the next year. Moreover, investors have different horizons, owing to differences in age, health, the ages of their children, and so on. To adequately take such diversity into account presents a huge challenge to anyone trying to build an analytic model or computer simulation of the equilibrium process. We do not attempt the feat but can at least provide a hint of the possible impact investors' horizons may have on asset prices and portfolio choice.

Imagine that in Case 1 the likely alternative catches of fish after date 2 differ, depending on the actual situation at date 2. For example, long-term prospects might be less desirable after a bad season in which more fish went south. This could well affect people's attitudes about consumption in that state at date 2, especially if some of the fish obtained at date 2 could be frozen for later use or kept alive and used to create more fish in the future. Moreover, the effect might differ between those with longer horizons and those with shorter horizons. These differences could be represented, albeit imperfectly, by assigning different discounts to states, as we did in Cases 12 and 13. Asset prices, portfolios, or (more likely) both could be affected. If prices are affected, expected returns may not be solely a function of consumption in the next period. And if portfolios are affected, some people will choose to take non-market risk.

Horizon effects are being actively investigated by financial economists. Few are so bold as to try to work from a complete model of equilibrium based on multiperiod production, consumption, and exchange. But such ideas provide a motivation for the widely held belief in the investment industry that investors should "tilt" their portfolios to some extent toward asset classes that have desirable characteristics for their particular horizons.

5.8. Summary

Investors are different. They have different preferences, different positions, and they often make different predictions. We consider the latter in the next chapter. In this chapter, we have explored the possible effects of differences in investor positions, including some that can be represented albeit imperfectly as differences in preferences.

Differences in investor positions present significant challenges to the standard conclusions of asset pricing theory. The greatest challenge arises when investors have diverse positions that generate large amounts of consumption outside the capital markets and such consumption is poorly correlated with the returns on traded securities. In such circumstances, the MRRT and MRRC might hold rather well if all sources of consumption were included in the analysis. But measurement of all of these variables is difficult, if not impossible, and rarely attempted. For better or worse, analysts focus instead on portfolios of traded securities and on the prices of such securities. In this narrower view, neither the MRRT nor the MRRC may hold.

What can then be said about investment portfolios and security prices in the presence of outside sources of income and consumption? Even with agreement, one cannot help but conclude that some investors should make their portfolio choices taking into account outside positions and hence take some non-market risk in their security portfolios to better complement their other sources of income and consumption. At least some investors should thus disregard the MRRC.

But this does not imply that there is a reward in higher expected return for taking some types of non-market risk. The MRRT may still hold. This could be the case if market risk is a good proxy for the risk associated with total consumption. The MRRT might also hold if security markets are dominated by individuals who depend on their portfolios for most of their income and consumption.

Some who study the financial markets have argued that there are rewards for bearing certain types of non-market risk. If so, such rewards may well come from assets that exacerbate the risks associated with investors' outside positions rather than mitigate such outside risks. In efficient capital markets there is no such thing as a free lunch.

SIX

PREDICTIONS

6.1. Disagreement

ALL OUR PREVIOUS CASES had one common aspect: investors agreed on the probabilities of future states. While people chose to hold different portfolios, in an important sense all their actions were based on the same predictions. There was no distinction between what our investors did and what they should have done. They correctly chose different portfolios because they had different preferences and/or positions.

Anyone who has observed or participated in the investment world knows that the assumption of agreement is a fanciful representation of reality. Much of the behavior of real investors can be explained only by acknowledging that they make *bets* with one another, whether they know it or not.

Betting is most obvious in circumstances in which people take risks that need not be borne. When you and I bet on a football game, it is because we have different views of the likely outcomes. No productive purpose is served by our wager unless one or both of us are hedging to have some good news ("I won") if the outcome inflicts emotional or other financial pain ("my team lost").

Betting in financial markets may be less obvious. When I hold less than my proportionate share of Hewlett Packard stock, someone must hold more than his or her proportionate share. Do our portfolios differ because we have different positions or preferences? Perhaps, but we may hold different portfolios because we have different predictions, or because we have faith in different people (investment managers) who themselves have different predictions.

Consider an investor who puts all of her equity money in a single mutual fund that holds stocks of only 200 companies. How could one possibly argue that her positions or preferences make it optimal to overweight these companies and underweight all the companies not represented in the portfolio? Absent very unusual circumstances, she was likely motivated in part by a belief that the manager of the mutual fund could find *mispriced* securities, and thereby "beat the market." Most mutual funds suggest that they can do so, but of course not all can. Given sufficient time, one would imagine that diversity in predictions would decrease. If you want to trade with me at a price that seems a bargain to me, I may question my own predictions. Bids, offers, and prices of actual transactions can carry information about others' predictions, although such information is difficult to infer owing to the influence of diverse positions and preferences as well as lack of complete information about others' portfolios. Economists sometimes justify a focus on a single set of predictions on the grounds that, given enough time, expectations will be *rational* in the sense that everyone agrees on probabilities. While this may be very sensible in some domains, people operating in financial markets simply do not have sufficient time to process information and converge to a single set of predictions before the information changes. Hence we need to try to understand the characteristics of equilibrium in markets in which there is significant disagreement about future probabilities. Such is the task of this chapter.

6.2. Active and Passive Management

It is helpful to remember that the laws of addition and subtraction have not been repealed. Imagine a world in which all the securities in a dollar-denominated market are held by two types of investors. *Passive investors* hold proportionate shares of all securities, while *active investors* do not. Now imagine that a year has passed. Before costs, the return on the average dollar invested in this market is X percent. So is the return on the average dollar invested passively. Given the laws of arithmetic, so too is the return on the average dollar invested actively. But investment costs money, and active investment management costs more than passive management. Hence the return *after costs* on the average actively managed dollar must be less than the return after costs on the average passively managed dollar. Some active managers can beat passive managers, but after costs, the average actively managed dollar will underperform the average passively managed dollar, as argued in Sharpe (1991).

The differences in performance are not trivial. There are now many types of index funds, each of which either purchases proportionate shares of all the securities in a designated market sector or attempts to replicate the results of doing so. Such funds can have very low costs since they need to do little research, have low turnover, and enjoy other economies. Well managed index funds available for purchase by individual investors have annual management and distribution costs as low as 0.08 to 0.10 percent of asset value (that is, 8 to 10 cents per year for each 100 dollars of asset value). Actively managed funds can have management and distribution costs of 0.75 percent to well over 2.00 percent of asset value per year (that is, 75 cents to 2 dollars per year for each 100 dollars of asset value). Actively managed funds also incur higher turnover and thus must bear additional costs; they may also impose greater tax burdens on investors owing to more frequent realization of capital gains.

By design, active fund managers diversify less than is possible. At base, their predictions about the future differ from the predictions reflected in current asset prices. Such managers have more or less idiosyncratic notions of how securities should be priced and look for divergences from those prices, holding disproportionately large shares of securities that appear to be underpriced and disproportionately small shares of securities that appear to be overpriced. At the end of the day, some such managers will win and some will lose, but net of costs the average actively-managed dollar (or euro or yen) will underperform the average passively managed dollar (or euro or yen).

6.3. Vox Populi

In a highly entertaining book, James Surowiecki summarizes a host of research that leads to the conclusion stated in the title: *The Wisdom of Crowds: Why the Many Are Smarter Than the Few and How Collective Wisdom Shapes Business, Economics, Societies and Nations* (Surowiecke 2004). He begins with the results of a small study performed by Francis Galton long before the dawning of formal asset pricing theory (Galton 1907). Galton, credited with developing regression analysis, correlation, and (sadly) eugenics, was an inveterate collector of empirical data. His analysis of bets made at a local fair has considerable relevance for the analysis of capital markets. Here are portions of his account, published under the title "Vox Populi":

> In these democratic days, any investigation into the trustworthiness and peculiarities of popular judgment is of interest. The material about to be discussed refers to a small matter, but is much to the point.
>
> A weight-judging competition was carried on at the annual show of the West of England Fat Stock and Poultry Exhibition recently held at Plymouth. A fat ox having been selected, competitors bought stamped and numbered cards, for 6d. each, on which to inscribe their respective names, addresses, and estimates of what the ox would weigh after it had been slaughtered and "dressed." Those who guessed most successfully received prizes. . . . The judgments were unbiased by passion and uninfluenced by oratory and the like. The sixpenny fee deterred practical joking, and the hope of a prize and the joy of competition prompted each competitor to do his best. The competitors included butchers and farmers, some of whom were highly expert in judging the weight of cattle; others were probably guided by such information as they might pick up, and by their own fancies. The average competitor was probably as well fitted for making a just estimate of the dressed weight of the ox as an average voter is of judging the merits of most political issues on which he votes, and the variety among the voters to judge justly was probably much the same in either case.

Galton borrowed and tallied the 787 tickets that were sold. His graph of 19 points on the cumulative distribution of the estimates is replotted in Figure 6-1, with the median and actual values added.

Galton's conclusion is striking. "According to the democratic principle of 'one vote one value,' the middlemost estimate expresses the *vox populi*, every other estimate being condemned as too low or too high by a majority of the voters. . . . Now the middlemost estimate is 1207 lb., and the weight of the

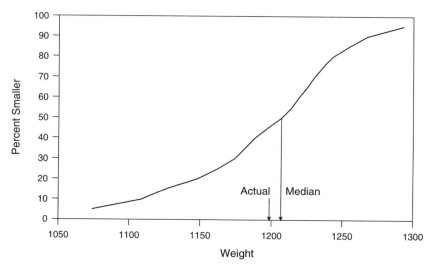

Figure 6-1 Estimates of weight of ox.

dressed ox proved to be 1198 lb. So the *vox populi* was in this case 9 lb., or 0.8 percent of the whole weight too high. It appears, then, in this particular instance, that the *vox populi* is correct to within 1 per cent of the real value. . . . This result is, I think, more creditable to the trustworthiness of a democratic judgment than might have been expected."

Galton did not explore the implications of this natural experiment for the determinants of the prices of financial assets when investors' predictions differ. But we can. The analogies are not difficult to make. Investing entails paying a fee (usually considerably more than a sixpenny). There is clearly the hope of a prize. Some investors are highly expert in judging the likelihoods of alternative outcomes, others are "probably guided by such information as they might pick up, and by their own fancies." Sadly, it may indeed be the case that "the average competitor [is] probably as well fitted for making a just estimate . . . as an average voter is of judging the merits of most political issues." Without question, there is ample variety among investors. Can investors do as well as the farmers and butchers at the Plymouth Fat Stock and Poultry Exhibition? As in previous chapters, we turn to simulation analyses to shed some light on this important question.

6.4. Case 14: Mario and Hue Disagree

People disagree because they have different information, process the information they do have differently, or both. Whatever the sources of the differences,

FIGURE 6-2
Case 14: Actual Probabilities

Probabilities:	Now	BadS	BadN	GoodS	GoodN
Probability	1	0.15	0.25	0.25	0.35

any given person's predictions can differ from those of another investor and from the "correct" predictions.

Case 14 provides our first illustration. It is yet another variant of Case 1. The securities are the same, and Mario and Hue have the same preferences and portfolios. But now their estimates of the probabilities of the alternative future states differ. Their estimates are also likely to be incorrect in the sense that they differ from the "true" probabilities.

The idea that there is a true set of probabilities is not without controversy. One might argue that an omniscient power would not have to deal with probabilities at all, since he, she, or it would know the actual future state of the world. But this degree of prescience is unattainable by ordinary mortals. Even if one had access to all knowable information about future prospects and the most efficient means for processing that information, it is unlikely that it would be possible to correctly predict which future state of the world would actually occur. Absent powers of clairvoyance, the best that can be said is that there is a set of probabilities for alternative states that would be estimated by one with access to the full set of relevant information and the ability to process it efficiently. Such "actual" or true probabilities are the ones shown in the probabilities table in our standard simulation inputs. For Case 14 they are the same as in Case 1, as shown in Figure 6-2.

In this case, however, individual investors' probabilities differ from actual probabilities owing to differences in their information and/or their abilities to process the information they have. We model this somewhat crudely by starting with the actual set of probabilities, drawing a sample of observations generated by that set, then mixing the resultant frequency distribution with the original set. Figure 6-3 shows the inputs for Case 14.

FIGURE 6-3
Case 14: Information

Information:	Prior Wt	Samples
Mario	0.01	100
Hue	0.01	100

To determine Mario's predictions we start by drawing 100 samples from the actual probability distribution. The procedure is similar to that used in Chapter 4 for *ex post* analyses. The simulator in effect creates an urn with 100 balls, 15 marked BadS, 25 marked BadN, 25 marked GoodS, and 35 marked GoodN. Then it draws a ball at random, records the state written on it, and returns it to the urn. In this case, the process is repeated 100 times. This provides a distribution of the percentage frequencies of trials for the states. To preclude the possibility of obtaining a zero probability that a state will occur, a weighted average of this frequency distribution and the actual probabilities is then computed. In this case, a 99 percent weight is placed on the frequency distribution and a 1 percent weight on the actual probabilities.

We use the same procedure and the same parameters to obtain Hue's predictions. Of course, she will reach different conclusions, since the simulator will draw a different set of 100 balls from the urn for her.

This approach makes it possible to simulate situations in which people are only partially informed and rely to at least some extent on different information. In Case 14 the investors have similar amounts of information, but this is not necessary. If Hue were able to draw 500 samples she would undoubtedly make better predictions—that is, her probabilities would be closer to the true values. Figure 6-4 shows the actual predictions made by our two protagonists. As can be seen, their probability estimates differ and neither set equals the actual probabilities in Figure 6-2. This is clearly a case with disagreement.

Figure 6-4 also shows the averages of Mario and Hue's predictions. They differ from the actual probabilities. But the average probabilities are closer to the actual probabilities than are those of either investor. Using the sum of the squared deviations from the actual predictions as a measure of error, both Mario's and Hue's probabilities are more than 2.5 times as far from the actual probabilities as the average set of predictions. Both our investors made *unbiased predictions* since we started with actual probabilities in our Monte Carlo calculations. If you had to make a single prediction about Mario's probabilities you would have written down the actual probabilities. You know that he will make *errors* but, given enough samples, such errors will be small. With a large

FIGURE 6-4
Case 14: Predictions

Predictions:	Now	BadS	BadN	GoodS	GoodN
Mario	1.00	0.15	0.26	0.31	0.28
Hue	1.00	0.08	0.23	0.28	0.41
Average	1.00	0.12	0.25	0.29	0.35

number of investors, each making unbiased estimates, many such errors will average out. In such circumstances, an average of all investors' predictions can be both unbiased and have relatively small errors. This would not have surprised Francis Galton. As we have indicated, the influence of an investor on overall asset prices will depend on both his or her wealth and willingness to bear risk. If these two characteristics are uncorrelated across investors, wealth will be the key element. And if (as is sometimes thought) wealthier investors are more tolerant of risk then wealth will be even more important. In any event, asset prices may well be relatively close to those that would prevail if everyone used all the available information about the future. If people make unbiased predictions, the better are investors at processing information, especially those who have more invested wealth and thus more reason to gather information and process it carefully, and the better will market prices reflect actual probabilities.

With only two partially informed investors, the equilibrium in Case 14 will differ from that in Case 1. In Case 1 Mario and Hue agreed on the probabilities of alternative future states of the world. As a result, when equilibrium was reached each chose to hold the market portfolio plus either borrowing or lending. But now they disagree and their portfolio choices reflect their different opinions about the future. This can be seen in Figure 6-5. Portfolio choices no longer conform to the Market Risk/Reward Corollary (MRRC), since each investor takes considerable non-market risk.

There is more. Although Mario and Hue are able to act on their differing opinions by holding idiosyncratic portfolios of the existing securities, they would like to have more alternatives. This can be seen in Figure 6-6. After equilibrium is attained their reservation prices differ for each future state.

This is not surprising. Investors who disagree wish to make bets with one another. To accommodate them the financial services industry provides a rich menu of vehicles, including such instruments as financial futures contracts, options, swaps, and many other exotica. In a world of agreement, some such securities would undoubtedly prove useful, but their numbers and popularity would be much smaller.

FIGURE 6-5
Case 14: Portfolios

Portfolios:	Consume	Bond	MFC	HFC
Market	98.00	0.00	10.00	10.00
Mario	48.23	2.56	5.78	3.79
Hue	49.77	−2.56	4.22	6.21

FIGURE 6-6
Case 14: State Prices

State Prices:	Now	BadS	BadN	GoodS	GoodN
Mario	1.00	0.17	0.34	0.19	0.22
Hue	1.00	0.16	0.36	0.20	0.21

6.5. Case 15: More Investors with Different Predictions

Francis Galton found that 787 forecasters could produce an excellent average estimate. We have argued that in typical situations a market with more investors will better incorporate information than one with fewer investors. Case 15 is designed to illustrate this possibility. It is a variant of Case 14, but there are now five people in Monterey and five in Half Moon Bay. All the people in Monterey (whose names begin with M) are exactly like Mario except for their predictions. And all the people in Half Moon Bay (whose names begin with H) are exactly like Hue except for their predictions.

Each makes predictions based on a sample of 100 draws from the simulated frequency distribution with a weight of 99 percent, as did Mario and Hue in Case 14. Each sample is obtained separately, however, reflecting investors' access to at least partially different information. Figure 6-7 shows the resulting prices for the three securities in Cases 14 and 15. Also shown are the prices from Case 1, which reflects the same situation with the key difference that all investors agree on the probabilities of the states.

In Case 1 security prices "fully reflect" the available information concerning the future states of the world, since every investor utilizes that information when making trades and choosing a portfolio. In Case 14, the prices do not fully reflect the information since there are only two partially informed investors. As a result the security prices are affected and, in a sense, wrong. In Case 15, however, the results are considerably closer to those in Case 1. With more investors, more information is available and prices differ less from those obtained in a market in which every investor utilizes all available information.

FIGURE 6-7
Cases 1, 14, and 15: Security Prices

Security Prices:	Consume	Bond	MFC	HFC
Case 1	1.00	0.96	4.35	4.89
Case 14	1.00	0.93	4.31	4.74
Case 15	1.00	0.96	4.31	4.91

In Case 1 the market is *informationally efficient,* since security prices reflect available information about the future. In Case 15, the market is not fully efficient in this sense; but it is very close. But as in Case 14, portfolio choices in Case 15 are very different from those in Case 1.

In a world of disagreement, every investor has his or her own view regarding state probabilities and hence of all statistics that incorporate such probabilities. Thus Mario calculates beta values, expected returns, portfolio standard deviations, and price per chance (PPC) values that differ from those calculated by Hue. Neither knows the "true" statistics calculated using the actual probabilities. But as creators of our simulated worlds we can observe the true values and investigate the conformance of the equilibrium results with the asset pricing theories described in Chapter 4.

Figure 6-8 shows the Security Market Line (SML) graph for Case 15. It departs only slightly from those encountered in many cases with agreement: expected returns are closely related to beta values. Despite investors' disagreement, in Case 15 the SML version of the Market Risk/Reward Theorem (MRRT) provides a very good approximation to reality.

Figure 6-9 shows the Capital Market Line (CML) graph for Case 15. Despite their different predictions, the ten investors hold portfolios with actual Sharpe Ratios only slightly inferior to that of the market portfolio. To some extent, this is due to their limited ability to make extreme bets on individual states since there are only three securities and markets are incomplete.

If every investor chose a portfolio comprised of the market portfolio plus borrowing or lending, all the points in Figure 6-9 would lie on the CML. Instead

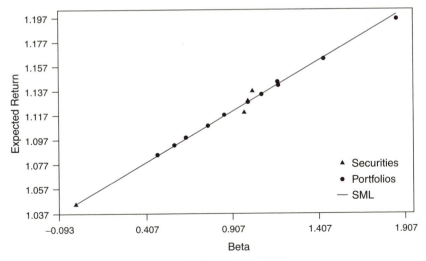

Figure 6-8 Case 15: The Security Market Line.

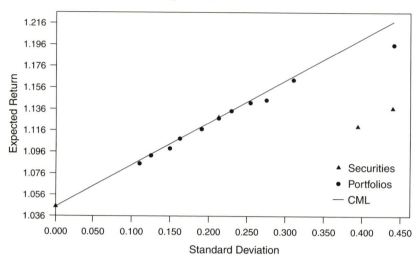

Figure 6-9 Case 15: The Capital Market Line.

they lie to the right of the line, reflecting the properties of strategies with re-turns not linearly related to the returns on the market portfolio. While this might indicate that investors chose nonlinear market-based strategies, this is not the case. Instead, the investors in Case 15 took varying amounts of non-market risk. They thus violated the MRRC. When investors disagree, they typically choose to take non-market risk.

In Case 15 markets are insufficiently complete, hence the equilibrium pric-ing kernel can be computed only by using averages of investors' reservation prices for state claims using the available securities. Figure 6-10 shows the re-sulting PPC and total consumption values. There is not a one-to-one relation-ship; the true PPC values differ for the two Bad states, which is also the case, but to a much smaller extent, for the two Good states. Nonetheless, the PPC values are considerably lower for the states of plenty (on the right) than they are for the states of scarcity (on the left). And the disparities in the PPC values for states with the same aggregate consumption are not huge. The basic pricing equation (BPE) is violated, but not egregiously.

6.6. Case 16: Correct and Incorrect Predictions

Case 15 does not provide much solace for active investment managers. Surely, they believe, someone must have superior information and/or the ability to better process information. Case 16 provides an example.

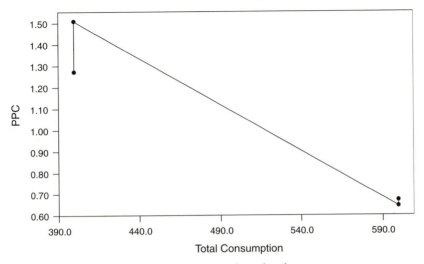

Figure 6-10 Case 15: The pricing kernel and consumption.

We start with Case 15. Again there are five people in Monterey and five in Half Moon Bay. All the people in Monterey are exactly like Mario except for their predictions and all the people in Half Moon Bay are exactly like Hue except for their predictions. In this case, we specify investors' predictions explicitly rather than using a Monte Carlo approach. With the exception of Mario and Hue, all the investors make the same predictions based on historic frequencies of different fish runs over the last 10 years. However, both Mario and Hue have done extensive additional research on the persistence of climate effects, ocean temperatures, and other relevant factors. They have both correctly concluded that the fish are more likely to go south than indicated by historic frequencies and that this will be the case whether the overall catch is large or small. Figure 6-11 shows the actual probabilities and the investors' predictions. Mario and Hue are right while all the other investors are wrong, and in the same way.

FIGURE 6-11
Case 16: Predictions

Predictions:	Now	BadS	BadN	GoodS	GoodN
Actual	1	0.20	0.20	0.30	0.30
Mario	1	0.20	0.20	0.30	0.30
Hue	1	0.20	0.20	0.30	0.30
All others	1	0.15	0.25	0.25	0.35

FIGURE 6-12
Case 16: Portfolio Returns

Portfolio Returns:	BadS	BadN	GoodS	GoodN
Mario	0.916	0.754	1.551	1.228
Other M's	0.798	0.838	1.317	1.397
Difference	0.117	−0.084	0.234	−0.169
Hue	0.966	0.872	1.345	1.157
Other H's	0.898	0.922	1.209	1.255
Difference	0.068	−0.049	0.136	−0.098
Probability	0.20	0.20	0.30	0.30

As in Case 15 we allow trading only of the bond and the stocks of the two fishing companies. When equilibrium is established, Mario chooses a different portfolio than his Monterey neighbors, all of whom choose the same portfolio. A similar situation prevails for the more conservative investors in Half Moon Bay. Figure 6-12 shows the resultant returns by state, along with return differences and the actual probabilities of the states.

Mario has chosen a portfolio that will do better than those of his neighbors in the states about which he is (correctly) more optimistic (BadS and GoodS) and will do worse in the states about which he is (correctly) more pessimistic (BadN and GoodN). Hue is in a similar position relative to her neighbors. Importantly, we compare each of the superior predictors with peers having the same risk tolerance. This avoids mixing differences due to preferences with those due to predictions.

What might happen to Mario next period? There is a 50 percent chance that he will substantially underperform his peers (by either 8.4 or 16.9 percent). On the other hand, there is a 50 percent chance that he will outperform them, and by even larger amounts (either 11.7 or 23.4 percent). Taking the probabilities of the states into account, Mario's expected outperformance is .026, or 2.6 percent.

Hue is in a similar situation but, true to her conservative nature, takes smaller bets relative to her peers. She also has a 50 percent chance of underperforming them but expects superior performance (.015, or 1.5 percent).

Figure 6-13 shows the expected returns and beta values for all the investors. Mario and Hue's portfolios plot above the line. The other investors' portfolios plot below the line, with all of Mario's peers at one point and all of Hue's at the other. Mario and his peers have higher betas owing to their greater risk tolerance and Hue and her peers have lower betas owing to their lower risk tol-

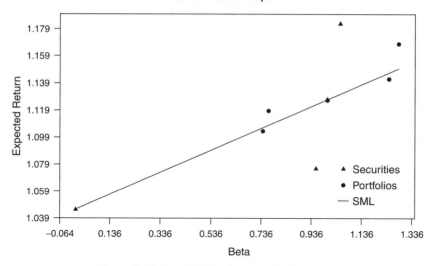

Figure 6-13 Case 16: The Security Market Line.

erance. The securities fall far from the line because of the erroneous predictions made by the majority of investors.

We know that Mario is expected to outperform his peers but some of the difference can be attributed to the slightly higher beta value of his portfolio. To adjust for this we compare his expected return with that of a combination of the market and the riskless security with the same beta value as that of his portfolio. As discussed in Chapter 4, this is termed an *alpha* value. The alpha values for the investors in Case 16 are shown in Figure 6-14.

Mario is expected to outperform an equal-beta market portfolio by 1.8 percent per year while Hue is expected to outperform her equal-beta market portfolio by 1.1 percent per year. In the long run, both Mario and Hue will outperform their benchmarks but their performance can be much worse or much better than their benchmarks in any single period or even over several periods.

FIGURE 6-14
Case 16: Alpha Values

Alpha Values	Alpha
Mario	0.018
Hue	0.011
Other M's	−0.005
Other H's	−0.003

All the other investors are expected to underperform their equal-beta market portfolios, although by relatively small amounts. In the long run they will underperform their benchmarks, but their performance can be much worse or much better than their benchmarks in any single period or even over several periods.

Mario and Hue are superior predictors. In the long run, this superiority will be evident. But, as Lord Keynes famously said, "In the long run we are all dead." Superior investors can underperform their benchmarks and their inferior brethren even over periods of many years. To repeat the warning from the U.S. Securities and Exchange Commission quoted in Chapter 4: "Past performance is not a reliable indicator of future performance."

6.7. Case 17: Biased and Unbiased Predictions

The superior active managers in Case 16 knew the correct probabilities and agreed with one another. The inferior active managers made different predictions but agreed with one another. This provided a useful illustration but was hardly realistic. A more interesting scenario is one in which superior managers make unbiased predictions that are nonetheless subject to error, while inferior managers make biased predictions with error. Case 17 provides an example. It combines features of Cases 15 and 16. As in Case 15, each investor makes predictions based on 100 samples drawn from a probability distribution mixed (99 to 1) with that probability distribution. But in this case, the distribution utilized for the Monte Carlo analysis for each investor is the one utilized in Case 16. As a result, Mario and Hue make unbiased but erroneous predictions while the other investors make biased and erroneous predictions.

Figure 6-15 shows the situation once equilibrium is attained. As luck would have it, Mario, whose portfolio plots at the highest point in the graph, is in an excellent position, with an alpha value of 0.044 (4.4 percent per year). Hue, whose portfolio plots slightly above the line at a beta of 1.14, is less fortunate. Her alpha value is positive: 0.003 (0.3 percent per year) but unremarkable. By chance, four other investors selected portfolios with positive alpha values and three of them actually had higher alpha values than Hue's. Only four of the ten investors selected portfolios with negative alphas, ranging from Haley's –0.003 (–0.3 percent) to Molly's 0.036 (–3.6 percent).

This example shows that skill can lead to superior expected performance, but so can luck, reinforcing the observation made in conjunction with Case 16. A great many periods of performance may be required to even begin to differentiate between managers with skill and those with good luck. It is easy to find investors with superior historic track records, but much more difficult to identify investors who can be expected to have superior performance in the future.

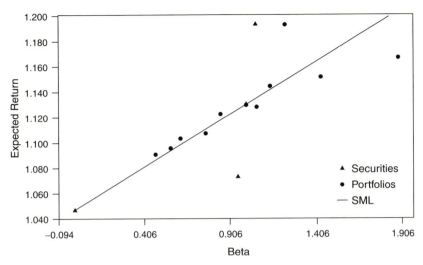

Figure 6-15 Case 17: The Security Market Line.

6.8. Case 18: Unbiased Predictions with Different Accuracies

In Cases 16 and 17, superior investors could be expected to be rewarded with superior performance over the long run. But their superiority depended wholly on an ability to make unbiased forecasts in a world populated by investors who were biased and in the same way. But what if inferior predictors are on average unbiased, but simply subject to greater errors? Case 18 provides an example.

We start with the situation in Case 16. Once again, there are five investors in Monterey with the same preferences and initial portfolios and five investors in Half Moon Bay with the same preferences and initial portfolios. Each makes predictions based on a sample drawn from a distribution, but in this case each investor is unbiased, drawing a sample from the actual probability distribution. However, two of the investors (Mario and Hue, of course) do better research; we use 1,000 trials to determine their probabilities. The other eight do less research; we allow them only 100 trials.

Figure 6-16 shows the resulting expected returns and beta values. Mario and Hue are above the line but just barely; so are four others, three of whom have higher alpha values than either Mario or Hue. Mario and Hue are among the winners because of their superior skill. But four other investors selected portfolios with positive alpha values due simply to luck. Moreover, alpha values reflect only expected performance. In any single period, actual results will differ even more.

Happily for superior managers, Figure 6-16 does not tell the entire story. It is important to recognize that alpha values describe only the expected difference

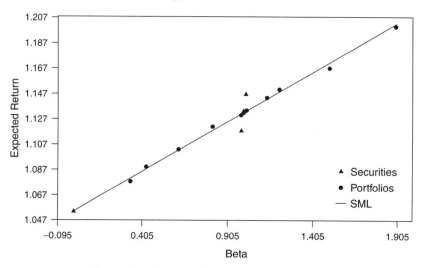

Figure 6-16 Case 18: The Security Market Line.

between a portfolio's return and that of an equal-beta market portfolio. A typical investor cares about more than this, since his or her utility depends on the entire distribution of portfolio returns. The best measure is, of course, expected utility. In Case 18 all the investors care about more than mean and variance since they have power utility functions. But mean and variance can still serve as approximate indicators of expected utility. Figure 6-17 shows each portfolio's expected return and standard deviation of return. Mario and Hue's portfolios plot slightly above the CML. Each has a Sharpe Ratio of 0.367, slightly better than the market's value of 0.366. The other investors' portfolios have lower Sharpe Ratios ranging from Holly's dismal 0.237 to Hannah's lucky 0.367.

In this case, better research leads to better portfolios, at least as measured by *ex ante* Sharpe Ratios. Nonetheless, simply investing in the market portfolio and the riskless asset can provide results that are almost as good. It is difficult to be a superior active manager in a world in which inferior active managers are plentiful, error-prone, but unbiased.

6.9. Index Funds

In the 1970s there was a sign on the wall at Wells Fargo Bank, which produced the first index fund. We repeat its inscription here, terming it the *Index Fund Premise*:

(IFP)   None of us is as smart as all of us.

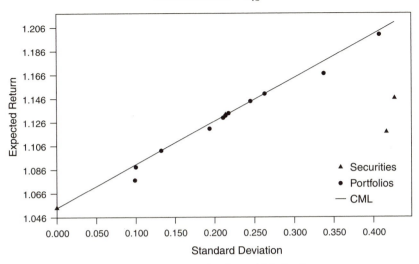

Figure 6-17 Case 18: The Capital Market Line.

In our terms, this holds that the average opinion about future probabilities is better than that of any single investor. But the average opinion (weighted by wealth and risk attitude) is to a considerable extent reflected in security prices. If the IFP is true, the best investment strategy for investors with preferences and positions that do not differ significantly from those of the average investor will be to hold risky securities in market proportions and combine the resulting market portfolio with the riskless asset in amounts commensurate with risk tolerance.

As indicated earlier, in its purest form, an index fund literally buys all the securities in a market in proportions equal to their relative values. Equivalently, it holds x percent of the outstanding shares (or certificates) of every security in the market. In practice, some index funds do just this; others hold a representative sample of the securities. The goal is to provide a before-cost return equal to that of the market in question.

It is not expensive to run a large index fund. As indicated in our discussion of active and passive management, this implies that the after-cost return on a low-cost index fund should be superior to that obtained by the average actively managed dollar in the same market. When comparisons are made correctly, history shows this to be so.

Case 18 illustrated the argument. Mario and Hue were smarter than the other eight investors. But the market was almost as smart since it combined the information obtained by all ten investors. Mario and Hue chose better portfolios than the others, primarily because they diversified more extensively.

Case 18 also shows how easy it can be for an index fund investor to "free ride" on the research done by other investors. In a market in which investors' predictions are erroneous but unbiased an index investor can concentrate on predicting the probabilities of various outcomes for the market portfolio as a whole (i.e., the probabilities for the market states), rather than the probabilities of the more numerous detailed states. Given these forecasts and the observable riskless return, an index fund investor can then come very close to achieving the expected utility attainable with large amounts of expensive research and analysis.

Of course the index fund premise is far too extreme. Among the more plausible variations that have been advanced (using more elegant language) in the financial economics and investment literature are these:

(IFPa)   Few of us are as smart as all of us.

(IFPb)   Few of us are as smart as all of us, and it is hard to identify such people in advance.

(IFPc)   Few of us are as smart as all of us, it is hard to identify them in advance, and they may charge more than they are worth.

IFPc is perhaps the most realistic argument for investing much (if not all) of one's money in index funds.

A case can still be made for active management by a minority of managers, but as we have seen, the case is much stronger if there is reason to believe that the majority of investors make predictions that are biased *in the same manner*. For example, some argue that many investors tend to assume that past trends in corporations' earnings will continue unabated, while both historic evidence and good economics suggest otherwise. If many investors do act in this manner, predictions can be biased, allowing a minority of clever managers to obtain superior returns by underweighting (relative to the market) high earnings-growth firms and overweighting (relative to the market) low and negative earnings-growth firms. In such a world, a few of us can be smarter than all of us. If this argument is true and if an investor can identify one of those few willing to share the fruits of his or her skills, it may be possible to be among the minority of investors with a prospect of "beating the market." But at best, such prospects will be available to only a minority of investors; not everyone can be above average.

6.10. Summary

We have examined a number of cases in which investors utilize different information, reach different conclusions about the likelihood of alternative future outcomes, and hence choose different portfolios. What do these examples imply about the relevance of standard asset pricing formulas in a world of disagreement? The good news is that most of the formulas will hold under most circumstances. Unfortunately this is also the bad news.

In Chapter 4 we showed that in the absence of arbitrage opportunities it is possible to find one or more sets of state prices that will make the Law of One Price (LOP) hold. What about the BPE? It follows directly from the LOP as long as probabilities that are positive and sum to 1 are employed. We could make up a BPE using randomly chosen positive numbers scaled to sum to one. Similar comments apply to the kernel beta equation (KBE), which is simply an algebraic transformation of the BPE. Up to this point, there is not much interesting economic content other than that resulting from the lack of arbitrage.

The main economic content of asset pricing theory comes when we (1) move from the KBE to an equation involving a relationship between a security or portfolio's return and that of some potentially observable variable or variables and (2) assert that the relationship holds with actual probabilities. In a one-period world of agreement with no positions or state-dependent preferences, either of two variables suffice: aggregate consumption or the return on the market portfolio. The relationship may be general, as in the market beta equation (MBE), or specific, as in the Security Market Line (SML). With outside positions, state-dependent preferences, and/or disagreement the situation can, however, be very different.

In this and the previous chapter we examined more complex cases and found that the simple SML relationship may be a good, fair, or poor approximation, depending on the nature of the factors that influence asset prices and portfolio choice. In some cases, the more general MBE, suitably parameterized, may provide a considerably better description of the relationship between expected returns and a relevant measure of covariance. In others it may be little better than the simpler SML relationship.

Broadly, our examples are consistent with Francis Galton's insight made almost a century ago. In our cases, the MRRT was bruised but not thoroughly beaten. The MRRC fared less well, at least as a description of actual investor behavior. The *vox populi* may be rather good at establishing asset prices that reflect available information, despite the choice of suboptimal portfolios by many of the contestants in the market game.

SEVEN

PROTECTION

7.1. Protected Investment Products

SHOULD ONE INVEST in stocks or in bonds? Stocks have *upside potential*, generating higher returns if markets go up. But they can generate losses if markets go down. Bonds offer *downside protection*, providing interest and principal repayment if held to maturity (absent default). But in good market environments, bonds generally underperform stocks. Wouldn't it be splendid if an investment offered both upside potential and downside protection? There are such investments and we will have much to say about them in this chapter. We will call them *protected investment products*, or *PIPs*.

Of course, in an efficient capital market one never gets something for nothing. PIPs are no exception. But they are created by financial services firms and purchased by investors (mostly individuals). The relevant questions for us concern their suitability for specific investors. We will see that these products may be appropriate for investors with particular kinds of preferences. This said, there is reason to believe that many of the investors who currently purchase protected products may be motivated more by predictions that differ from those reflected in market prices than by preferences that differ from those of the average investor.

7.2. Principal Protected Equity Linked Minimum Return Trust Certificates

There are many protected investment products in the United States and in other countries. They are usually sold directly to investors by banks and brokerage firms. Such instruments are intended to be held to maturity, although transactions prior to that time may be made on an exchange or directly with the initiating bank or brokerage.

In the United States, many PIPs are listed on the American Stock Exchange under the rubric *structured products*. For example, in April 2003, the exchange listed more than 100 issues offering downside protection and upside potential, with maturity dates ranging from the years 2003 to 2011.

A prototypical example is provided by a series of instruments created for U.S. investors in the first years of the twenty-first century by Citigroup Global Markets, Inc. A typical prospectus for instruments in the series (e.g., Citigroup

2004a) starts with the heading "Safety First Investments," followed by the caption "Safety of Principal, Opportunity for Growth." The general characteristics of these products are described in a publication (Citigroup 2004b) with the somewhat legalistic title *Principal Protected Equity Linked Minimum Return Trust Certificates*. We use this as our source for the details that follow.

As an example of the securities in the series, Citigroup uses a Certificate (SNJ) issued in November 2002, tied to the performance of Standard and Poor's 500 stock index (the S&P 500). At issuance the certificate had a maturity of five years and an issue price of $10 per certificate. At the maturity date (December 2007) the investor would receive one payment, providing the "Principal plus an Additional Payment [equal to the] . . . greater of (i) 9% Minimum Return or (ii) Index Return."

The Index Return was to be calculated by compounding 60 monthly total returns. If in a given month the S&P 500 price appreciation (not total return) was less than 1.045 (4.5 percent per month), the price appreciation on the index would be used. In any month in which the price appreciation was more than 4.5 percent, a value of 1.045 would be used instead. Subtracting 1.00 from the product of the resultant 60 total returns would then give the *capped index return*. If this were, say, 15 percent, the investor would receive $11.50 per certificate, realizing the promised "opportunity for growth." If the capped index return were less than 9 percent, however, the investor would receive $10.90 per share, thanks to the guaranteed "safety of principal." SNJ clearly offered upside potential and downside protection.

To illustrate the possible outcomes that an investor in such a certificate might obtain, Citigroup backtested the formula for all possible 60-month periods beginning in February 1985 and ending in February 2004. These 170 overlapping periods were then used to compute historic statistics for the total return on the SNJ certificate and other investments. A number of mean/variance analyses were reported, including one leading to a finding that "A portfolio that is weighted 80% in the Bond Fund and 20% in SNJ has the highest Sharpe Ratio."

The overall conclusions of the publication were that:

> In the current market environment, where investors are not willing to assume principal risk for potential equity gains, Safety First Investments offer a viable alternative. These Certificates offer investors the opportunity to enhance the returns on low yielding cash balances and fixed income securities without taking the downside risk of the stock market. Finally, by adding the Certificates to an existing asset mix of stocks and/or bonds, investors are able to tilt their asset allocation toward a more conservative risk/return profile through greater diversification.

The initial phrase ("In the current market environment . . .") suggests that the authors might have felt that their Safety First products would be most suitable for investors with especially pessimistic views concerning the future prospects of the stock market. If so, the certificates were intended more for those with divergent predictions than for those with divergent preferences.

7.2.1. Historic Returns from Safety First Products

Backtests raise a number of questions. First, investment results are usually time period–dependent. Statistics from one historic period may differ significantly from those taken from another period. Second, as in this case, overlapping time periods are often used to increase the sample size. If so, the results are not independent. For example, only two wholly independent 60-month periods can be created using the data from the period utilized in the Citigroup study. Third, our previous caveats about the dangers of using historic average returns as proxies for future expected returns apply. Finally, there is also the possibility of selection bias. One wizened investment professional has said, "I've never met a backtest I didn't like."

Another concern relates to the analysis. Mean/variance analysis has a limited ability to fully capture the advantages or disadvantages of financial products designed to provide probability distributions of returns with very different shapes than those of traditional instruments, and this is especially true for long holding periods.

Protected investment products are members of a class known as *derivative securities*, since the return on such a product is derived from a stated relationship with another security or economic variable. For the SNJ certificate, the *underlying* variable is the price return on the S&P 500.

Figure 7-1 (prepared by the current author) shows the relationship between the total return on a PIP with the characteristics of the SNJ certificate and the total return on the S&P 500. Each point represents one of the 170 sixty-month periods used in the Citigroup study. Overall, the period was a good one for stocks. The S&P 500 index would have outperformed a SNJ certificate in 89.5 percent of the periods. In several of the later periods, however, the protected investment product would have provided a significantly better outcome, returning $10.90 for each $10 invested, while the S&P 500 returned as little as $8.25. One can see why an investor fearing a likely continuation of recent trends might be attracted to such a product in early 2004.

Given the manner in which this particular certificate's return is calculated, the ending value is not a one-to-one function of the ending value of the index. Rather, the total return on the certificate depends on both the ending value of the index and the path that the index takes to reach its final value. Over a five-year holding period, such a certificate will thus have non-market risk for which there may not be a commensurate reward for the reasons given in the earlier chapters of this book.

Nonetheless, some investors might prefer to hold an appropriately priced PIP in a world in which everyone agreed on the probabilities of alternative

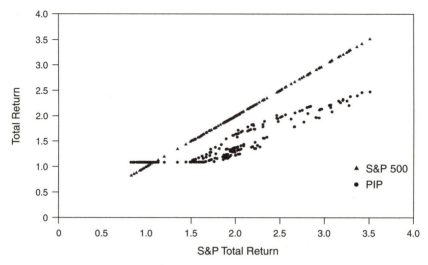

Figure 7-1 Backtested returns on SNJ certificate.

future outcomes. Not all can do so, of course, so these investors would have to have non-average positions, preferences, or both. We will not consider the effects of diverse positions or predictions in this connection, but will explore the possibility that a demand for PIPs could arise from diverse investor preferences.

7.3. Options

Some protected investment products are more complex than the SNJ certificate. However, each offers a return related in a nonlinear manner to the performance of an underlying investment, with greater sensitivity on the upside than on the downside. But how can the provider of such a product guarantee the ability to deliver the promised return? The Citigroup publication provides a hint:

> Safety First Investments are economically similar to an investment portfolio consisting of a zero coupon bond and an option on the underlying index. The zero coupon bond component provides the investor with principal protection and the minimum return payable at maturity. The option component provides the investor with the return, if any, tied to the performance of the underlying index.

A *zero coupon bond* provides a single payment at maturity and no intermediate payments (coupons). Zero coupon bonds with different maturity dates backed by the full faith and credit of the U.S. government are generally available.

An *option* is a contract that gives the holder the right but not the obligation to buy or sell a security at a price determined in advance. A *call option* allows the holder to purchase a security at a specified future date for a price determined today. A *put option* allows the holder to sell a security at a specified future date for a price determined today. Put and call options with different maturity dates that use the S&P 500 index as the underlying asset are routinely traded on options exchanges.

If instruments with the desired maturity dates are available, an investor can easily construct a homemade protected investment product by combining (1) a zero coupon bond that will provide a minimum return (e.g., $10.90) with (2) a call option that is worth exercising only if the total return on the underlying index is greater than the amount that would provide that minimum return.

If such instruments are available, a financial services company can offer a protected product and use the proceeds to purchase a portfolio of zero coupon bonds and options that will replicate the promised payments. If the price paid by the purchaser of the protected product is greater than the cost of such a *replicating portfolio*, the issuing company can also be rewarded for its efforts.

Unfortunately, traded call options on broad market indexes usually have relatively short maturities (less than three years in most cases), making it difficult for small investors to create long-term protected strategies themselves. This also makes it expensive and/or difficult for financial services companies to offer the longer maturities associated with protected investment products. Usually several parties are involved, with obligations only partially hedged explicitly.

7.4. Cases 19 and 20: Quade and Dagmar with Options

Derivative securities can allow an investor to hedge against preexisting risks, thus lowering his or her overall risk—an ability often cited by proponents. Options can definitely fulfill such a role. But, like other derivative securities, they can also serve as potent instruments for placing speculative bets. In any event, the availability of options and other derivative securities can help complete a market, allowing investors to better take advantage of their differences in preferences, positions, or predictions.

To illustrate, we return to Quade and Dagmar. Their preferences are the same as in Case 6. To focus on essentials we give them two traditional securities: a riskless bond (STBond) and a market index fund (MIF). As in the earlier case, there are ten states of the world but only five market states. The securities table for Case 19 is shown in Figure 7-2. Quade starts out with 500 MIF shares, no bonds, and a current consumption of 515 units, as does Dagmar. After our investors have finished trading, they hold quite different portfolios because of the significant differences in their preferences. Dagmar borrows money from Quade

FIGURE 7-2
Case 19: Securities Table

Securities:	Consume	STBond	MIF
Now	1.00	0.00	0.00
Depression1	0.00	1.00	0.87
Depression2	0.00	1.00	0.87
Recession1	0.00	1.00	0.92
Recession2	0.00	1.00	0.92
Normality1	0.00	1.00	1.07
Normality2	0.00	1.00	1.07
Prosperity1	0.00	1.00	1.17
Prosperity2	0.00	1.00	1.17
Boom1	0.00	1.00	1.22
Boom2	0.00	1.00	1.22

to obtain more MIF shares. She thus will do better than Quade in good markets and worse in bad markets, as shown in Figure 7-3.

In this case, the investors must be content with linear market-based strategies. But we know from Case 6 that when Quade and Dagmar were allowed to trade state claims they chose nonlinear market-based strategies. Absent this ability, our investors have done the best they can but a certain amount of frustration remains. Their reservation prices differ considerably. Across states, the ratio of Dagmar's reservation price to Quade's ranges from 0.90 to 1.31.

To help our investors achieve better results, we create Case 20 which adds two new securities, a put and a call, to those available in Case 19. The call allows the holder to purchase an MIF share at the future date by paying 1 (dollar) at that time. The put allows the holder to sell an MIF share at the future date for a price of 1 (dollar).

A rational holder will exercise a call option only if the value of the security received is greater than the amount that must be paid. Similarly, a rational holder will exercise a put option only if the value of the security given up is less than the amount to be received. Figure 7-4 shows the securities table for Case 20. The payoffs for the traditional securities are the same as before; the payoffs for the options are based on the assumption that the holder makes an optimal choice as to whether or not to exercise the option.

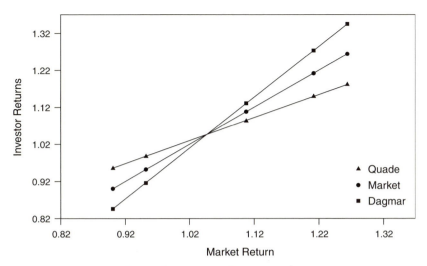

Figure 7-3 Case 19: Returns graph.

FIGURE 7-4
Case 20: Securities Table

Securities:	Consume	STBond	MIF	Put	Call
Now	1.00	0.00	0.00	0.00	0.00
Depression1	0.00	1.00	0.87	0.13	0.00
Depression2	0.00	1.00	0.87	0.13	0.00
Recession1	0.00	1.00	0.92	0.08	0.00
Recession2	0.00	1.00	0.92	0.08	0.00
Normality1	0.00	1.00	1.07	0.00	0.07
Normality2	0.00	1.00	1.07	0.00	0.07
Prosperity1	0.00	1.00	1.17	0.00	0.17
Prosperity2	0.00	1.00	1.17	0.00	0.17
Boom1	0.00	1.00	1.22	0.00	0.22
Boom2	0.00	1.00	1.22	0.00	0.22

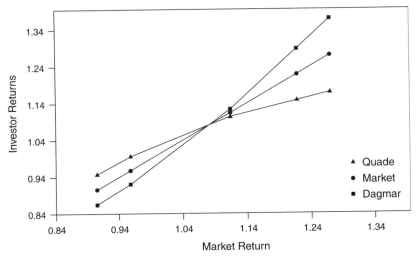

Figure 7-5 Case 20: Returns graph.

Quade and Dagmar's initial holdings are the same as in Case 19. As usual, the net supply of the derivative securities is zero. At the outset, neither investor has an option position. If one is to hold ("be long") an option, the other must create it ("be short"). This is exactly what happens in the real world, often using the services of organized exchanges that set standard terms for such agreements.

In Case 20, our investors are delighted to use their newfound ability to take options positions. As shown in Figure 7-5, they are now able to adopt nonlinear market-based strategies, coming much closer to the positions that they would choose in a complete market setting. The presence of markets for derivative securities greatly reduces Quade and Dagmar's malaise. Across states, the ratio of Dagmar's reservation price to Quade's now ranges from 0.98 to 1.003. While formally the market is not sufficiently complete, as a practical matter it is very close to being so.

7.4.1. The Put/Call Parity Theorem

Case 20 involves a bit of overkill. Our investors could have achieved the same results with only one of the two options. To see why, it is useful to present a famous no-arbitrage theorem.

Using the securities from Case 20, consider a portfolio consisting of a long position in one bond, a long position in one call option, and a short position in one put. Figure 7-6 shows the associated payoffs in each state. Compare this with the payments for the index fund in Figure 7-2. Each entry is precisely the same. The portfolio offers the same prospects as a MIF share. From the Law of

FIGURE 7-6
Case 20: Returns on a Portfolio
of Bonds and Options

Payments:	Portfolio
Now	0.00
Depression1	0.87
Depression2	0.87
Recession1	0.92
Recession2	0.92
Normality1	1.07
Normality2	1.07
Prosperity1	1.17
Prosperity2	1.17
Boom1	1.22
Boom2	1.22

One Price they should sell for the same amount; in the equilibrium in Case 20 they do.

In this case, the options had an exercise price of 1 unit. But we could have constructed a bond plus options portfolio equivalent to the MIF shares with options having a different (but equal) exercise price (E). The general principle is to combine a bond position that will provide E at the future date with a long position in a call with an exercise price of E and a short position in a put with an exercise price of E. Letting X_{iz} represent the payment received in state i from one security of type z (where z is B for the bond, C for the call, and P for the put), we then have:

$$X_{iS} = EX_{iB} + X_{iC} - X_{iP}$$

where the bond is assumed to return 1 (dollar) at the options' exercise date.

Since this equation holds for every state i, the portfolio of one stock (on the left of the equal sign) offers the same payments as the portfolio of the positions in the three instruments on the right. But investments that offer the same future payoffs will sell for the same price, so that:

$$P_S = EP_B + P_C - P_P$$

where P_S, P_B, P_C, and P_P are the prices of the stock, bond, call, and put, respectively. This is known as the *put/call parity theorem*.

More generally, we can say that in terms of both prices and payoffs there is an equivalence among the instruments of the form:

$$S = EB + C - P$$

where S, B, C, and P are the stock, bond, call, and put, respectively.

This equation can be rearranged, moving items from one side of the equality sign to the other. For example:

$$P = EB + C - S$$

This shows that the both the payments and the price of a put can be replicated with a combination of E bonds, a long position in a call, and a short position in the underlying security. Quade and Dagmar could have achieved their goals with only the call.

Financial engineers love nothing more than discovering relationships among financial instruments similar to this one. If it is possible to replicate a set of payments across states with a portfolio of existing securities then a financial services company can offer a single instrument with that set of payments, perfectly hedge it with a replicating portfolio, and hopefully charge an explicit or implicit fee for its effort.

7.5. Case 21: Karyn in a Crowd

Options can definitely help investors such as Quade and Dagmar achieve their desired nonlinear market-based strategies, as can protected investment products. But these investors had smooth marginal utility functions and thus chose portfolios with returns that were relatively smooth functions of the return on the market portfolio. PIPs offer more dramatic payoffs; a plot of their returns versus market returns has a substantial kink. For whom might such an investment be particularly attractive? The question almost answers itself.

In Case 21 we introduce Karyn, who has a kinked marginal utility curve. She would very much like to consume an amount between 98 and 98.98. Over that range she has a constant relative risk aversion of 50. For amounts of consumption below 98 or above 98.98 she has a constant relative risk aversion of 3.

Karyn is unique among the investors in Case 21. There are 16 other investors, each of whom has a constant relative risk aversion; their coefficients range from 1.75 to 4.00. Available investments include a riskless bond and a market index fund. There are 24 future states of the world. We assume that the market is complete in order to see what our investors would choose if they could trade state claims.

Figure 7-7 shows the returns for the 17 investors and the returns on the market portfolio. Karyn stands out in this crowd; her returns fall on the kinked curve, to which we have added thickness and diamonds for emphasis. She has

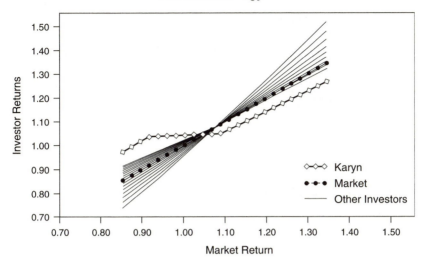

Figure 7-7 Case 21: Returns graph.

chosen a strategy that provides consumption within her preferred range (98 to 98.98) as long as the market portfolio's total return is within the range from 0.92 to 1.09. Only in a major bear market would she be worse off. And only in a major bull market would she be better off.

Figure 7-8 provides insight into the reasons for Karyn's choice. It shows the relationship between her consumption and the pricing kernel after equilibrium

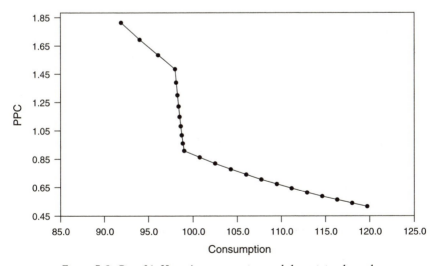

Figure 7-8 Case 21: Karyn's consumption and the pricing kernel.

is attained. Substantial differences in price per chance (PPC) values are required to get her to budge from her narrow reference range. If the cost of consumption in a state is high enough she will economize. And if the cost is low enough she will splurge. But over a wide range she adjusts her consumption very little to differences in cost.

This picture is familiar. Except for the numbers on the vertical scale, it is a plot of Karyn's marginal utility function. But this is precisely what we would expect based on the discussion in Chapter 4. Absent binding constraints, when an investor has achieved an optimal portfolio in a complete market, the marginal utility of consumption in each future state will equal a constant times the PPC for that state:

$$d_j m(X_j) = m(X_1)PPC_j$$

Karyn's consumption plots as a kinked function of PPC because her marginal utility function does.

The situation is very different for the market as a whole, as shown in Figure 7-9. Even though Karyn's consumption is included, the other 16 investors dominate the overall market equilibrium.

Since there are no outside positions in this case, the market's return is proportional to total consumption and Karyn's return is proportional to her consumption. Figures 7-8 and 7-9 would look the same had returns been plotted on the horizontal axes.

One way to obtain a figure such as Figure 7-7 is to combine the return versions of Figures 7-8 and 7-9. In this case, since the relationship between market

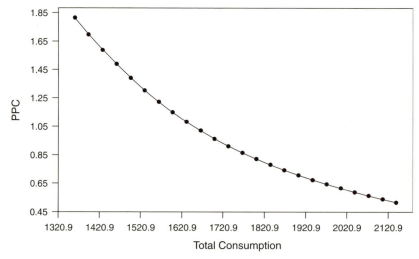

Figure 7-9 Case 21: Total consumption and the pricing kernel.

returns and PPC values is smooth, Karyn's return function looks very much like her marginal utility function rotated 90 degrees. Since she has little price sensitivity within her reference range and is able to obtain such levels of consumption in a number of states she chooses very similar returns over a rather wide range of market returns. Her preferences differ from those reflected in market prices, and thus so does her portfolio.

Since we require that marginal utility curves be downward sloping, Karyn's return graph has a section that is almost but not completely flat. Aside from this minor discrepancy, her graph has a shape known in option circles as a "Travolta" after the stance of the actor of the same name in the film *Saturday Night Fever*.

Risk-averse investors such as Karyn with one reference range can be quite happy with portfolios that have this classic *up-flat-up* pattern if the reference range is not far above or below the amounts of consumption they can afford. In other cases, only one or two of the three segments may be within the relevant range, as we will see.

7.6. Case 22: Karyn and the Crowd with Options

In a complete market, investors can adopt diverse nonlinear market-based strategies. But real markets do not allow trading in every possible state claim. Happily, in many cases investors may be as well served by a relatively small number of options and/or protected investment products.

Case 22 provides an illustration. It differs from Case 21 only with respect to the securities that can be traded. There is no trading in state claims. However, two options are available: a put with an exercise price equal to the payoff at which the MIF security has a total return of 0.92 and a call with an exercise price equal to the payoff at which the MIF security has a total return of 1.09.

With only the resulting four securities, the investors achieve returns that are indistinguishable from those shown in Figure 7-7 (and hence there is no need for us to show the graph). Karyn's portfolio consists primarily of a long position in bonds, a long position in the call, and a short position in the put. Collectively, the other investors provide the options positions that Karyn desires, but no single investor takes a large position in either option.

A single protected investment product could also appeal to Karyn. Consider a security offering a base return with upside potential for higher returns if the market return exceeds a given threshold. If there were also a possibility that the return could fall below the base return in especially bad markets as a result of "credit risk" the product might replicate the returns on the portfolio of bonds and options positions that Karyn chose in this case. An issuing financial institution could sell such a product to Karyn, use the proceeds to take the appropriate positions to hedge its obligation, and possibly charge Karyn an additional fee for its services.

7.7. Case 23: Karyn and Her Friends

What if every investor had a kinked marginal utility function? Case 23 provides an example. Here each person's preferences are described by such a function but their reference ranges occur at different points (perhaps because they purchased their current portfolios at different times and prices). The reference ranges of eight investors are lower than Karyn's and the ranges of eight are higher. Each of the 17 investors has a constant relative risk aversion of 50 within his or her reference range and 3 above and below it.

The securities in Case 23 are the riskless bond and the market index from Cases 21 and 22 but investors can trade state claims to achieve the most desirable allocations of the amounts of consumption available in different states.

Figure 7-10 shows that when equilibrium is reached the pricing kernel is not unusual; asset prices are affected by the investors' preferences but not dramatically. However, no investor chooses a portfolio that is equivalent to a simple combination of the market portfolio and the riskless asset. Dramatic evidence of this is seen in Figure 7-11: expected returns depart significantly from the Security Market Line (SML).

Not only are many of the differences from the SML significant, they are far from random. Kathryn, with the lowest reference point, chooses a strategy that is similar to a levered market portfolio and has the highest beta value. Kimball, with the next-to-lowest reference point, picks a strategy with the next highest beta value. If the investors' reference ranges were shown alongside the points in Figure 7-11 the lowest value would be at the upper right, then the values

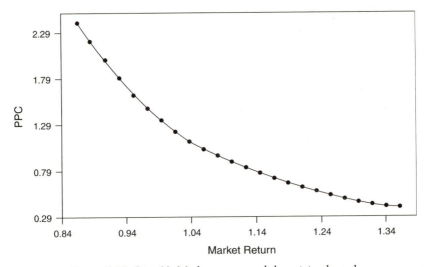

Figure 7-10 Case 23: Market return and the pricing kernel.

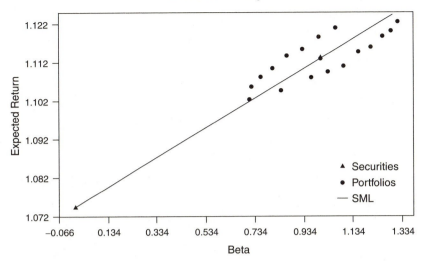

Figure 7-11 Case 23: The Security Market Line.

would increase moving clockwise around the oval formed by the dots that surround the market portfolio, which plots at the center of the oval.

Some reflection will show why this is the case. An investor's greatest risk aversion occurs in his or her reference range. For some this is mostly below the range of affordable outcomes; for others it is near the middle of that range, and for yet others it is mostly above it.

The reasons for some of the radical departures from the SML are best illustrated by examining the strategies chosen by Kong, who has a negative alpha, and Krishna, who has a positive alpha. Their returns are shown in Figure 7-12, along with those of the market portfolio.

Kong's goals are modest; he can obtain consumption within his reference range and afford substantially more consumption in the cheaper states in which the market does well. Krishna's situation is very different. His goals are high; he can afford only to obtain consumption within or above his reference range in the cheaper states in which the market does well. In the other states he must settle for less.

Kong could be happy with a protected investment product; he wants downside protection and upside potential. Krishna is very different; he is willing to accept downside losses but to limit his upside gains.

One might think that although positive-alpha strategies such as Krishna's plot above the Security Market Line they would involve sufficient added risk to make them inferior when expected return and standard deviation of return are considered. But, as shown in Figure 7-13, strategies such as Krishna's also plot above the Capital Market Line (CML) and thus have higher Sharpe Ratios than

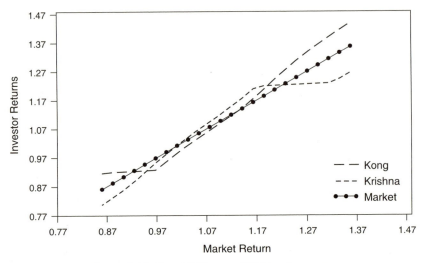

Figure 7-12 Case 23: Kong and Krishna's returns.

the market portfolio. On the other hand, strategies such as Kong's plot below the SML and well below the CML, with Sharpe Ratios considerably
lower than that of the market portfolio. Since we know that each of these investors has chosen an optimal portfolio, these relationships emphasize the fact
that comparisons based only on mean and variance may be insufficient in a
world in which investors' marginal utility curves have significant curvature.

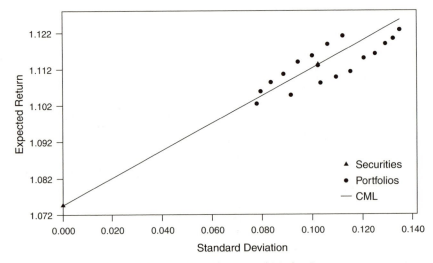

Figure 7-13 Case 23: The Capital Market Line.

These very special investors were able to pursue nonlinear market-based strategies by trading state claims. But they could have accomplished their goals using options, although a rather large variety with different exercise prices would have been required. In more realistic cases involving both investors with smooth marginal utility curves and others with kinked curves fewer options might be required to make the market sufficiently complete.

7.8. Protection Demand and Supply

In Case 23, protected investment products could have been attractive for some investors. But in a well-functioning capital market one cannot expect to get something for nothing. Return diagrams that are steeper for up markets than for down markets offer good news and bad news. The good news is the softer blow delivered by a bad market. The bad news is that taking all possible markets into account, protected investment strategies may offer lower expected returns than available from equal-beta linear market-based strategies. The opposite holds for diagrams that are steeper for down markets than for up markets.

7.8.1. m-Shares

Diverse preferences can provide a demand for PIPs, but they must also provide a supply. This rather obvious point can be seen most clearly by considering a simple institutional product that can internalize both aspects.

Most PIPs are complex. The Citigroup product (Citigroup 2004a) involves six parties: an underwriter, a trustee, a co-trustee, a depositor, a swap counterparty, and a swap insurer. The trustee invests in a set of term assets (in this case floating rate notes backed by credit card debt), then pays the proceeds to the swap counterparty. In return, the swap counterparty is obligated to make the required terminal payments to holders of the certificates. In the event of default by the swap counterparty, the swap insurer is obligated to cover any shortfall. Nonetheless, the prospectus indicates, there could be circumstances in which holders of the certificates will receive less than the promised amount at the expiration date.

It might seem as though the swap counterparty is providing the downside protection for the certificates. Legally it is. But in all likelihood it is hedging most of its obligation so that, in effect, other investors are the primary providers. The prospectus provides some indication of the nature of such activity, stating that initially the swap counterparty "directly or through its subsidiaries will hedge its anticipated exposure . . . by the purchase or sale of options, futures contracts, forward contracts or swaps or options on the index, or other derivative or synthetic instruments related to the index." Subsequently, depending on market conditions (including the market price of the index) one or more of the parties may use "dynamic hedging techniques and may take long or short positions in the index, in listed or over-the-counter option contracts in, or other derivative or synthetic instruments related to the index."

It seems unlikely that, unaided, the typical purchaser of such a certificate would be able to estimate the true risk and return of the investment. But even a sophisticated purchaser could not follow the full chain of transactions to determine the ultimate providers of the certificate's protection. From whom might the swap counterparty buy an option? Does the seller of the option hold the underlying securities, some other derivative, or some set of derivatives? If derivatives are involved, what counterparty is on the other side? And what are the assets and liabilities of that counterparty? The chain could be very long indeed, with each link adding counterparty risk and cost.

Might there be a better way to provide such payoffs? Possibly. A trustee could hold a set of assets and issue two or more sets of claims, at least one of which provides downside protection. We illustrate with a prototypical version in which a trust issues securities that we will call *m-shares* (for "market shares"), although the procedure could be used with any set of trusteed assets. We build on the concept of a *superfund* that issues *supershares*, proposed by Hakansson (1976). In 1992 Leland, O'Brien, and Rubinstein created vehicles derived from Hakansson's approach (Rubinstein 1990). Included were the first two exchange-traded funds ("superunits") traded on the American Stock Exchange and four claims ("supershares") traded on the Chicago Board Options Exchange. Two of the supershares were backed by one of the superunits and two by the other. All six securities were scheduled to expire at the end of 3 years.

Unfortunately, these securities were not a great success. Investors had to take the initiative to create supershares from superunits. The idea of an exchange-traded fund (but without an expiration date) clearly caught on, although the creation of separate claims on such a fund did not. This may have been due to the complex legal structure required at the time, insufficient interest in the particular payoff patterns incorporated in the securities, inadequate incentives for brokers and others to sell the products to individual investors, or all three factors. The simple version we will describe may be impractical as well. Even so, it provides a convenient metaphor for thinking about protected investment products and other market index derivatives.

Figure 7-14 shows the payoffs from a simple set of m-shares. A current amount of $100 is used to buy a portfolio that tracks a market index. The portfolio is held in trust until a stated expiration date, with all stock dividends and bond coupon payments reinvested in the interim. At expiration the portfolio is sold and a total amount equal to that shown by the dark gray area paid to those who hold shares of *m-share1*. The remaining money is then distributed to those who hold shares of *m-share2*.

The payoffs from m-share1 have a familiar pattern. Within the range of market values from 50 to 200 it provides a payoff pattern similar to that of a capped

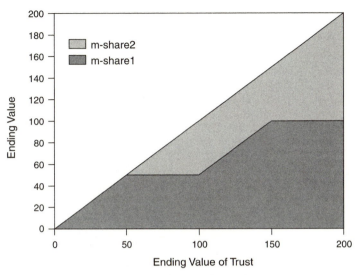

Figure 7-14 m-share ending values.

product with downside protection (*flat-up-flat*). This is known in the options business as an *Egyptian* (think of images on ancient tombs) or a *collar*. Within the range from 0 to 150, m-share1 offers the Travolta pattern desired by Karyn in case 21 (*up-flat-up*). Over the entire range it provides participation in very bad markets (0 to 50) and good markets (100 to 150) with protection for bad to medium markets (50 to 100) and a cap for very good markets (150 to 200).

The other part of this story is the payoffs to holders of m-share2. The amounts are shown by the light gray area in Figure 7-14 but the pattern can be seen more clearly in Figure 7-15. The pattern for the range from 50 to 200 is another Travolta. Taking the entire range, both m-share1 and m-share2 have two flat areas, which could be appropriate for an investor with two reference ranges and the associated kinks in marginal utility curves.

In each range, a change in the value of the trust goes entirely to one of the two m-shares. Thus a given percentage increase in the ending value of the trust will lead to a greater percentage increase for one share and no increase at all for the other. More generally, in every range of market returns in which one m-share's returns increase less than one-for-one with market returns, some other m-share (or m-shares) must increase more than one-for-one. If one investor wants downside protection, someone else must provide it.

Such m-shares might have many advantages. Overhead costs could be low, there could be almost complete transparency, and there would be no counterparty risk in the conventional sense. On the other hand, they might be too transparent to be sold profitably since there could be little magic to promote.

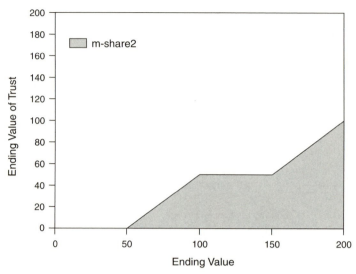

Figure 7-15 m-share2 ending values.

Nonetheless, the m-share construct makes very clear the fact that investors collectively share the market. One could also carve the market into more than two pieces, each of great or little complexity. Eventually each piece would sell at an equilibrium price. If the sum of the values of the pieces were greater than the value of the underlying portfolio, there would be a rush to create new funds. If the sum were less, anyone wishing to hold the market portfolio could simply buy proportionate shares of all the pieces and get the market portfolio at a discount—a situation unlikely to prevail for long.

The goal of an m-share provider would be to profit by designing m-share payoff functions that could help complete the market in ways that some investors crave. This might or might not be as efficient as using other financial vehicles (such as options) but if done cleverly some investors might pay for securities that would provide such payoffs. Some might have different views about the chances of alternative market outcomes than are reflected in market prices and thus choose to bet against the market. Others might be simply unaware of the extent to which they are sacrificing upside potential to get downside protection. But, as we have seen, there is reason to believe that people may have sufficiently diverse preferences so that some should have downside protection and others should provide it. It is conceivable that half the people could fall in one of the two camps and half in the other. More likely, a minority of investors should get protection, a minority of a similar size should provide it, and the majority of investors should do neither. To know how large the minorities might be, we need evidence about the preferences of real investors—our next topic.

7.9. Measuring Investors' Preferences

In a simple two-date setting an investor allocates his or her wealth to obtain current consumption and state-contingent amounts to be consumed in future states. Absent outside positions or state-dependent preferences, the future prospects for any allocation can be summarized in a *probability distribution* of future consumption. In a complete market setting such an investor's decision process can be summarized as follows:

$$\text{Budget} + \text{Prices} + \text{Preferences} \rightarrow \text{Distribution}$$

Given a budget, a set of state prices, and his or her preferences, the investor will choose the most desirable distribution—formally, the one that maximizes his or her expected utility.

Assume that an investor has chosen a distribution and that an outsider can observe the budget, state prices, and the selected distribution. From this information it may be possible to infer the investor's preferences:

$$\text{Budget} + \text{Prices} + \text{Distribution} \rightarrow \text{Preferences}$$

This is the approach taken in a series of studies reported in Sharpe, Goldstein, and Blythe (2000), Sharpe (2001), and Goldstein, Johnson, and Sharpe (2005) using a set of software known as the *Distribution Builder*. Here we focus on the results obtained in the study reported by the authors of the latter paper (hence, GJS).

In 2003 GJS enlisted a number of paid participants to make choices about retirement income using the Distribution Builder software. The participants also answered a number of questions regarding risk attitudes, investment portfolios, and personal characteristics. The usable responses from 304 participants will be used for our analyses.

7.9.1. The Distribution Builder

The Distribution Builder is a Web-based program that allows the user to place 100 markers on a simulated game board. Figure 7-16 shows the user interface. Each marker represents a person, one of which is the user. The user does not know which marker represents him or her, but is told that the odds are 1 out of 100 for each marker. Each row corresponds to a given standard of living in retirement. For example, if the user's marker is in the row marked 75 percent, he or she will retire with a total real income each year (until death) equal to 75 percent of income just prior to retirement. The user is told that retirement incomes of 20 percent or below may be painful and that a level of 75 percent is recommended by many retirement advisors. Both these ranges are highlighted for emphasis.

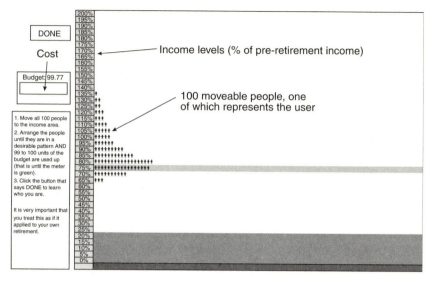

Figure 7-16 The Distribution Builder interface.

The user can place as many people in a row as desired, or none. For every pattern, a cost is calculated. This cost, expressed as a percentage of the user's budget, is shown prominently. Only if it is between 99 and 100 percent of the budget is the user allowed to declare that the current pattern represents the preferred feasible choice. The user is told that costs are not symmetric, so that moving a marker down from the lowest occupied row will save enough money to move a market up a greater distance from the highest occupied row. The user's task is to experiment with different patterns to find a preferred one that does not exceed the budget.

7.9.2. *The Underlying Economy*

It will come as no surprise to readers of this book that this is a setting with 100 states of the world, each of which is equally probable. There is (forced) agreement on probabilities and, as we will see, it is possible to buy state claims. The focus on total retirement income attempts to exclude the influence of outside positions. We thus have a case of agreement and complete markets with no participants' outside position. By design, this is an excellent setting for investigating individuals' preferences.

Internally, the software uses a set of state prices, no two of which are the same. While the participants did not need to think of probabilities or probability distributions, we know each did, in fact, choose a probability distribution of consumption.

After each move, a financial advisor determines the least-cost way to provide the current distribution and reports the associated cost as a percentage of the participant's budget. The procedure is simple enough. The list of a participant's 100 desired levels of consumption is arranged from the lowest to highest values. Then the smallest consumption is allocated to the most expensive state, the next-smallest consumption to the next-to-most expensive state, and so on. The resulting portfolio provides the desired distribution at the lowest possible cost.

It is important to emphasize that many of the subsequent results are dependent on this procedure and that they may not represent choices that would have been made by the participants without the benefit of rudimentary financial advice. The advisor does no more than ensure that each investor obtains a given probability distribution of consumption at the lowest possible cost. This may seem innocuous, but as we will see, it is inconsistent with upward-sloping marginal utility curves. An investor who wishes to obtain a probability distribution of return at the lowest cost does not exhibit behavior consistent with risk preference over any range of outcomes. This rules out some aspects of the prospect theory preferences first documented in Kahneman and Tversky (1979).

For the purpose of estimating an investor's marginal utility it does not matter how the state prices are determined, as long as they differ. However, to make the survey results as meaningful as possible an attempt was made to provide prices consistent with traditional views concerning long-run return distributions.

The next three paragraphs briefly describe the procedure for those conversant with related literature. Others may pass them by.

Assets were assumed to be invested for 10 years. Two securities were available: a riskless bond with a real return of 2 percent per year and a market portfolio with an annual Sharpe Ratio of 1/3. Returns and state prices were assumed to be independent and identically distributed (IID); that is the possible returns and probabilities of those returns were the same each period.

Given these assumptions, with a large number of short periods (say, weeks) state prices for payoffs after 10 years will be very close to lognormally distributed, as will terminal values for the market portfolio and all buy-and-hold combinations of the market portfolio with a 10-year investment in the riskless bond. If returns on the market portfolio are assumed to take on only two values (up and down) in each of a great many very short periods, there will be a one-to-one relationship between the logarithms of terminal values of the market portfolio and 10-year state prices. But for each of these variables to be lognormally distributed the relationship between the logarithms of their values will have to be linear.

These assumptions are used to derive a lognormal distribution of state prices, which is then approximated with 100 discrete state prices, each of which is a probability-weighted average of the prices within a range having a probability of 0.01. The most important aspect of the resulting set of state prices is that they are very different. The most expensive state costs 325 times as much as the cheapest! This reflects the fact that in actual capital markets it can be extremely expensive to purchase consumption or portfolio return in a state in which the economy is in terrible shape (e.g., deep depression). On the other hand, it can be very inexpensive to buy consumption or return in a state of great plenty.

7.9.3. Estimating a Participant's Marginal Utility

The survey participants varied in wealth: roughly half were given budgets sufficient to obtain a retirement income of 75 percent of pre-retirement income without risk while the remainder could only obtain 60 percent without risk. For any chosen distribution, the lowest possible cost was calculated using the state prices, compared with the initial budget and the resulting ratio shown in the user interface. Any value lower than 99 percent or above 100 percent was shown in red and any value between 99 and 100 percent shown in green, indicating that the participant could, if desired, choose the current distribution.

Since the probabilities of all states are the same, each state price can be divided by 0.01 to determine the associated price per chance. Moreover, given a participant's chosen distribution and the assumption that he or she wants to obtain it at the lowest possible cost we can plot desired consumption and PPC values directly.

Figure 7-17 shows the distribution chosen by Bin, one of the participants. Figure 7-18 shows the relationship between PPCs and Bin's chosen levels of consumption. As we know, this has the same shape as his marginal utility function. Except for scaling, Figure 7-18 can thus be considered the marginal utility of a real person.

The information in Figure 7-18 is replotted using logarithms in Figure 7-19, along with a fitted regression line. This shows that Bin's preferences can be well represented by a marginal utility function with constant relative risk aversion, since an investor with such preferences will choose consumption so that there is a linear relationship between the logarithm of price per chance and the logarithm of consumption. In this case, the actual relationship is almost linear (the regression line fit to the data has an R^2 value of 0.99). Bin appears to be very much like Mario, Hue, and many of the other investors in our simulation cases who have constant relative risk aversion.

7.9.4. Aggregate Consumption and the Pricing Kernel

It is a simple matter to compute the relationship between the pricing kernel and the aggregate consumption chosen by the participants in this small econ-

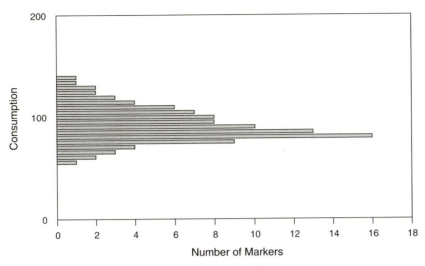

Figure 7-17 Bin's selected distribution.

omy. For each state, we simply sum the retirement consumptions chosen by the individual investors. The resulting relationship, shown in Figure 7-20, is very similar to many we have seen in the simulated worlds of our cases.

The data from Figure 7-20 are replotted using logarithms in Figure 7-21. The overall relationship is quite well approximated by a constant relative risk

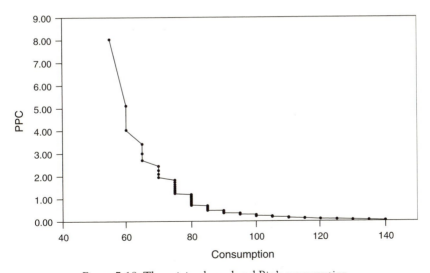

Figure 7-18 The pricing kernel and Bin's consumption.

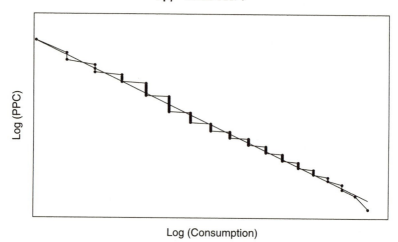

Figure 7-19 Logarithms of the pricing kernel and Bin's consumption.

aversion function. A straight-line fit to the logarithms of the variables has an R^2 value of 0.99. There is a slight indication of greater risk aversion for very low levels of aggregate consumption (corresponding to an average retirement income below 50 percent of pre-retirement income) and for very high levels of aggregate consumption (corresponding to an average retirement income above 125 percent). This might reflect a feeling on the part of some participants that an income of 50 percent is a bare minimum and that one of 125 percent is suf-

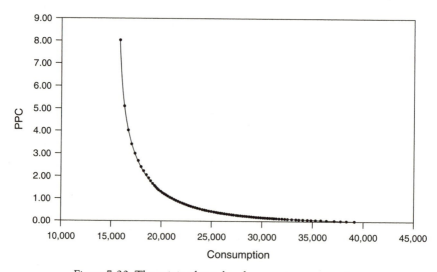

Figure 7-20 The pricing kernel and aggregate consumption.

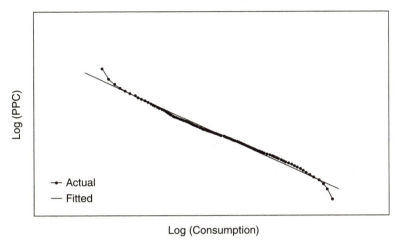

Figure 7-21 Logarithms of the pricing kernel and aggregate consumption.

ficient to achieve most goals. It might thus be fruitful to explore the possibility that some investors' preferences could be represented by a marginal utility function with three segments, each with constant relative risk aversion, with larger coefficients for the left and right segments than for the middle segment.

7.9.5. Portfolio and Market Returns

Given a participant's budget and choice of a set of consumption levels it is a simple matter of division (of the latter by the former) to determine the corresponding set of 100 portfolio returns. Similarly, dividing the aggregate consumption amounts chosen in each state by aggregate wealth gives the market returns by state.

Figure 7-22 shows the relationship between Bin's returns and the market's returns, along with a line showing the returns provided by an equal-beta combination of the market portfolio and the riskless asset, using the beta value determined by regressing the portfolio's returns on the market returns.

Not surprisingly, the curve relating Bin's returns to the market's returns is flat in each range in which the curves in Figures 7-18 and 7-19 were vertical. In Bin's case, the flat spots are likely due more to the granularity of the available choices than to substantial kinks in his utility function. But there were investors who chose distributions with return graphs that were decidedly nonlinear. Figures 7-23 and 7-24 show two extreme examples.

Compared to an equal-beta market strategy, Arthur has chosen higher returns in several of the worst (lowest aggregate consumption and market return) states of the world and several of the best (highest aggregate consumption and

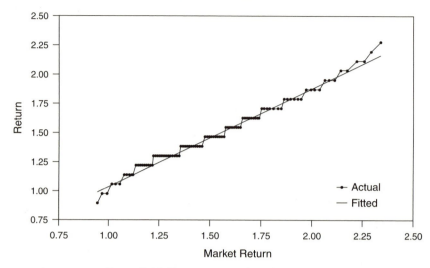

Figure 7-22 Bin's returns and market returns.

market return) states of the world. He has covered the cost of doing so by accepting lower returns relative to an equal-beta market strategy in all the intermediate states of the world. Patricia has done just the opposite. They should definitely meet. Neither Arthur nor Patricia is a prospect for a traditional PIP. But each of them would clearly be interested in a market-based strategy other

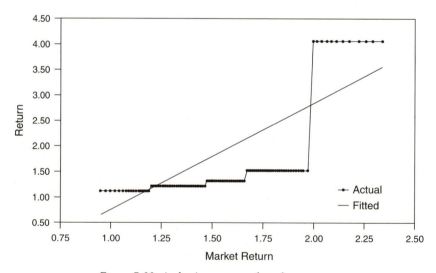

Figure 7-23 Arthur's returns and market returns.

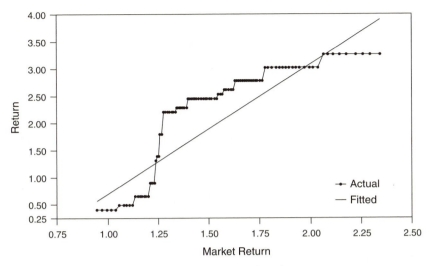

Figure 7-24 Patricia's returns and market returns.

than one that could be obtained by combining the market portfolio with a risk-less asset.

7.9.6. Expected Returns and Beta Values

One more graph completes this picture. Figure 7-25 shows the expected returns and beta values for the strategies selected by the participants. It is the experimental counterpart to the SML figures from our simulation cases. Many of the chosen portfolios plot above or below the SML. Since every portfolio is, of necessity, a market-based strategy, this provides clear evidence that a number of the participants chose nonlinear market-based strategies.

An indication of the nonlinearity of a participant's chosen strategy is provided by the R^2 value obtained when regressing the participant's return on the market return to obtain its beta value. An R^2 value of 1 indicates that the variation in market returns explains 100 percent of the variation in the participant's returns, as would be the case with any upward-sloping linear strategy. A value of 0 indicates that none of the variation in a participant's returns is explained by a linear relationship with market returns. As indicated earlier, the R^2 value for Bin was 0.99. For Arthur and Patricia the values were, respectively, 0.59 and 0.77.

As we have suggested, some of the nonlinearities in these results are undoubtedly due to the granularity of the experiment. Nonetheless, approximately 25 percent of the participants who took risk had R^2 values smaller than 0.80. The patterns varied. Only a few participants appeared to be likely candidates

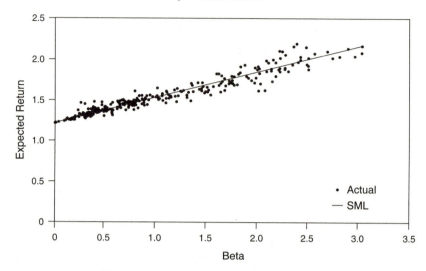

Figure 7-25 Expected returns and beta values.

to buy or to sell simple protected products, but there were definitely a number who, like Arthur and Patricia, chose substantially nonlinear strategies. Overall, roughly one out of four of the participants might possibly be interested in the offerings of an options exchange or a financial services firm offering a market-based product with nonlinear payoffs if there were no additional costs. In a more realistic setting, the portion of likely buyers and sellers could be much lower.

7.9.7. Other Applications

The results from this experiment are at best suggestive. Much more can be done with the Distribution Builder. More extensive studies may provide better evidence concerning investors' preferences. Normative applications are also possible, with an investor crafting a preferred distribution and then a financial institution providing the needed investment strategies to approximate it.

More broadly, experimental and survey techniques hold great promise for financial economists interested in investors' preferences. Inferring people's preferences from the *ex post* results of their choices is at best a difficult task. Empirical analyses can and should be supplemented with carefully designed experiments to find and analyze individuals' *ex ante* choices when probabilities are known.

7.10. Dynamic Strategies

Absent extensive disagreement about likely market outcomes, the demand for preference-based downside protection may be too idiosyncratic to warrant large numbers of costly new financial products. But there are other ways to affect the way in which returns relate to market returns. In long-run settings it is possible to create a nonlinear return function with a *dynamic strategy* that follows decision rules for changing asset mixes based on previous returns. The final results will be less than perfect because of transactions costs and differences between assumptions about the ways in which returns can move and the ways in which they actually do move (as the purveyors of dynamic strategies designed to provide "portfolio insurance" discovered in the U.S. stock market crash in 1987). But it may be possible to achieve results that will have general shapes that will please the likes of Arthur and Patricia.

Figure 7-26 can help fix ideas. It shows the return relationships for three strategies. The straight line represents a standard combination of the market portfolio and a riskless asset. The curve that increases at a decreasing rate represents a strategy designed to appeal to the Arthurs of this world. The curve that increases at an increasing rate is designed for the Patricias. Mathematicians call these convex and concave strategies. To avoid confusion we will give them simpler names. Relative to the market-based strategy, one curve appears to be smiling while the other one frowns. Arthur would favor a smiling strategy and Patricia a frowning one. While Arthur may smile at the prospect of downside protection while Patricia may frown at the prospect of downside disaster, we know that in capital markets good news often accompanies bad news. Often the downside protection offered by the smiling strategy (good news) comes at the price of lower expected return (bad news). The converse holds for the frowning strategy.

How can one achieve these results with dynamic strategies? It need not be complicated. Imagine a strategy that sells shares in securities that have had the worst recent performance (relative losers) and buys shares in securities that have had the best recent performance (relative winners). Such an approach, often termed a *momentum* or *trend-following* strategy, will perform well if markets trend. Figure 7-27 provides an illustration. Assume that the market falls from a to b. Afterwards, the momentum investor sells some risky securities and buys some riskless ones. Then the market falls from b to c. With a lower beta,

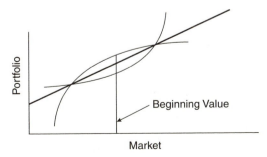

Figure 7-26 Dynamic strategy results.

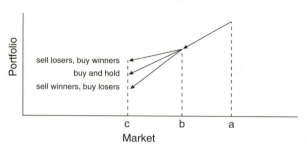

Figure 7-27 Dynamic strategies.

our momentum investor does better than one who initially bought the market and held the shares through both periods.

The other prototypical strategy is just the opposite. It buys relative losers and sells the relative winners. Since this is counterintuitive to some, it is termed a *contrarian* strategy. In a market that continues in the same direction, as in Figure 7-27, such an approach suffers relative to both the momentum strategy and a simple buy and hold approach. Following the initial market decline our contrarian buys additional risky securities, using either previous holdings of riskless securities or borrowed money. When the market falls again, the contrarian's portfolio falls more than the others' because of its increased beta value.

In a market that reverses itself, the story is just the opposite. This is illustrated in Figure 7-28, in which the market falls from a to b, then rises back to c, which is the same as a. Now the contrarian is the winner, the buy and hold investor is in the middle (as always), and the momentum investor brings up the rear.

It is not hard to see why these strategies can produce long-horizon results that are similar to those in Figure 7-26. If the market ends up near its beginning level, there will have been more reversals (Figure 7-28) than trends (Figure 7-27). When all the results are in, the contrarian will likely be the winner, the momentum player the loser, and the buy and hold investor's return will fall between theirs. On the other hand, if the market ends up well above or well below its beginning level there will have been more trends than reversals. The contrarian will likely be the poorest of the three, the momentum player the richest, and the buy and hold investor once again in the middle.

In the context of Figure 7-26, contrarians produce frowns but have the highest expected returns, momentum players produce smiles but have the lowest expected returns, and buy and hold investors remain resolutely in the middle on all counts. No strategy dominates any other— you pay your money and take your choice.

In practice, dynamic strategies produce at best fuzzy versions of diagrams such as Figure 7-26. Because transactions cost money, portfolio changes should not be made after every small market move. Moreover, sometimes the market

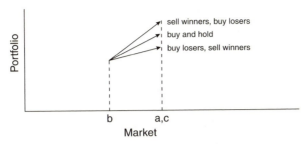

Figure 7-28 Dynamic strategies.

moves too rapidly to make desired adjustments (as it did in October 1987). Finally, trading costs lower net returns. For all these reasons, dynamic strategies are a less-than-perfect substitute for explicit contracts. In many cases, it will be better to use options, PIPs, or other derivatives that provide returns explicitly related in a nonlinear manner to the returns on an underlying index.

7.11. Buyers and Sellers of Downside Protection

Investors who desire a smiling pattern must find other investors who will accept a frowning pattern, whether outcomes are achieved with dynamic strategies or using explicit financial instruments such as options or PIPs. Those who buy PIPs get dramatic downside protection while others may settle for less extreme patterns of the sort shown in Figure 7-26. We can identify at least some of the buyers of downside protection, but who are the sellers? Are there many, each taking a little extra downside risk or a few, each taking a substantial amount? Most likely the answer is a mix of both possibilities. However, one can identify some financial institutions that specialize in strategies that can bring disaster in very bad markets. Directly or indirectly they supply downside protection to others. Many of these firms, organized as *hedge funds*, use long and short positions, leverage, and exotic investment strategies in the pursuit of high expected and realized returns. While specifics differ, such funds take positions that will pay off well in all but the worst states of the world, but may well crash and burn if markets experience substantial distress. Some observers have said that the typical hedge fund "picks up nickels in front of a steamroller."

In a market characterized by a pricing kernel that decreases at a decreasing rate, such strategies may offer higher expected returns and higher Sharpe Ratios than strategies with similar betas that participate symmetrically in both up and down markets. Over long periods they will thus produce positive alpha values using conventional measures of beta. But hedge funds do not provide something for nothing. Even after a commendable run of performance there may well be danger lurking in the background, as those who invested in Long Term Capital Management discovered during the liquidity crisis in the summer of 1998.

A situation that provides extraordinary returns in most states of the world and disastrous returns in a few states of the world gives rise to what is known as the *peso problem*. The name stems from a period many years ago when the Mexican peso fell slowly against the U.S. dollar due to currency controls. Month after month one could convert dollars to pesos, invest the pesos in a Mexican bank, then reconvert the principal plus interest into dollars, achieving a higher return than could be obtained from a U.S. bank. Something for nothing? Hardly. Eventually the day came when the Mexican authorities could no longer continue to prop up their weak currency. The exchange rate changed radically and American investors with money in Mexican banks suffered large losses. A similar fate befell some large hedge funds years later when European currencies were suddenly revalued.

The peso problem is a serious impediment for anyone attempting to evaluate the abilities of managers who intentionally expose their clients to a small probability of a large loss. Unless and until the disastrous event occurs, such a managers' performance will be even better than its overall expected return, which is itself above average.

Not all hedge funds follow strategies that suffer greatly in bad markets, but many do. With such managers it is more important than ever to "investigate before you invest."

7.12. Summary

While we began this chapter with protected investment products, we have gone substantially farther to consider the broader class of nonlinear market-based strategies. There is a case to be made that such strategies can provide gains through trade even if investors agree on the probabilities of future states. If investors have sufficiently diverse preferences it will be desirable for them to have access to a set of investment vehicles with returns that are nonlinearly related to market returns in different ways. If, in addition, investors disagree about the probabilities of alternative future market returns, derivative securities based on broad market portfolios will be in even more demand.

Not surprisingly, reality differs substantially from the pictures painted in this chapter. While some derivative products are based on broadly diversified portfolios, most are not. This is true as well for protected investment products. The underlying asset for a PIP might be a relatively broad index such as the S&P 500 but it might instead be a narrow index of as few as five stocks, typically all from a single industrial sector. Some of the purchasers of such products may wish to complement outside positions, but most probably have views about future prospects that differ from those reflected in current market prices.

Unfortunately, it is also possible that some buyers of protected investment products simply do not understand the underlying economics of these investments. There is anecdotal evidence that financial firms issue more PIPs when interest rates are high, making the cost of locking in the minimum promised payment low. If buyers do not realize that the present value of a dollar five years hence is less in a high interest rate environment, they may be unduly attracted to protected investment products. Not everyone reads the quotations for five-year zero coupon bonds.

There is also evidence that more PIPs are issued when the projected volatilities of the underlying assets are low, making the costs of call options small. If buyers do not realize that upside potential is worth less when there is less likelihood of a major upward move, they may be excessively enthusiastic about protected investment products. Not all read the quotations for long-term options.

Some protected investment products seem, at first glance, to be too good to be true. At one time a major brokerage firm offered a product that provided an upside potential of 100 percent of the total return on an index of Japanese stocks with a downside protection equal to the return of the investor's total investment. On closer examination, one found that the payment in dollars would be based on the return on the underlying index in yen. At the time, Japanese interest rates were substantially below rates in the United States. Had the underlying instrument been a zero coupon Japanese bond the implication would have been clear, since the upside would have been, say, 1 percent per year in dollars rather than 5 percent available from U.S. bonds. With stocks the impact of interest differentials and the associated currency exchange rates is more subtle, but the issuer presumably planned to use a series of transactions in currency forward markets to make a tidy profit no matter what happened to Japanese stocks. Even sophisticated investors might be forgiven for failing to see the driving force behind this product.

Protected investment products may indeed be appropriate for some investors. But they may be dangerous for the naïve or the gullible. Caveat emptor.

EIGHT

ADVICE

MOST OF THIS BOOK has focused on positive economics. We have created investors; given them preferences, predictions, and positions; let them trade with a set of available securities until they would trade no more; and then examined the relationships among security and portfolio prices, expected returns, and various measures of risk. Our focus was on the properties of equilibrium in capital markets.

But the actors in our plays made normative decisions as they sought to maximize their expected utilities. And they made these decisions by themselves. In the real world, only a minority of investors can and should attempt such difficult feats alone. In this domain, as in many others, the principle of comparative advantage dictates a division of labor. An individual investor can be aided by professionals with deep understanding of financial markets and the needed supporting technology and databases. Broadly, we will call such experts and expert systems *financial advisors* or simply *advisors*.

8.1. Investment Advice

In some cases a person or firm will only make recommendations that the investor can accept or reject, then make the appropriate trades. Terms for advisors who operate in this manner include *investment advisors, financial planners,* and *consultants*. In other cases, an investment organization or individual will provide both the needed advice and its implementation. Terms for those who operate in this manner include *personal investment managers* and *family offices*. For convenience, we subsume all these approaches under the heading "advisor."

This chapter is normative in nature, focusing on the ways in which advisors can help investors make the best possible financial decisions. We will argue that the need for personal investment advisors is growing in much of the world. And we will contend that it is imperative that such advisors make their recommendations or decisions in the context of logically consistent and well reasoned models of equilibrium in financial markets. We thus return to the theme introduced at the outset: asset pricing and portfolio choice are not two subjects, but one.

8.2. Demographics and Individual Investment Decisions

In most developed economies, people pass through three fairly distinct stages of life. First they mature and go to school; then they work; finally, they retire. To finance consumption for people in the third stage requires sacrifice of consumption on the part of those who are more productive. Until recently, most developed economies facilitated life-cycle consumption by paying workers less than their contributions to output, then providing them with income after retirement. The prototypical scheme centered on the concept of a *defined benefit* (DB) in which retirement payments are a function of salary, years worked, and other variables, but not of investment returns. Traditional corporate and government employee pension plans in the United States and other countries were of this type, as were public plans such as the U.S. Social Security system. In most cases, the worker had no decisions to make. The amount "saved" (in forgone wage or salary) was predetermined, as was the formula determining benefit payments.

Now, however, most developed economies are in the midst of dramatic changes in population age distributions. Figure 8-1 shows the distribution of population by age and sex in the United States in 1950 and 2005 plus an estimate for 2050. In 1950 the graph conformed to its classic name; it was a "population pyramid." In 2005 it had a shape more like that of the French Michelin man. By 2050 it is projected to become a population blob. Those interested in graphs for other countries can find them at the U.S. Census Bureau Web site (U.S. Census Bureau 2005). The changes in the situations of most developed countries are similar to or even more dramatic than those shown in Figure 8-1.

These profound changes in population demographics have been accompanied by major shifts in the ways in which people save and invest for retirement in many countries. There is an increasing reliance on schemes involving *defined contributions* (DC). In a standard system of this type an employee decides how much to deduct from wages or salary each month. This amount, plus a possible contribution by the employer, is then invested in investment vehicles (such as mutual funds) selected from a list provided by the employer. The employee is responsible for allocating funds among the investment vehicles. When the employee reaches retirement, he or she has access to the ending value of the money that has been invested. At that point, the money can be re-invested, used to purchase an annuity, or both. Unless funds are fully annuitized, the individual will then have decisions to make about the amounts to be spent each year until he or she (and often a partner) dies.

Why the movement away from a defined benefit toward a defined contribution system? Part of the answer lies in the fact that the former provides only fixed claims on societal output while the latter allows variable claims for those who desire them. As the composition of the population has changed, the

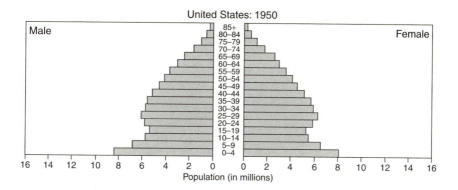

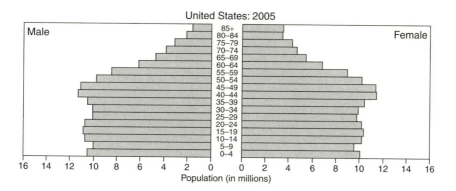

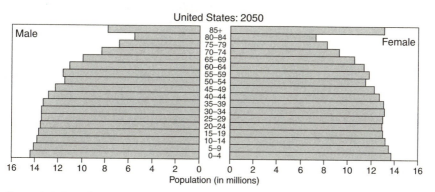

Figure 8-1 Distribution of the population of the United States, 1950, 2005, and 2050.
Source: U.S. Census Bureau, International Data Base.

inability of the traditional system to provide a variety of methods for sharing productive outcomes has become a greater and greater impediment.

In a defined benefit regime, retirees have a prior claim on the economy's output: a claim that is fixed in either nominal or real terms. Economically, those currently working are residual claimants after the retirees have been paid. Economic output is distributed to satisfy the claims of traditional providers of capital, to retirees, and then current workers. Retirees have bond-like claims (nominal or real) while workers have claims similar to levered equity holdings. Such an approach may have provided a reasonable distribution of societal risk and reward when there were few retirees per worker, but it would almost certainly result in an unreasonable distribution of risk with current and projected higher ratios of retirees to current workers.

Defined contribution plans provide the flexibility to allow better sharing of economic outcomes. They do not preclude the ability of a person to replicate a defined benefit plan by investing in low-risk investments during the working years, then purchasing an annuity at retirement. Those with little tolerance for risk may do this, but others need not do so. As in the cases in this book, the overall risk of an economy should be allocated among people based on their positions and preferences.

In the United States, many employers have switched from defined benefit to defined contribution plans. Social security (the government retirement system) remains a defined benefit system as this book goes to press but proposals are frequently made to change it to a system that would include features of both defined benefit and defined contribution plans.

For good or ill, individuals increasingly have the responsibility to make savings and investment decisions that will determine their welfare over decades of their later life. The more a person saves, the less he or she will consume before retirement. The larger a person's savings and the better the performance of his or her investments, the more can be consumed after retirement. But bad choices and/or bad luck can lead to highly unfortunate outcomes. Those who fail to make sensible financial decisions can run out of money and be forced to rely on children, charity, or government welfare in their later years.

We have entered an era in which many millions of people need to make informed savings and investment decisions. The majority should not do so alone. A personal investment advisor or manager can help.

8.3. The Investor and the Advisor

Figure 8-2 portrays a possible division of labor between an investor and an advisor, using terms from our earlier analyses. The investor knows the most about his or her outside financial positions and preferences. He or she also brings to the process an initial portfolio, or overall level of wealth.

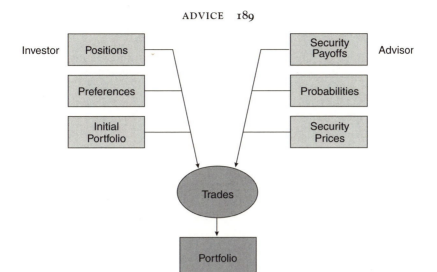

Figure 8-2 Investor and advisor roles.

The advisor's task is to contribute expertise about financial markets and securities. This includes forecasts of the possible outcomes from different types of investments and the associated probabilities. In our approach this is captured in the securities table showing the payoffs from various investments in alternative states of the world and the probabilities table, indicating the probabilities of those states. The advisor also is likely to have better access to the prices of securities, especially the more exotic types such as options and other derivative securities.

To determine the best investment program requires that information about investor positions, preferences, and wealth be brought together with information about security prices, payoffs, and probabilities (in conventional terms, security risks and expected returns). This can be accomplished by the investor, armed with an efficient means to interact with the results of the advisor's work. In many cases, however, it can be done more efficiently by the advisor, after sufficient interaction with the investor to establish the latter's positions, preferences, and current holdings. Whatever the process, the goal is to ensure that the ultimate decisions take into account both the personal situation of the investor and the opportunities available in financial markets.

More broadly, the set of key decisions includes not only the choice of an investment portfolio but also plans for the amounts to be saved (until retirement) or spent (after retirement). In some cases, decisions about housing, mortgage borrowing, insurance, and years of employment may be included as well.

8.4. Portfolio Optimization

In the simple procedure depicted in Figure 8-2 someone needs to determine the set of trades that will create the best portfolio for the investor in question. The advisor (or the advisor's computer) should best be suited to fill this role. The goal is to maximize the investor's expected utility, taking into account all relevant information, including any constraints on holdings. The objective is to find the *optimal portfolio* for the investor in question.

Much of the material covered in the first seven chapters of this book is relevant in this connection. But there are differences.

Any change in an investor's holdings requires that trades be made with another investor or institution, and such trades will change the equilibrium situation and affect security prices. However, for all but the wealthiest investors and the least liquid stocks the impact on security prices of changes in one person's portfolio holdings will be sufficiently small that it can be ignored. Thus investment advisors typically assume that each security can be bought or sold at a price very close to that of the most recent trade or the average of the currently quoted bid and ask prices. The investor is thus assumed to be a *price taker*—able to trade any desired amount of any security or asset class with "the market" at the current market price. The goal is to maximize the investor's expected utility by making possible trades with this compliant partner.

While our simulation program is not designed to solve such a problem directly, our basic approach can easily be adapted to accomplish the task, as follows. Each security is considered in turn, with a "paper trade" made to bring the investor's reservation price in line with the market price (or until a constraint is reached). The process is repeated for every security, completing a round. If no paper trades were made in the first round, the initial portfolio is optimal and no more computations are required. If, however, some paper trades were made, another round is conducted. The process is continued until an entire round has been completed with no further paper trades. At that point, the initial portfolio is compared with the final portfolio and actual trades made to move from the former to the latter.

In the special case in which an investor's utility function is quadratic, a simpler approach can be employed. As we have shown, such an investor will be concerned only with the mean and variance of portfolio return. Efficient computational procedures have been developed for selecting portfolios under such conditions using only the expected returns for the securities, the standard deviations of their returns, and the correlations among the returns. Simple cases can be solved using the gradient method of Sharpe (1987). The critical line method developed by Markowitz (1952) can be utilized for more general problems. The solver procedure included with Microsoft's Excel program may also be utilized.

Of course an "optimal" portfolio is only as good as the forecasts used to determine it. Most of the remainder of the chapter is devoted to a discussion of useful ways to forecast security payoffs and probabilities.

8.5. Past and Future Returns

When making forecasts, most advisors begin by looking at history. For seasoned securities, one can analyze a number of periods of realized returns. This sort of approach is often used when recommending the allocation of an investor's portfolio among asset classes. An historic period is selected and a limited number of such classes chosen. Historic mean returns, standard deviations of return, and correlations are computed, then used as estimates of future expected returns, risks, and correla, Optimal portfolios are chosen assuming investors care only about portfolio expected return and standard deviation of return, then possible results over many future periods are computed, typically using Monte Carlo techniques.

If each of the historic periods was a realization of an unchanging probability distribution and many periods are available, past frequencies of various outcomes could provide a useful approximation of future probabilities. But, as we saw in Chapter 4, even under these ideal conditions history may be an imperfect guide to the future. Worse yet, current probabilities may differ significantly from historic frequencies. Some possible future events may have never occurred in the past. Moreover, the longer the historic period, the less likely it is that future probabilities are similar to those that gave rise to the past outcomes. Fortunately, we will see that the dangers are smaller for some estimates than for others, and additional information can be used to mitigate the problem.

To illustrate the problem, we take summary statistics from Dimson, Marsh, and Staunton (2002), a monumental study of returns from bonds, stocks, and cash in 16 countries from 1900 through 2000. We focus on the performance of the broadest aggregates: "world bonds" and "world stocks," computed by taking country-weighted averages of returns in the 16 countries. Summary statistics for real returns for a U.S. investor are shown in Figure 8-3. The correlation of the decade-by-decade real returns for world bonds and stocks was 0.52.

FIGURE 8-3
Historic Real Returns for World Bonds and Stocks

	Arithmetic Mean	Standard Deviation
World bonds	1.70	10.30
World stocks	7.20	17.00

To investigate possible relationships between past and future returns we conduct an experiment with these statistics. We assume that these are in fact the correct predictions of bond and stock expected real returns and risks and that the correlation between them equals the historic value. Moreover, we assume that the current values of bonds and stocks are in the ratio of 40 percent bonds and 60 percent stocks (very close to the average in the United States over the last 25 years). We then use standard mean/variance procedures to find the risk tolerance of an investor (Richard) with quadratic utility for whom a 60/40 stock/bond portfolio would be optimal.

Now, imagine that Richard is not privy to our knowledge of the true risks, returns, and correlation but that he does have 25 years of annual data. If he computes historic average returns, standard deviations, and a correlation coefficient, then proceeds to select an optimal portfolio using only historic statistics he will almost certainly choose to invest too much or too little in stocks. How far off might he be? We can get an idea by analyzing a thousand possible 25-year histories with a computer program that draws annual returns from a joint normal probability distribution with the true expected returns, risks, and correlations.

The results show that that Richard could end up with a decidedly suboptimal portfolio. In more than half of the 1,000 possible simulated scenarios he chooses a portfolio with either less than 40 percent or more than 80 percent in stocks, rather than 60 percent (the correct amount).

By looking only at history, Richard had two problems: (1) his estimates of future expected returns were almost certainly faulty and (2) his estimates of future risks and correlations were also likely wrong. To see the contribution of each of these components to erroneous portfolio choices we repeated the experiment two more times, assuming that he was able to contract with a seer to get one or the other aspect right. Figure 8-4 shows results for the three simulations, as well as those obtained by the seer.

In this case, using only historic average returns to estimate future expected returns led to larger errors in portfolio choice than did using historic data to

FIGURE 8-4
Range of Errors for 1,000 Trials

Expected Returns	Risks and Correlations	Percentage of Cases with <40% or >80% Stocks
True	True	0.0
True	Sample	35.0
Sample	True	47.1
Sample	Sample	55.7

estimate only risks and correlations. There are two reasons. First, history is generally a better guide for risks, correlations, beta values, and other measures that involve variation than it is for averages. Second, optimization exacerbates forecast errors and optimization procedures are typically more sensitive to variations in expected returns than to variations in risks and correlations.

Sensible portfolio choice requires more than a simple projection that the future will be like the past. Other information must be utilized as well. We deal with two approaches designed to obtain better forecasts. The first involves the use of factor models, the second the incorporation of information about current asset market values.

8.6. Factor Models

In all the cases that we have examined, a portfolio that includes all marketable securities occupies center stage, although it may not be the only star. This suggests that there should be strong demand for an index fund holding the *world market portfolio* of all marketable securities, including bonds, stocks, and other vehicles, in proportions equal to their relative outstanding values. At the time of this writing, no such fund does this nor attempts to provide a close approximation. Instead, each available index fund attempts to replicate the overall return from a particular set of securities. Some have broad coverage, targeting the entire U.S. stock market, the entire U.S. bond market, the entire non-U.S. stock market, and so on. Others are narrower, targeting large-capitalization U.S. stocks, long-duration government bonds, stocks with high price-to-book value ratios, and so on. And some are very narrow; for example, replicating returns on stocks of companies in one industry.

This suggests that even some investors who disdain attempts to find mispriced individual securities still wish to allocate funds among such index funds in proportions that differ from those in the market as a whole. Accordingly, many widely used analytic procedures rely on some sort of *factor model* of security returns. The prototypical form is given by the *factor model equation*:

$$\tilde{R}_i = b_{i1}\tilde{F}_1 + \ldots + b_{in}\tilde{F}_n + \tilde{e}_i$$

Here, R_i is the return on a security or portfolio; F_1 through F_n are the values of factors 1 through n, b_{i1} through b_{in} are constants, and e_i is the *residual return*: the part of the return on i not attributable to the joint effects of the factors (F's) and the sensitivities (b's) to those factors. The squiggly curves (tildes) indicate variables whose values are not known in advance. In most applications, it is assumed that the e_i values are uncorrelated with both the factors and with each other. The non-factor or *residual risk* due to uncertainty about the outcome for the e_i term is considered to be *idiosyncratic* to the security or portfolio in question. Given this assumption, it follows that a portfolio with a large number of securities will have relatively little idiosyncratic risk, owing to the effects of diversification.

Factor models form the core of much current investment practice. In many applications, the factors are the returns on portfolios or on hedged portfolios of long and short positions. For example, an equity security or portfolio might be characterized as equivalent to a *benchmark portfolio* with 80 percent invested in a value stock index and 20 percent in a growth stock index plus a residual return. In factor model terms:

$$\tilde{R}_i = 0.8\tilde{V} + 0.2\tilde{G} + \tilde{e}_i$$

Of particular interest in our context are such *asset class factor models*, in which each factor is the return on a subset of all available securities, with (1) every security included in one and only one such factor or asset class and (2) the securities in each asset class included in proportion to their outstanding market values. If factors are formed in this way it is straightforward to construct an index fund for each factor and to create a market portfolio, if desired, by combining the asset class index funds in their market proportions.

8.6.1. Performance and Risk Analysis

Asset class factor models can be used to measure an active investment manager's performance. The goal is to find a set of *factor loadings* (*b* values) summing to 1 that constitutes a mix of asset classes that reflects the manager's *investment style*. The sum of the corresponding terms in the factor model equation then represents the return on a passive portfolio that serves as an appropriate benchmark for the manager in question. The final (e_i) term will then measure the part of the manager's return due to active management.

To determine the relevant factor loadings for a manager, and hence a relevant benchmark portfolio, one can investigate the manager's portfolio holdings or, more easily, analyze the historic co-movement of his or her returns with those of the asset classes using the technique known as *returns-based style analysis* (Sharpe 1992).

In addition to providing performance benchmarks, factor models can be used to estimate the overall risk of a portfolio, the sources of that risk, and the effects of small changes in holdings on overall risk. To be as effective as possible, the factors should capture the major sources of risks that affect more than a few securities. Models used for this purpose in the investment industry range from those with a few factors (for simple asset allocation analyses) to those with a great many (for some types of risk analysis).

There is no doubt that certain groups of securities move together. Returns on the stocks of two large companies are likely to be more highly correlated than the returns of a large and a small company. Stocks selling at similar prices relative to book values per share tend to move together more than stocks selling at disparate price-to-book ratios. Stocks in the same industry tend to move together, as do stocks issued in the same country. And so on.

The best choice of factors for purposes of benchmarking and risk analysis depends on the ultimate application, an understanding of the underlying economics of companies and industries, and possible effects of investor preferences and positions. There are clearly risk factors in modern capital markets. Nothing in this book is inconsistent with that fact, and factor models can be extremely valuable in measuring such effects.

Expected returns are a separate issue. What can theory and empirical data tell us about the expected returns on factor portfolios, and hence the expected returns of securities? We describe two approaches, one based on the characteristics of a competitive capital market, the other based primarily on empirical observation.

8.6.2. The Arbitrage Pricing Theory

In a world with a finite number of states, the factor model equation can only approximate the true return-generating process since residual returns cannot be truly uncorrelated. To see why, consider a portfolio that includes all the securities in an asset class factor portfolio. If the equation holds for each of the securities, a value-weighted combination will hold as well. It should have a loading (b_i) of 1 on that factor and zero on all others. And it will have little residual risk because of the inclusion of a number of securities with uncorrelated residual returns. But mathematically there will still be residual risk, which is conceptually impossible since the portfolio is exactly that of the asset class. This subtlety can be disregarded for large portfolios but may cause problems in settings with a small number of asset classes (e.g., the factor model equation will imply that the market portfolio has at least some non-market risk). This discrepancy also makes it difficult to fully reconcile traditional factor models with our approach in which residuals returns result from dividing up the pie representing a given level of market return.

This issue aside, it is often argued that in equilibrium the only sources of expected return for a security or a portfolio are the factors and exposures thereto. The general idea is that the expected return on an investment should equal that of an equivalent mix of factor portfolios. Thus:

$$E_i = b_{i1}E_1 + \ldots + b_{in}E_n$$

This obviously requires estimates of the equilibrium expected returns for the factor portfolios (E_1 through E_n). In a capital market in which the Security Market Line (SML) holds, the expected return of any security or portfolio will be a linear function of its beta with respect to the market portfolio. This will be true for security or portfolio i and for each of the factor portfolios. But the beta of security or portfolio i will equal the weighted average of the betas of the factors, using the loadings (b_i values) as weights. Thus in a Capital Asset Pricing Model (CAPM) world we can calculate the expected return of a security or portfolio either directly, based on its market beta, or indirectly, using the expected returns of the factor portfolios based on their market betas.

The well-known *arbitrage pricing theory* (APT) advanced by Ross (1976) assumes that returns are generated by a factor model and that differences in security and portfolio expected returns are explained wholly by differences in their loadings on factors and on the factor expected returns. However, the APT does not specify the identity of the factors or the determinants of their expected returns. Factor expected returns could be linearly related to their market beta values or not. Identification of the appropriate factors and measurement of their expected returns is left for empirical, macroeconomic, and industrial organization analyses.

8.6.3. The Fama/French Three-Factor Model

In recent years, some researchers have concluded that the expected returns on some factors may not depend wholly on their beta values. Prominently, Fama and French (1992) have studied the performance of portfolios of securities grouped on the basis of market capitalization and price-to-book ratios. Commercial risk models have used similar factors for many years, but Fama and French commendably make their results (French 2005) available to all without charge, and this has led to their widespread use in the academic community.

There is no doubt that the Fama/French factors are valuable for risk and performance analyses. On the other hand, their use in estimating expected returns has stirred controversy. Fama and French find that relative to their beta values, small stocks seem to have performed better than large stocks and that low price-to-book (value) stocks seem to have performed better than high price-to-book (growth) stocks.

Some have argued that the empirical record on which such statements are based provides evidence that human behavioral traits lead to biases in asset prices. Others have suggested that this may not be the case since, relative to likely future possibilities, the record contains too few disastrous outcomes in which small stocks and value stocks crashed or disappeared entirely. Other explanations also deserve consideration. We know that historic average returns can easily differ from forward-looking expected returns, even over relatively long time periods. Such discrepancies may be especially great for portfolios representing a small part of the total value of the economy. Moreover, any possible gains to be achieved by investing in small and/or value stocks may be lost due to high execution costs. Finally, even though the relationship may have been true in the past, once it is recognized and publicized, prices may adjust so that it will not occur in the future.

FIGURE 8-5
Fama/French Portfolio Performance, July 1926–December 2004

	Small Growth	Small Neutral	Small Value	Big Growth	Big Neutral	Big Value
Average percentage of market	2.35	2.85	2.06	51.65	31.10	9.99
Average excess return	1.04	1.33	1.52	0.93	1.01	1.24
Beta	1.28	1.19	1.32	0.97	1.02	1.20
Alpha	−0.10	0.25	0.36	−0.01	0.04	0.15
Tracking standard deviation	3.60	3.05	4.12	1.17	1.79	3.23
t-Statistic	−0.82	2.56	2.69	−0.29	0.74	1.41

The Fama/French factors are constructed from six portfolios formed based on market capitalizations and book-to-price ratios. The assignment process does not result in portfolios with similar value since it focuses on security names rather than values. As a result, the small and value portfolios consistently represent very small parts of the overall market portfolio's value. Figure 8-5 provides statistics for the six portfolios over the period from July 1926 through December 2004. The first row shows the average percentages of total market value for the portfolios. The second indicates the portfolio average monthly excess returns (over one-month treasury bills). The third row shows the portfolio market betas, based on regressions of excess returns on the excess returns of Fama and French's stock market portfolio. The fourth row shows the portfolio alpha values—the average differences between each portfolio's average excess return and its beta times the market portfolio's average excess return. Each alpha value indicates a portfolio's average performance above (if positive) or below (if negative) an *ex post* security market line. The fifth row shows tracking standard deviations, which indicate the extent to which each portfolio's excess returns deviated over the months from those of a comparable-beta combination of the market portfolio and bills. The final row shows t-statistics, indicating the statistical significances of the departures of the alpha values from the SML value of zero. Average excess returns and alpha values are in units of percent return per month (e.g., the average excess return for the Small Growth portfolio was 1.04 percent per month).

Using the standard rule that requires a t-statistic with an absolute value greater than 2.0 for statistical significance, only two portfolios (Small Neutral and Small Value) departed significantly from the SML predictions of a zero alpha. On average, these portfolios represented less than 5 percent of the total value of the market (2.85 percent for the Small Neutral portfolio and 2.06 percent for the Small Value portfolio).

Fama and French construct three factors from the returns on these six portfolios. Each factor is the return on a zero-investment hedge portfolio with the same amount invested in the long positions as in the short positions. The first factor represents the returns obtained with a long position in the market portfolio and a short position in treasury bills. The second factor (SMB: Small minus Big) represents the returns from equal dollar amounts of long positions in the three Small portfolios, financed by equal dollar amounts of short positions in the three Big portfolios. The third factor Fama and French term HML for high minus low book/price ratios. We call it VMG (Value minus Growth) since it represents the returns from equal dollar amounts in long positions in the Small Value and Big Value portfolios, financed by equal dollar amounts of short positions in the Small Growth and Big Growth portfolios.

Figure 8-6 shows balance sheets representing the three factors, with the average proportions of total market value for the components shown in parentheses. As can be seen, for the second and third factors the long positions include stocks representing relatively small portions of the value of the market while the short positions include stocks representing large portions of overall market value.

To capture the returns on the Fama/French factors an investor would need to post funds to serve as margin. A typical hedge fund requires margin equal to the size of the long (and short) position. In some cases interest equal to the treasury bill rate can be earned on such funds; in other cases, the interest earned is somewhat less. In any event, the net return in any given month from investing in either the Fama/French SMB or VMG factor would almost certainly be considerably less than the sum of the return on the factor and the riskless rate of interest due to the costs involved. The composition of each of the six portfolios is changed every June, based on prices, book values, and shares outstanding at the time. Moreover, to track each factor would require changing the holdings in the underlying portfolios each month to return to the proportions shown in Figure 8-6. Considerable expense could be incurred buying and selling the relatively small and illiquid stocks held in the long positions. Changing the short positions could also be costly, even though the securities are large and relatively liquid securities. It is possible that the costs associated with implementing the investment strategies required to obtain the returns on the second and third Fama/French factors could easily be greater than any associated advantages.

This aside, the record shows that the Fama/French SMB and VMG factors provided historic average gross returns greater than those of equal-beta linear market-based strategies. But what about their *future expected returns?* Are small and value stocks likely to have positive future alpha values? And if so, is this

FIGURE 8-6
Composition of the Fama/French Factors
Percentage of equity market value in parentheses

Factor 1: Market—Bills				
Market	(1.000)	1.0000	Bills	1.0000

Factor 2: Small—Big				
SG	(.0235)	0.3333	BG	(.5165)	0.3333
SN	(.0285)	0.3333	BN	(.3110)	0.3333
SV	(.0206)	0.3333	BV	(.0999)	0.3333

Factor 3: Value—Growth				
SV	(.0206)	0.5000	SG	(.0235)	0.5000
BV	(.0999)	0.5000	BG	(.5165)	0.5000

consistent with an equilibrium in which asset prices reflect the best possible estimates of future probabilities or is it predicated on market inefficiency?

As we have seen, there are market equilibria in which prices fully reflect available information and some assets have positive or negative alphas. It could be that returns from value stocks and small stocks would be particularly poor in very poor markets. Perhaps small and downtrodden companies are more likely to fail (with a return of –100 percent) in a serious depression than are large and profitable companies. In a world in which the pricing kernel decreases with market return at a decreasing rate, assets with "frowning" return graphs can have positive alphas and those with "smiling" return graphs can have negative alphas. And if disastrous market outcomes are more probable in the future than they were frequent in the historic record, average past returns will be higher than expected returns, leading to historic alpha values greater in magnitude than should be expected in the future.

There is also the possibility that small and value stock returns are more highly correlated with human capital than are growth stocks. The chance, however remote, that widespread layoffs will coincide with the bankruptcy of many small and low-priced companies may lead investors to require higher expected returns on the stocks of such companies than would be indicated by their beta values relative to a portfolio of traded equities.

It is still possible that the historic record of seeming outperformance of securities representing a small part of the overall equity market reflects market inefficiency. If so, such performance might continue, since transactions costs may deter those attempting to exploit it. But the superiority of small stock returns diminished substantially after 1980 following widespread attention to the phenomenon. More recently, the superiority of value stocks has been broadly publicized. If this truly reflected market inefficiency, some future diminution might be anticipated. Methods for beating the market often carry the seeds of their own destruction. Some have argued that the performance of the Fama/French factors shows that security markets are inefficient and that this signals the "death of beta." The empirical record may indicate that markets are more complex than posited by the simple CAPM. But it seems highly unlikely that expected returns are unrelated to the risks of doing badly in bad times. In this broader sense, announcement of the death of beta appears to be highly premature.

8.7. Investing and Betting

Some of the discussion about the Fama/French results concerns the extent to which the *vox populi* leads to asset prices that reflect available information about future prospects. Advisors who believe that prices do reflect such information concentrate on aligning a client's portfolio with his or her preferences and positions. Those who believe otherwise go farther, attempting to exploit their hopefully superior predictive abilities. The former *invest* their clients' money. The latter choose to both invest and to *bet* against other investors.

Investors are clearly diverse and choose different portfolios. As we have seen, some diversity in portfolio choice would be observed in a market in which everyone shared a single set of predictions (in our terms, "agreed"). Preferences and positions differ; investors can and should divide up available securities to accommodate such differences. Investing allows for gains through trade that can improve everyone's situation (at least *ex ante*).

But even the casual observer of financial behavior must admit that a great many differences in portfolio holdings and a great many trades arise from diverse predictions. In addition to investing, financial markets facilitate betting. In a world in which everyone had access to all available information and processed it in the same way, much current activity would not occur.

Most people's portfolios reflect a combination of investing and betting. Sometimes this is explicit: one may invest in index funds and make bets using long/short hedge funds. More frequently, the split is at least partly implicit, involving investment in funds with holdings that have non-market risk that is not intended to compensate for outside positions.

Advisors who believe that their predictions are much better than those reflected in market prices may make large bets with their clients' money; those with more modest assessments of their abilities may show more restraint.

If some version of the index fund premise applies to actual capital markets, a wise advisor will make either very small bets or none at all. But if markets fail to reflect actual probabilities because of significant biases in the same direction on the part of a majority of investors, it may make sense for at least a minority of well-informed investors to bet (in moderation) against the market.

In either case, one cannot make sensible investment or betting decisions without a notion of the determinants of asset prices. Absent a concept of the "correct" price for a security, it is impossible to decide whether it is underpriced or overpriced. Some sort of equilibrium model is a prerequisite for responsible investment advice.

8.8. Macroconsistent Forecasts

Whatever an advisor's views about equilibrium in financial markets, it is imperative to form a set of predictions consistent with a view of investors' preferences and positions as well as current asset prices. Such predictions can be said to be *macroconsistent*.

The question that should be posed to an advisor who claims to foreswear betting and only invest his or her clients' money is this:

If you advised everyone in the world, would markets clear?

If the answer to the question is yes, the advisor's forecasts are macroconsistent. If the answer is no, they are not.

An advisor who wishes to bet against the market will choose a set of predictions that is not macroconsistent. But to know which bets to take requires comparison of the advisor's predictions with a set that is macroconsistent. Before investing or betting it is crucial for an advisor to construct a set of forecasts consistent with a view of equilibrium in which current asset prices reflect available information about the uncertain future.

It is impossible to construct a set of macroconsistent forecasts without explicitly taking into account the current market values of various assets. If European stocks have a current value equal to 20 percent of the value of the world market portfolio, to be consistent with market clearing (i.e., for demand to equal supply) the sum of the portfolios that would be recommended to all world investors must have 20 percent of its value allocated to European stocks. If the advisor would recommend 30 percent be invested in European stocks he or she is assuming that European stocks are undervalued. This may be correct, warranting the corresponding bet on European stocks and against other asset classes. But it is a bet nonetheless and should be recognized as such.

Clearly one cannot even know if a set of forecasts (and more broadly a system for giving advice) is macroconsistent without knowing current asset values. Surprisingly, many investment advisors fail to monitor such values, let alone take them into account when making forecasts. Such advisors are likely to make bets without even knowing the magnitudes or possibly the directions of those bets.

It is one thing to call for an advisor to produce a set of forecasts consistent with both current asset values and a set of investor preferences and positions. It is another to do it. Different advisors may adopt different procedures. There is ample room for competition among financial firms that choose to invest their clients' money, even if they disdain any betting. To illustrate a possible approach we describe a procedure that utilizes information about historic returns, current asset prices, and conditions in a manner consistent with mean/variance assumptions and the results of the simple CAPM.

8.8.1. Reverse Optimization

The first procedure, known as *reverse optimization,* builds on the fact that, reduced to its fundamentals, mean/variance portfolio optimization solves a problem of the form:

Covariances + Expected Returns

+ Investor Preferences → Optimal Portfolio

The known variables are on the left side of the arrow, the variable to be determined on the right side.

In a CAPM equilibrium the optimal portfolio for the representative investor will be the market portfolio. Thus:

Covariances + Expected Returns

+ Representative Preferences → Market Portfolio

Now, assume that we know covariances, the preferences of the representative investor, and the composition of the market portfolio. With a minimum amount of additional information, we can then infer the set of expected returns consistent with equilibrium. Schematically:

Covariances + Representative Preferences

+ Market Portfolio → Expected Returns

In effect, this procedure reverses the optimization process; hence the name.

This approach is described in Sharpe (1985). A similar procedure is part of an asset allocation method advocated by Black and Litterman (1992); the remainder of their procedure modifies the equilibrium expected returns to reflect an advisor's views concerning asset mispricing.

As we have seen, historic return covariances are likely to better predict future return covariances than average returns are to predict future expected returns. Those who use mean/variance reverse optimization typically exploit this relationship, using historic covariances as estimates of future covariances, then inferring expected asset returns from a combination of current asset prices, assumptions about the preferences of the representative investor, and the equilibrium conditions of the CAPM.

Given a set of covariances and the current relative values of assets in the market portfolio one can calculate a set of asset beta values using both history and the forward-looking predictions implicit in current market prices. If expected returns are linearly related to beta values (that is, if the SML relationship holds), one only needs to "pin" the location of the SML to compute implied asset expected returns. The current riskless rate of interest provides the vertical intercept for the SML. The slope is usually determined by specifying an expected return for the market portfolio—often based on the average of the risk premia in many countries over extended periods of time. The resulting set of forecasts, expressed in terms of covariances and expected returns, will be macroconsistent if investors fulfill the conditions of the simple CAPM with the representative investor choosing to hold the market portfolio.

In effect, reverse optimization computes a beta value for each security using historic covariances and the current market values of assets in the market portfolio. Expected excess returns proportional to security beta values are then added to the current riskless rate of interest to produce forward-looking estimates of expected returns. The premise is that beta values computed in this manner will provide better estimates of future expected returns than will historic average returns.

To illustrate this claim we perform another experiment, starting with a known equilibrium, then using Monte Carlo methods to generate a number of sample outcomes drawn from the set of possible outcomes in accordance with their actual probabilities. Our example uses the securities, probabilities, and equilibrium expected returns from Case 7. As was shown in Figure 4-28, in this case the equilibrium expected returns do not all lie on the SML but the divergences are not great.

For each simulated case we generate 25 years' returns by randomly choosing one state for each year, using the underlying state probabilities. We then compute the historic risks and correlations for the 25 annual returns, combine this information with the current market values of the assets, and compute estimated beta values. We also compute the average returns for the securities over the 25 years. Finally, we calculate two correlation coefficients. The first indicates the correlation between the true forward-looking expected returns and the historic average returns, the second the correlation between the forward-looking expected returns and the beta values computed using historic covariances and

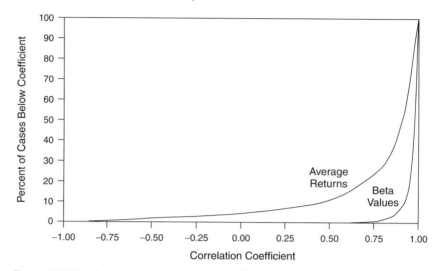

Figure 8-7 Correlations of expected returns with average returns and with beta values using historic covariances and current market values.

current market values. We then repeat this procedure, creating 1,000 25-year simulated histories.

Figure 8-7 shows the results. The vertical axis shows the percentages of the 1,000 cases with correlation coefficients below the amounts shown on the horizontal axis. For example, in roughly 5 percent of the cases historic average returns were actually negatively correlated with true future expected returns. This was never the case when the beta values using historic covariances and current market prices were utilized. On average, the correlation of the expected returns with the computed beta values was 0.18 greater than the correlation of expected returns with historic average returns; moreover, the beta values provided better predictions in more than 81 percent of the cases.

Although the conditions of the CAPM were not fulfilled in the equilibrium used for these simulations, it was clearly better to base forecasts of expected returns on historic asset covariances and current market values than on historic average returns. Current market values contain valuable information about investors' predictions about the future. It would be foolish indeed to ignore such information when making one's own predictions.

8.8.2. Calibrating a Pricing Kernel

The reverse optimization procedure works well if the world is populated by investors who care only about the mean and variance of portfolio return. An advisor can then use the resulting expected returns and historic covariances with a standard mean/variance optimization procedure to determine the best port-folio for a client, based on his or her willingness to accept higher portfolio vari-ance in order to obtain higher expected return. But much of this book has been about more complex worlds. How might an advisor select a set of macro-consistent forecasts in a more general setting?

An overall approach involves the *calibration* of an equilibrium model to make it consistent with current relative asset values. In some cases this can be achieved solely by altering historic security returns; in other cases more must be done. The reverse optimization procedure is a case of the former type. We address it again, focusing on the calibration of the pricing kernel. Assume, for example, that we have a table of 25 annual total returns for each of several as-set classes as well as the current market values of those assets. The composi-tion of the current market portfolio is calculated by dividing each asset's mar-ket value by the sum of the asset values. Next, a return on the market (R_m) is computed for every year, using the asset returns in that year and the cur-rent composition of the market portfolio. Absent any reason to presume other-wise, we treat each of these annual results (for the assets and the market) as a state of the world and assume that each state is equally probable.

The next step is to alter the market returns by adding a constant (d_m) (that may be negative) so that the expected total return on the market will equal a prespecified value (E_m). For each state s we compute a revised market total re-turn (R'_{ms}):

$$R'_{ms} = R_{ms} + d_m$$

where the constant d_m satisfies:

$$\bar{R}_m + d_m = E_m$$

where the first term represents the average of the R_m values.

We have shown that in a simple mean/variance world asset prices will be consistent with a pricing kernel that is a linear function of the total return on the market portfolio. In this case:

$$p_s = a + bR'_{ms}$$

where b is negative.

The pricing kernel must meet two conditions. First, when used to price the returns on the market portfolio, it must give a result equal to 1. Second, the sum of the state prices must equal the current discount rate (the present value of a riskless security paying $1). These conditions provide two linear equations in two unknowns (a and b). Solving this simple set of equations provides values for a and b and hence all the state prices.

Given the resulting pricing kernel, it is straightforward to adjust the total returns for each of the assets to provide macroconsistency. For each asset a constant (d_i) (that may be positive or negative) is chosen to be added to the total return in each state:

$$R'_{is} = R_{is} + d_i$$

The constant is chosen so that when the kernel is used to price the returns on the security the result will equal 1. These revisions provide a set of asset total returns consistent with the linear pricing kernel and with the revised market returns.

This procedure produces the same asset expected returns and covariances as those obtained with standard reverse optimization methods. This is easily seen by noting that adding a constant to each asset's returns does not change the covariance matrix, since each covariance measures the probability-weighted average value of the product of deviations of returns from their expected values. Moreover, the same relative asset values in the market portfolio are used in each approach, so the asset beta values are also the same. Further, when the pricing kernel is a linear function of market total return, expected returns will be linearly related to beta values. This is also the case with the reverse optimization procedure. Finally, since the riskless rate of interest and the specified expected return on the market are the same in each case, the expected asset returns will be identical.

Unlike reverse optimization, this approach provides detailed returns in different states making it possible to find optimal portfolios that maximize expected utility for investors who do not have mean/variance preferences and/or who wish to take outside positions into account. However, this may be at variance with the underlying assumption that the equilibrium asset prices are consistent with a linear pricing kernel.

Unfortunately it may not be a simple matter to alter historic returns so that they conform with a specified type of pricing kernel that is a nonlinear function of market return. But there is ample room for advisors to experiment and to develop sophisticated approaches. Whatever procedure is utilized, a key ingredient should be the explicit use of current market values.

8.9. Asset Allocation and Investment Advice

Many of those who manage large pension, endowment, or foundation funds or who serve as consultants to such funds approach portfolio choice in a stepwise manner. First the investment universe is divided into a relatively small number of *asset classes*. Next an "optimal" allocation of funds among those asset classes is determined. Managers are then hired to provide funds, each of which holds securities in or associated with one of the asset classes. Some of these funds are passive: intended to mirror the performance of a designated market sector or sectors. Others are active: intended to exceed the performance of a designated market sector. The goal is to have the sum of the managed funds' styles (benchmarks) correspond to the predetermined optimal asset allocation.

Similar procedures are used by many who provide investment advice to individuals or who manage the entire portfolio of an individual. An optimal asset allocation or "model portfolio" is determined then mutual funds or similar vehicles are used to implement the allocation. First comes the division of the investor's pie (asset allocation), then the filling of the pieces with actual investments (fund choices).

8.9.1. Asset Allocation Policies

Institutional investors engage in asset allocation studies or, if liabilities are taken into account, asset/liability studies. Such studies normally involve members of an investment board, which selects a *target policy mix* (asset allocation) and establishes allowable ranges around the target values. Between studies, staff members are directed to ensure that the fund's actual asset allocation stays within the prespecified ranges. Since such studies are time-consuming and expensive, they are performed infrequently, typically at intervals of one to three years. Those working with individuals typically review asset allocations more frequently—at least annually and often quarterly or even monthly. In some cases, the portfolio is changed to conform to the most recent optimal allocation. In others, changes are made only if the divergence between actual and optimal allocations exceeds a predetermined threshold.

While simple to execute, such stepwise procedures are likely to be inferior to a more integrated approach to the problem. In a typical two-stage approach, the preferred asset allocation is selected on the assumption that all funds will be invested in passive and costless index funds. But actual investment vehicles typically have costs, added risks, and more complex relationships with the underlying asset classes. The result is likely to be inferior portfolio choices and overly optimistic forecasts of future performance.

A far more rational approach uses only one stage, dealing directly with the actual investment vehicles, with all their attractive and unattractive features. This does not imply that asset classes should not play a role. Quite the contrary. As we have seen, asset classes can serve well as risk factors. Whether or not their expected returns are assumed to differ from those implied by their beta values depends on one's view of market equilibrium. But approaching the problem in two separate stages can only lead to inferior results.

8.9.2. Asset Allocation and Constant Mix Strategies

Despite the drawbacks, many advisors continue to advocate asset allocation policies. A number of investment funds designed to serve as complete investment solutions follow a similar approach. *Balanced* mutual funds often have explicit allocation targets. *Lifecycle funds* specify target allocations that change very gradually over many years but the allocations are not intended to respond to market moves.

However determined, asset allocation targets are almost always expressed in terms of percentages of total portfolio value. Thus a recommended mix might call for 60 percent of the portfolio's total market value to be invested in stocks and 40 percent in bonds.

In many cases asset allocation policies are selected without considering the characteristics of equilibrium. Far too many advisors fail to take current market values of asset classes into account when making forecasts to be used for choosing asset allocation policies. Another manifestation of this failure to consider market equilibrium arises when asset values change, as they frequently do. Since target asset allocations are expressed in value terms, a portfolio must be rebalanced to avoid so-called drift from the optimal allocation. For example, assume that a portfolio starts at its policy allocation, with 60 percent of its value in stocks and 40 percent in bonds. Subsequently, stocks fall relative to bonds so that 55 percent of the market's value is in stocks and 45 percent in bonds. To continue to conform to the optimal asset allocation policy, stocks must be purchased and bonds sold. Using the terms discussed in Chapter 7, this is a contrarian strategy, buying (relative) losers and selling (relative) winners. In principle, every investor with a predetermined policy mix should do just this. But of course not everyone can buy relative losers and sell relative winners. Contrarians must find momentum investors with whom to trade.

An investor who rebalances asset holdings to conform to a policy stated in terms of percentages of total value can be said to follow a *constant mix strategy*. As indicated in Chapter 7, this is a dynamic strategy that will provide a fuzzy version of a frowning return graph. But it is at best an inefficient way to obtain such a payoff function. To a considerable extent, constant mix strategies involve bets with other investors. If assets that are relative winners tend to become relative losers and relative losers tend to become relative winners, constant mix investors will profit at the expense of the investors with whom they trade. If assets that are relative winners tend to continue to win and relative losers continue to lose, constant mix investors will provide profits for other investors. Even if a constant mix policy is macroconsistent at the outset, it will lose this property once asset prices change significantly.

Rightly or wrongly, constant mix investors make bets against markets. A truly passive strategy intended only to invest in markets cannot follow an unchanging policy stated in terms of percentages of asset values. Those who wish to avoid betting should periodically use current market values to form new macroconsistent forecasts, then determine an up-to-date set of asset holdings. Not surprisingly implementation of such an approach will tend to require relatively few security purchases and sales, resulting in both more efficient port-folios and lower transactions costs.

8.10. Other Aspects of Equilibrium

This book has focused heavily on the properties of equilibrium in financial markets. While we have explored many aspects of such equilibria, many more remain to be considered (but in other places and at other times).

Our most glaring omission is the lack of more time periods. While we can interpret our framework as applying to a long, medium, or short period, our analyses cannot fully take into account interactions among periods. We addressed this set of issues crudely by suggesting that state discounts could proxy for differential subsequent investment opportunities, but it would be far better to model a multiperiod process explicitly.

This is not an easy undertaking. There are very rich models dealing with the behavior of returns over sequential periods, but they generally represent the assumed results of an equilibrium process, not the determinants of asset prices and returns in such a process. It should be possible to create a simulation program with multiple dates and states of the world that follow conditionally after prior states. But a realistic multiperiod model would need to include production opportunities. Cases involving insufficiently complete markets might be especially difficult, requiring very complex decision making on the part of individual investors. None of our cases took into account the costs associated with transactions, security creation, investment advice, mutual fund management, or other functions provided by the financial services industry. To do so would not be easy. As we have indicated, there are often many ways for investors to achieve a given allocation of claims on future outcomes, so one would have to either represent many alternative securities with different costs and have the investors shop for the best ones or predetermine the cheapest structure and include only the associated securities and trading procedures.

Finally we have left out two important issues associated with some financial contracts: adverse selection and moral hazard.

Adverse selection arises when an individual who wishes to make a financial transaction has relevant information not available to the other party. The classic case is found in the market for life insurance. If an insurance company announces a premium for life insurance coverage and invites people to buy policies, it is likely to find that is has insured an excessive number of people with poor health. This can be and often is mitigated by requiring physical examinations, but the process is imperfect.

Whenever there is asymmetric information between two parties wishing to make a contract there is a danger that an agreement that would be in both parties' interests will not be made. There is also the opposite danger—that an agreement will be made that one party would have refused had he or she known the facts—a situation not unknown in the hedge fund world. *Moral hazard* arises when an individual's or organization's behavior is changed by some contractual relationship. The classic case comes again from insurance. A driver with liability insurance may be more reckless than one without it. This may be an important aspect of other financial transactions as well.

Consider a simple case in which there are five people. If the economy turns bad, one (but only one) of them will be unemployed, with no salary income at all. There are thus five "bad" states, one in which the first person is out of work, one in which the second is out of work, and so on. In a complete market setting, the five investors would pool their unemployment risk, so that each had the same total income in each of the bad states. The equilibrium conditions would be familiar. The Market Risk Reward Theorem could hold, as could its corollary, and the market risk premium could reflect the fact that even in a bad state, the economy as a whole does not suffer a disastrous decline.

But who would agree to pay Mario a substantial sum of money if he is unemployed? Not Hue or Daniel or Arthur or Patricia. Once covered by generous unemployment insurance, Mario might well decide to slack off enough to get fired, no matter what the state of the economy. In practice, unemployment insurance is usually provided, if at all, by the government, comes with restrictions, and covers only a fraction of lost wages. In our terms, markets are not sufficiently complete and bad states of the economy carry far more risk to individuals than indicated by aggregate output and consumption. As a result, the market risk premium could be higher than it would be were moral hazard not a fact of life.

While it would be difficult to include some or all of these aspects of financial markets in an integrated equilibrium model or a simulation program this does not diminish their potential influence on asset prices—a caveat that should be kept in mind when making assertions about the real world.

8.11. Sound Personal Investment Advice

It is time to conclude this chapter and the book. We do so with four pillars of sound personal investment advice. Stated as verbs they are:

Diversify
Economize
Personalize
Contextualize

8.11.1. Diversify

We have shown that in many settings expected return is associated predominantly or exclusively with market risk. This implies that many investors should take non-market risk only if can help offset risk from positions outside the capital markets or satisfy preferences that are state-dependent. While few investors would be well advised to invest solely in the world market portfolio, extensive diversification is still highly desirable. For many investors a few highly diversified low cost index funds may suffice.

8.11.2. Economize

In this book, we have ignored transactions costs, investment management fees, and the like. But the real world is not as benign. Some mutual fund managers charge extremely low fees (under 10 cents per year for each $100 invested) and incur very few transactions costs because of low turnover. Others charge high fees (well over $1.00 per year for each $100 invested) and bear high transactions costs because of rapid turnover of holdings. Some high-cost investment strategies may be justified if the managers are sufficiently superior bettors. But capital markets are competitive and only a minority of investors and investment managers can beat the market. Absent compelling evidence to the contrary, it behooves an investor and an investor's advisor to economize on unnecessary investment costs.

8.11.3. Personalize

Investors differ in many ways. Some may have preferences consistent with a focus on portfolio mean and variance but many do not. Many individuals have positions outside the financial markets that should be taken into account when selecting investment portfolios. Asset prices reflect a diversity of investor preferences and positions as well as a diversity of predictions on the part of individuals, investment managers, and advisors. Good personal investment advice takes into account the specific preferences and circumstances of the individual for whom it is designed.

8.11.4. Contextualize

Asset prices are not set in a vacuum. As we have seen, they result from the interactions of many investors and investment professionals trading securities that provide payments that usually differ in different states of the world. Most investors assume that their choices will not significantly affect asset prices. But it is impossible to choose an appropriate portfolio without a coherent view of the determinants of asset prices. As we have argued, sound investment advice requires a well thought out concept of the nature of equilibrium in the financial markets. If the goal is only to invest an individual's money without making bets, this suffices. If bets are to be made as well, more needs to be done but a model of equilibrium remains a key ingredient. In either case, every advisor should be able to justify differences between holdings recommended for a particular individual and the proportions of assets in the overall world market portfolio. A sound portfolio choice must be made in the context of the determination of asset prices in capital markets.

We have argued throughout this book that asset prices and portfolio choice are not two subjects but one. The social scientist concerned only with understanding financial markets should study both, as should the investment professional interested in providing sound investment advice. If this book has helped those with both positive and normative interests address this subject its goal will have been achieved.

REFERENCES

Arrow, Kenneth J. 1951. "An Extension of the Basic Theorems of Classical Welfare Economics." In *Proceedings of the 2nd Berkeley Symposium on Mathematical Statistics and Probability*, edited by J. Neyman. Berkeley: University of California Press.

———. 1953. "Le Rôle de valeurs boursières pour la répartition le meillure des risques." *Econométrie, Colloques Internationaux du Centre National de la Rechereche Scientifique* 11:41–47.

Black, Fischer, and Robert Litterman. 1992. "Global Portfolio Optimization." *Financial Analysts Journal*, September–October, 28–43.

Citigroup. 2004a. *TIERS Principal-Protected Minimum Return Asset Backed Certificates Trust Series Russell 2004-1.*

———. 2004b. *Principal Protected Equity Linked Minimum Return Trust Certificates.*

Cochrane, John H. 2001. *Asset Pricing.* Princeton: Princeton University Press.

Constantinides, G., J. Donaldson, and R. Mehra. 2002. "Junior Can't Borrow: A New Perspective on the Equity Premium." *Quarterly Journal of Economics* 117(1):269–96.

Debreu, Gerard. 1951. "The Coefficient of Resource Utilization." *Econometrica* 19(3): 273–292.

Dimson, Elroy, Paul Marsh, and Mike Staunton. 2002. *Triumph of the Optimists: 101 Years of Global Investment Returns.* Princeton: Princeton University Press.

Fama, Eugene, and Kenneth R. French. 1992. "The Cross-Section of Expected Stock Returns." *Journal of Finance* 47(2):427–65.

French, Kenneth R. 2005. Data Library. http://mba.tuck.dartmouth.edu/pages/faculty/ken.french/data_library.html.

Galton, Francis. 1907. "Vox Populi." *Nature*, March 7, 450–51.

Goldstein, Daniel G., Eric J. Johnson, and William F. Sharpe. 2005. "Measuring Consumer Risk-Return Tradeoffs." October 3, 2005. http://ssrn.com/abstract=819065.

Hakansson, Nils. 1976. "The Purchasing Power Fund: A New Kind of Financial Intermediary." *Financial Analysts Journal*, November/December, 49–59.

Kahneman, D., and A. Tversky. 1979. "Prospect Theory: An Analysis of Decision Under Risk." *Econometrica* 47:263–91.

Lintner, John. 1965. "The Valuation of Risky Assets and the Selection of Risky Investment in Stock Portfolios and Capital Budgets." *Review of Economics and Statistics* 47:13–37.

Markowitz, Harry. 1952. "Portfolio Selection." *Journal of Finance* 7:77–99.

Mossin, Jan. 1966. "Equilibrium in a Capital Asset Market." *Econometrica* 34:768–83.

Ross, Stephen A. 1976. "The Arbitrage Theory of Capital Asset Pricing." *Journal of Economic Theory* 13(3):341–60.

———. 1977. "Return, Risk, and Arbitrage." In *Risk and Return in Finance*, edited by I. Friendand and J. Bicksler, pp. 189–218. Cambridge: Ballinger.

———. 2005. *Neoclassical Finance.* Princeton: Princeton University Press.

Rubinstein, Mark. 1976. "The Valuation of Uncertain Income Streams and the Pricing of Options." *Bell Journal of Economics and Management Science* 7(2):407–25.

———. 1990. "The Supertrust" (with historical note, 2000). www.in-the-money.com/artandpap/SuperTrust.doc.

———. 2006. *A History of the Theory of Investments: My Annotated Bibliography.* New York: John Wiley & Sons.

Sharpe, William F. 1964. "Capital Asset Prices: A Theory of Market Equilibrium under Conditions of Risk." *Journal of Finance* 19:425–42.

———. 1970. *Portfolio Theory and Capital Markets.* New York: McGraw-Hill.

———. 1978. *Investments.* Upper Saddle River, N.J.: Prentice-Hall.

———. 1985. *AAT: Asset Allocation Tools.* Redwood City, Calif: The Scientific Press.

———. 1987. "An Algorithm for Portfolio Improvement." In *Advances in Mathematical Programming and Financial Planning,* edited by K. D. Lawrence, J. B. Guerard, Jr., and G. D. Reeves, pp. 155–70. Greenwich, Conn.: JAI Press.

———. 1991. "The Arithmetic of Active Management." *Financial Analysts Journal,* January–February, 7–9.

———. 1992. "Asset Allocation: Manager Style and Portfolio Measurement." *Journal of Portfolio Management* 18(2):7–19.

———. 2001. "Individual Risk and Return Preferences: A Preliminary Survey." September 2001. www.stanford.edu/~wfsharpe/art/rrsurvey/vienna2001.htm.

Sharpe, William F., Gordon J. Alexander, and Jeffery V. Bailey. 1999. *Investments,* 6th edition. Upper Saddle River, N.J.: Prentice-Hall.

Sharpe, William F., Daniel G. Goldstein, and Philip W. Blythe. 2000. "The Distribution Builder: A Tool for Inferring Investor Preferences." October 2000. www.wsharpe.com/art/qpaper/qpaper.html.

Stevens, Stanley S. 1957. "On the Psychophysical Law." *Psychological Review* 64(3): 153–81.

Surowiecke, James. 2004. *The Wisdom of Crowds: Why the Many Are Smarter Than the Few and How Collective Wisdom Shapes Business, Economics, Societies and Nations.* New York: Doubleday.

Treynor, J. L. 1999. "Toward a Theory of Market Value of Risky Assets." In *Asset Pricing and Portfolio Performance,* edited by Robert A. Korajczyk, pp. 15–22. London: Risk Books.

Tversky, A., and D. Kahneman. 1992. "Advances in Prospect Theory: Cumulative Representation of Uncertainty." *Journal of Risk and Uncertainty* 5:297–323.

United States Census Bureau. 2005. http://www.census.gov/ipc/www/idbpyr.html.

Wikipedia, the free encyclopedia. www.wikipedia.org.

INDEX

Page numbers followed by *f* indicate figures.